"Drew Hart has prophetic fire and pastoral grace. He is one of America's sharpest young theologians. For far too long, some Christians have tried to dissect elements of the faith that were never meant to be separated—like faith and works, the great commandment and the great commission, social justice and personal salvation. Dr. Hart reminds us that Jesus and justice are like the blades of a scissors, like two sides of the same coin. In this book, you see that God is both personal and social. God is healing our hearts, and our streets, and our world. Let this book stir up in you a holy indignation and put a fire in your bones. May it birth in you the audacious hope that, with the Spirit's help, we can change the world from what it is into what God wants it to be."

—**Shane Claiborne**, author, activist, and cofounder of Red Letter Christians

"Drew Hart is an important rising voice in American Christianity. His theology and ethics are rooted in a powerfully productive combination of black prophetic Christianity and Anabaptism. His new book, *Who Will Be a Witness?*, offers a searching critique of compromised American Christianity and a richly detailed proposal for a better way forward in theology, church life, and social justice practice. I strongly recommend this book!"

—**David P. Gushee**, Distinguished University Professor of Christian Ethics and director of the Center for Theology and Public Life at Mercer University, and former president of the American Academy of Religion and the Society of Christian Ethics

"Drew Hart has done it again! *Trouble I've Seen* compellingly and revealingly challenged Christian churches to confront and address their own complicity and participation in racist systems and structures. In *Who Will Be a Witness?*, Hart courageously, compassionately, and prophetically urges Christians to follow Jesus faithfully by living fully into the radical implications of his teaching, rather than attempting 'to go halfsies on very serious social concerns' in the misguided effort to claim that 'truth always lies somewhere in the middle.' An excellent, accessible introduction to Christian activism—and, indeed, its necessity—this book is thoroughly biblical, theologically rich, engagingly practical, and tremendously urgent."

—**Michael Barram**, professor of theology and religious studies at Saint Mary's College of California and author of *Missional Economics*

"Drew Hart's deep passion for humanity, the gospel, and the calling to alleviate the suffering of people disinherited is on full display. This brilliant public intellectual, preacher, and cultural critic is uniquely gifted to cross denominational, racial, political, and class lines to offer a vision of hope and healing our nation is yearning to hear. Do yourself a favor and purchase this book."

—**Otis Moss III**, senior pastor of Trinity United Church of Christ in Chicago

"Drew Hart's *Who Will Be a Witness?* is a clarion and prophetic call for the church to not remain satisfied with an impotent and disembodied theology of justice within our communities. Hart's writing is sermonic as he masterfully enfolds justice and Scripture to point us toward the enfleshed, boundary-transgressing, and power-shifting life of Jesus as its center. This book is a must-read—offering a tangible and compelling way forward for everyone who claims to be a follower of Jesus."

—**Gail Song Bantum**, lead pastor of Quest Church

"With heart and soul, careful attention to Scripture, and piercing candor about human relationship, Drew Hart summons us to a beautifully holistic vision of Christian witness. He urges us toward holy discomfort. He warns of the danger of individualism. He reminds us of the character of faithful Christian community. And he helps us reimagine what love must be—and do—in a world desperately in need of God's justice, true healing, and life-giving good news."

—**Jeff Chu**, cohost of Evolving Faith Conference and author of *Does Jesus Really Love Me? A Gay Christian's Pilgrimage in Search of God in America*

"Drew Hart is fast becoming a go-to voice for articulating a practical and prophetic Christianity in our time. Dubbed 'AnaBlacktivism' by some, Hart's vocation is the jazz improvisation of two prophetic critiques of Christendom: the Black church and peace church traditions. Here is a revolution more radical than that of Barabbas. A liberation that rejects all violence for the militant love of Calvary. In these pages, Hart wields these influences to unmask oppressive economics, white supremacy, and imperialism while revealing what it is for us to take up our cross and follow Jesus for the liberation of others."

—**Jarrod Mckenna**, award-winning peace activist, pastor, founding CEO of Common Grace, and cohost of *InVerse* podcast

"Using powerful imagery and a historical framework, Drew Hart challenges the church to roll up our sleeves. The church of today must reflect our roots and dive deep into responding to the injustice and oppression in our communities. It is time to answer our divine call."

—**Glen Guyton**, executive director of Mennonite Church USA and author of *Reawakened: How Your Congregation Can Spark Lasting Change*

"Drew Hart has written the most challenging and enriching book that I have read in a very long time—a book brimming over with moral urgency, uncommon wisdom, and spiritual insight. At its core, it summons the church to do what the American church has seldom done—to discern and then burst the bonds of nationalism, capitalism, American exceptionalism, and white supremacy, and to embrace instead the revolutionary vocation of Jesus on behalf of marginalized people. But it goes beyond that summons to give us the tools we need to accomplish that task—a richer understanding of Jesus and the entire biblical text, penetrating insights into both Euro-American history and popular culture, and practical strategies the church can use if it hopes to serve as a liberating, redemptive force in our world."

—**Richard T. Hughes**, author of *Myths America Lives By: White Supremacy and the Stories That Give Us Meaning*

"The call to follow Jesus is a revolutionary one. It's a call to reimagine a world often marked by dominance in order to embrace deliverance; a call to embody the prophetic mandate to liberate the world from the shackles of systemic sin in all the forms it takes. Drew Hart offers us a powerful vision to be a people on the liberating journey. I'm inspired by his depth of insight, social and spiritual analysis, and the demanding—yet accessible—ways he names for living faithfully to God. I highly recommend this book!"

—**Rich Villodas**, lead pastor of New Life Fellowship in Queens, New York, and author of *The Deeply Formed Life*

WHO WILL BE A WITNESS?

WHO WiLL BE A WiTNESS?

iGNiTiNG ACTiViSM FOR GOD'S JUSTiCE, LOVE, AND DELiVERANCE

DREW G. I. HART

FOREWORD bY MiCHAEL MCBRiDE, PASTOR AND COMMUNiTY ORGANiZER

HERALD
P R E S S

Harrisonburg, Virginia

Herald Press
PO Box 866, Harrisonburg, Virginia 22803
www.HeraldPress.com

Library of Congress Cataloging-in-Publication Data
Names: Hart, Drew G. I., author.
Title: Who will be a witness : igniting activism for God's justice, love,
    and deliverance / Drew G. I. Hart.
Description: Harrisonburg, Virginia : Herald Press, 2020. | Includes
    bibliographical references.
Identifiers: LCCN 2020009959 (print) | LCCN 2020009960 (ebook) | ISBN
    9781513806587 (paperback) | ISBN 9781513806594 (hardcover) | ISBN
    9781513806600 (ebook)
Subjects: LCSH: Communities--Religious aspects--Christianity. | Social
    justice--Religious aspects--Christianity. | Jesus Christ--Example. |
    Church and social problems. | Christian life--Anabaptist authors.
Classification: LCC BV625 .H38 2020 (print) | LCC BV625 (ebook) | DDC
    261.8--dc23
LC record available at https://lccn.loc.gov/2020009959
LC ebook record available at https://lccn.loc.gov/2020009960

Study guides are available for many Herald Press titles at www.HeraldPress.com.

WHO WILL BE A WITNESS?
© 2020 by Herald Press, Harrisonburg, Virginia 22803. 800-245-7894.
All rights reserved.
Library of Congress Control Number: 2020009959
International Standard Book Number: 978-1-5138-0658-7 (paperback);
    978-1-5138-0659-4 (hardcover); 978-1-5138-0660-0 (ebook)
Printed in United States of America
Cover and interior design by Reuben Graham

Unless otherwise noted, Scripture text is quoted, with permission, from the *New Revised Standard Version*, © 1989, Division of Christian Education of the National Council of Churches of Christ in the United States of America.

Scripture quotations marked (NIV) are taken from the Holy Bible, New International Version®, NIV®. Copyright © 1973, 1978, 1984, 2011 by Biblica, Inc.™ Used by permission of Zondervan. All rights reserved worldwide. www.zondervan.com The "NIV" and "New International Version" are trademarks registered in the United States Patent and Trademark Office by Biblica, Inc.™

Scripture quoted by permission. Quotations designated (NET) are from the NET Bible® copyright © 1996–2018 by Biblical Studies Press, L.L.C. All rights reserved.

24 23 22 21 20   11 10 9 8 7 6 5 4 3 2

To Vincent Hart and his namesake, Vincent Harding

CONTENTS

FOREWORD

An Oakland-based Muslim mentor encouraged me early in my public justice ministry to stay committed to organizing the people because "a disorganized truth will find it difficult to defeat an organized lie." As I read Drew Hart's words, I am reminded of why I fell in love with organizing the power of faith congregations, particularly black churches. I think Drew agrees with me that when truths are organized, they defeat organized lies.

In an era obsessed with bigness, I hear Drew's words holding out hope for local congregations willing to unleash the power of organizing to change the world. I resonate with his conviction that Christians formed after the ways of Jesus can be consequential in changing the course of our churches, communities, and nations. I see his commitment to speak boldly to these faithful ones, stirring in neighborhoods and communities sprinkled across the breadth of this country and planet. And in a time when many are looking anew for instruction from new and familiar voices who can help uncouple faith from a failed American religious project called American evangelicalism, Drew is up to the task.

As a trained theologian raised in evangelicalism, who has since transitioned into Anabaptist Christianity, Drew possesses needed experiences that afford him the ability to discern and expose some of these organized lies at work. I appreciate the gestures to history as well, since so much of our challenge in this contemporary moment is a misremembered history that allows idiocy and falsehoods to flourish. We need more Christ followers committed to interrogating and reflecting on their faith in ways that call the faithful forward into bold and public stewardship of all creation.

Such a call to action, and not more paralysis of analysis, is an urgent and needed one among Christ followers in the world. Much is at stake in our adrift nation, led by an immoral political leader, while multiple pandemics run side by side. Truth is in desperate need of being organized to defeat the big lies of human hierarchy, state violence, ecological disaster, and religious fundamentalism. I do believe the future is yet to be written and it is in our hands, with the help of the Lord to do what is necessary to redeem our public witness as the church of Jesus Christ in the United States.

In the second chapter of the book of Joel, the prophet declares that in the last day, God will pour out the Spirit on all flesh. Sons and daughters will prophesy. Old men will see dreams and young men will see visions. Even servants will receive the Spirit. And everyone who calls on the name of the Lord shall be saved (Joel 2:28-32). Obviously, the prophet felt like witnesses would abound during the last days. All Flesh. Prophesy. Imagination. Dreams. Salvation. I hear these themes calling forth witnesses among and around us. May you who read this text raise your hand to be a witness, less in words and more in deeds. For they who know the truth will indeed be free.

—Michael McBride,
director of urban strategies and the LIVE FREE campaign for Faith in Action and founder and lead pastor of The Way Christian Center in West Berkeley, CA

INTRODUCTION

On Thursday, April 11, 1963, as Rev. Dr. Martin Luther King Jr. and the Southern Christian Leadership Conference (SCLC) sought to galvanize Project C and the freedom movement in Birmingham, Alabama, they found that very few people were willing to volunteer to get arrested and go to jail. During the mid-1950s, the black church[1] in Montgomery, Alabama, rallied black residents to boycott the Jim Crow segregationist busing system, leading to a yearlong battle and eventual victory. Almost a decade later, King had matured in his understanding of nonviolent struggle and shifted philosophically toward a more confrontational model, which applied direct pressure at strategic targets and required that participants accept the social and often physical consequences of those actions. King was especially influenced by the student movements that set the South ablaze beginning in 1960 when student activists put their very bodies on the line by physically disrupting and occupying Jim Crow spaces that denied them access. Consequently, Dr. King, along with many of his key strategists, made the shift from boycotts to more direct non-violent action.

Project C stood for *confrontation*, and that is exactly what King and his collaborators were hoping to spark. Confrontation and mass disobedience would expose the hidden injustices that shaped everyday life in Birmingham. It is often said that Birmingham was the most segregated city in the South, and it had a reputation for maintaining that segregation through violence. Birmingham's nickname was "Bombingham" because so many black churches, homes, and businesses were bombed, and without any repercussions for the perpetrators.

Birmingham was not a place people wanted to get arrested. Despite the honor of being arrested alongside King, there were many social and economic costs one would have to pay, alongside the very real possibility of facing white supremacist violence. And so, as Passover and Easter weekend approached, the movement stumbled and seemed to be dwindling to a standstill. Not only were there not enough volunteers to fill the jails (or to even have a real presence at all), but there were other troubles. The city had filed an injunction against marching. The injunction was said to be illegal, but that mattered little since an opportunity to challenge it in court wouldn't be available before the demonstration. And there was the issue of bail funds; they had none. Who would be willing to risk getting locked up in the Birmingham jail indefinitely? And finally, the timing was difficult. Easter is the most significant celebration in the Christian calendar, and is certainly a big event for black churches. Most of the SCLC's leaders, including King, were pastors and ministers of congregations. How could they demonstrate and risk being away from their pastoral responsibilities on the most significant Christian holiday of the year? They probably had already prepared great sermons for their congregations.

On April 12, Good Friday morning, Martin Luther King Jr. and over twenty freedom movement leaders gathered in his room at the famous Gaston Motel, which served as headquarters for civil rights work in the city. King shared his own tension about his conflicting obligations before listening quietly as everyone else spoke. They all had an opinion. Some, of course, thought that, injunction or not, they needed to move forward courageously. Others thought it was a bad idea for King, particularly, to get arrested at this time, since they believed that King was the only one who could quickly raise the money needed by making visits around the country to key supporters and holding rallies. How could he raise money while in jail? Daddy King, who had come down from Atlanta, thought it was a bad idea for his son to go against the injunction. And of course, some believed they should be in church services on Sunday morning, because Easter! Spirits were low and movement leaders were feeling defeated and cornered, without any good solutions.

As his collaborators shared their views one after the other, King sat quietly and listened. He didn't express in any way that one particular option resonated with him. After a bit of time, King suddenly got up, left the living room area of his hotel suite, went into the bedroom, and closed the door behind him, leaving everyone else to continue pondering what to do. Minutes went by with no sight of him. Then, suddenly, the door opened and out came Martin Luther King Jr. But something was different about him now—he had changed his clothes. In most images we have of him Dr. King is wearing a clean black suit with a white shirt and a black tie. It is simple apparel that suggests he expects to be taken seriously, and it reflected the respectability practices in the black church at the time. The look appeared to work for a young man caught in such an intense crucible of history while challenging the soul of America.

But on this day, when Martin Luther King Jr. emerged from the bedroom, he had changed his clothes—not to a suit and tie, but to something entirely different. He came out of the bedroom dressed in a blue work shirt and a pair of blue jeans, with his sleeves rolled up. The moment his collaborators saw him they knew exactly what that meant.

When Dr. King put on his blue jeans, he was indicating that they were not going to get dressed up for an Easter church service. When he put on his blue jeans, he meant that it was time to get to work and do the mundane and real labor of demonstrating in Birmingham against the injunction, knowing full well that the consequences would place him in the Birmingham jail. And by putting on his blue jeans to engage in civil disobedience over Passover and Easter weekend, Dr. King also revealed something about his understanding of the deeper meaning of the holiday, of Christianity in general, and of the significance of Jesus' revolutionary action on that first Good Friday. Dr. King knew that he "had to make a faith act" even though the circumstances were not aligned in his favor. The response to Jesus' clash with the establishment and his willingness to lay down his life should lead to more than just worshiping and celebrating him for what he did—it should also ignite a revolutionary, grassroots, Jesus-shaped witness in society. Those who follow Jesus should love our neighbors to such a degree that we are willing to accept the consequences that come from struggling for shalom and true justice in the public square.[2]

Who Will Be a Witness? has that goal in mind. It was written to ignite and mobilize the church into faithful and revolutionary Jesus-shaped work for justice as we join God's delivering presence in a world haunted by the legacy of Christendom (societies shaped by Christian supremacy) and colonialism and racism (societies organized by white supremacy). Every Sunday, people gather and proclaim that they have put their faith in Jesus, yet our domesticated discipleship fails to produce followers who embody, as Jesus modeled, a faithful witness in our society. This book suggests that restoring our public witness requires us to return to the root of our faith, the gospel of Jesus, to take responsibility for our legacy of a mangled Christianity, and to discover methods that are faithful and conducive to local churches seeking God's justice and deliverance in their neighborhoods. The church's methods must align with our ecclesial vocation while also taking forms that are uniquely designed for a capitalist, democratic republic nation-state with a long legacy of oppression.

WHITE MAN'S RELIGION

"Christianity is the white man's religion," said my neighbor. My friend from two doors down was intentionally trying to provoke a reaction from me. He is a black Muslim who was raised Baptist. While he is no theologian or church historian, he does have firsthand experience with Christianity, and for him, ultimately, that proved to be a problem. I hadn't expected him to bring up this specific point, but he probably figured that we knew each other well enough to wade deeper into the waters of religious and political discussion. He and I generally got along well. We talked about almost anything over the years that we lived on the same block in Philly. We played ball together occasionally, and he was always generous with the food he threw on the grill out front. We got along, but occasionally he would intentionally say something abrupt and pejorative about Christianity to me. These comments were never mean, but he was clearly interested to see how I would respond. A comment like his was unlikely to rile me up, but I did have thoughts on the subject. My response included comments that fell into two main points.

The first point I shared with my friend has to do with the roots of Christianity. I explained that Christianity is not indigenous to Western Europe, but derived from regions we now call Asia and Africa. I talked about Africa's presence throughout the biblical narrative, how even the Septuagint was an ancient African translation of Hebrew Scripture, and more importantly, that Jesus, according to the book of Matthew, lived in Africa for a time while hiding out from Herod's violent regime, which sought to snuff out his messianic reign. I named some of the early African Christian thinkers who shaped ancient and contemporary Christian theology: Tertullian, Cyprian, Clement, Origen, Athanasius, and Augustine were all African Christian leaders and theological giants in church history who have guided and shaped Christian belief and practice. Contemporary theology is indebted to these Africans. To bring home my point, I mentioned that Christianity was present in parts of Africa before Europeans ever set foot there, and while some of those distinctly African strands are very small today, they still exist. Plus, today, all sorts of indigenous forms of African Christianity continue to emerge that reject the imposed Western assumptions and practices for understanding Christianity. Christianity is once again being interpreted and understood from within African contexts, lived experience, and customs. The motherland and Christianity have long been creatively intertwined in ancient and contemporary manifestations.

My second point probably surprised my friend. After narrating some of the Christian history that black people in this land ought to hold to tightly, I admitted that he is also right. Yes, you read that right: I agreed with my friend that Christianity has at times become the white man's religion. It is an undeniable fact that Christianity was weaponized by Europeans to justify their conquest of land and plundering of resources, as well as their enslaving, physically brutalizing, and subjugating black and Indigenous people's bodies all around the globe. In the fifteenth century, the church, through its official doctrines, gave its blessing to Portugal and Spain's mission of conquering and dominating the "heathen" worlds under the banner of Jesus. In the United States, like other places around the world, there is a direct correlation between racial oppression and white people's use of Christianity to justify their behavior by claiming divine sanction. In this land, slavery, black codes, Jim Crow, convict leasing, and other forms of neo-slavery, as well as lynching and local terrorism of black communities, could not have existed without preachers, biblical scholars, theologians, and Christian presidents of prestigious universities who used their explanatory power to produce pseudo-scholarship that made white supremacy over black and other nonwhite people appear divinely ordained. And so, with a sigh, I acknowledged that Christianity has too often been manipulated and weaponized against black people and used as a religion that bolsters white supremacy. Christianity has been used as a white man's religion, even if that wasn't faithful to its origins seen in the person of Jesus. It is these facts with which I knew I had to contend.

I had one last thing to say to my friend. The essential question for me is not whether Christianity has been used to justify white supremacy. Anyone who hasn't insulated themselves with a false narrative of white American innocence or a myth of Western exceptionalism understands that wherever colonialism took root, the presence of "white man's religion" is an undeniable and devastating historical fact. A careful exploration of history reveals that Western Christianity aided colonial conquest and the death-dealing forces it unfolded on nonwhite people around the globe. The core question for me is whether the Christianity that was practiced in these contexts was genuinely the way of Jesus, or if the religion of white Christians was distorted on behalf of their own social mission, one contrary to the vocation of the Messiah. Was the practice of Christianity in the West a reasonable expression and consequence of discipleship to Jesus and membership in the church? Did its faith and habits have a substantive relationship with the One revealed in Matthew, Mark, Luke, and John? Or did it (d)evolve into a religion of the status quo and the powerful, who were able to sleep well at night while engaging in brutality because they had convinced themselves that God had commanded them to subdue non-Christian lands and peoples?

You can safely assume that since I am writing this book, I do not actually believe that the way of Jesus correlates with that kind of oppression and violence. I believe Jesus' name has been vandalized every time people have slapped it onto their own ambitious projects of domination, just as one might slap a sticker onto the back bumper of a car. When someone asks me whether Christianity is the white man's religion, I respond in both the affirmative and the negative. Just as some enslaved Africans dared to distinguish between true Christianity and the religion of this land, so I too recognize that Christianity has been weaponized, but I reject any claim that its weaponized form is a faithful witness to the way of Jesus. The way of Christ has been distorted and domesticated, leaving too many people following after a whitened and westernized Jesus that bolsters the status quo. God, of course, will be the final arbiter of which ways of living align with the way of Jesus and which do not. For now, I simply invite us all to read Scripture together, to immerse ourselves in the story of Jesus, which is the culmination of our sacred Scripture, and to understand our lives within the context of church history and its traditions. I believe doing so will provide a lens for the church to discover its liberative and justice-oriented vocation in society.

THE MANGLED WITNESS OF THE CHURCH

When observing the public witness of the church in the United States today, it is hard not to conclude that something is terribly wrong. Those who take seriously the responsibility of the church to bear witness to, and make visible to our neighbors, the life and teachings of Jesus on earth probably already agree with this diagnosis. I do not write this as someone who has given up on the global body of Christ or as someone who no longer gathers locally with other followers of Jesus. I am committed to the church. Yet something is terribly amiss. I refuse to accept that what typically passes for Christianity in America is the actual embodiment of the faith. If it is, then something must be deficient, shallow, and harmful about Christianity itself. I'm not convinced that what we practice is what Jesus desired for us and passed on to the disciples and earliest Christians. Nor is the comfortable Christianity of today consistent with the wisdom that flows from wrestling with the Hebrew Scriptures, which Christians profess culminate in the person of Jesus. Something is wrong with our practices, our understanding, our hearts, and our sense of vocation in the world. And this (misin)forms how we disciple local congregations into a life of justice in their neighborhoods—or fail to do so altogether.

The church's witness is not all gloom and doom, though. There are churches that embody God's justice, love, and deliverance for their neighbors. And encounters with actual communities that take Jesus seriously—those that love their neighbors, incorporate practices for redistributing wealth, and confront and speak truthfully to those who unjustly abuse power, as Jesus himself did—are simply breathtaking and inspiring. They offer living hope. An encounter with a community living out their baptismal identity as followers of Jesus, and opting out of power dynamics that exercise domination over others, can surprise those who witness what God is doing. Jesus desires to lead us into a better way of living with others, and when people actually live that out in community, their shared life is compelling and contagious. Too often, though, we each see only small glimpses of this counter-witness.

For too many people, our experience with church offers nothing more than a lot of what we have already known and seen in the rest of society. Capitalist and corporate structures and principles dominate worshiping communities. And then there is the hierarchical way we understand and practice leadership in the church. Our communities are often extremely clergy-centric, which disempowers the whole congregation to pursue deep-rooted Christian formation that leads to justice. Celebrity, ego, and power frequently run rampant among Protestant Christian leaders. Sometimes clergy are expected to present themselves as set apart and holier than the rest of the congregation (or at least they allow the local community to put them on a pedestal as God's elite) and then advise parishioners on how to merely tweak their lives while awaiting an eternity with God. This creates unhealthy expectations with often few accountability measures for pastors and low expectations and structures for faithful discipleship for congregations. Everyday comfortable Americanized spirituality emphasizes hyper-individualism through a personal relationship with God, private devotions, internal interrogations of one's inner thoughts, and assurance of individual salvation while clergy are solely responsible for being a visible presence in the world.

Hyper-individualization coupled with a faith marginalized to the redlined boundaries of our hearts results in a church whose discipleship is crippled in the public square. It is no wonder that conservative Christianity has been easily hijacked and used as a puppet by the Moral Majority movement in their quest to manipulate the Christian vote. These manipulations have involved concocting a voting ethic for Christians focused on the single issue of abortion while enticing other voters with racially coded rhetoric. The mainline church has tended to have more understanding that justice is a part of the calling of the church, but its clergy-centric posture rarely leads to on-the-ground discipleship in the work of justice for the whole congregation. It is not hard to find mainline clergy marching, usually while wearing a collar and stole to distinguish themselves from ordinary people and visibly mark themselves in the public square. Often, in an attempt to revive the moral high ground assumed to belong to clergy during much of Christendom's run, the visibility of clergy in public demonstrations is emphasized, but little emphasis is given to how clergy can lead all their congregants toward the way of Jesus' justice and peace in their neighborhood. It can be easier at times to mobilize clergy together as the representation of Christianity's public witness, but mobilizing and empowering congregations for justice is harder work that is frequently skirted. Whether evangelical or mainline, every Sunday Christians pack the pews, passively expecting to receive a therapeutic teaching that will help them go about their American lives with ease while leaving their ethical commitments and social witness untouched. At most, the preacher will preach to the choir in line with the obvious partisan platforms with which their church is already closely associated. Beyond that, God has been shoved into the corners of our privatized spirituality and is only allowed out when it is time to battle once more in partisan or culture wars.

There is no shortage of Christians ready to fight partisan battles. It is hard to distinguish Christianity's commitments from the political parties of our day. Christian ethics appear at times to be nothing more than the current platform of Republicans or Democrats. Partisan politics seems to determine our ethics and social witness. When entering a new church, it usually takes only a few minutes to tell whether the congregation is Democratic, Republican, or some kind of wishy-washy political moderate. The unspoken clues are everywhere. And by "moderate" I don't mean politics that have escaped from mainstream political mindsets; I mean a church that tries to play the middle-ground fence and avoids risking critical conversations about how systems and policy affect their neighbors. These congregations are no more courageous than partisan churches. They believe that being centrist is the answer to polarization. For a brief second they may almost seem right, until you realize they like to go halfsies on very serious social concerns and want to meet in the middle between the conservative and the progressive. They are likely to say that "truth always lies somewhere in the middle." To recognize the problem in this logic, imagine if someone wanted to go halfsies on the Holocaust, or to be centrist about Jim Crow segregation, or to meet in the middle on allowing children to be molested. Those things would not fly for anyone with a meaningful moral compass. There are many social issues for which being centrist ends up being neutral to the violation of the inherent dignity of people made in the image of God. Silence on the challenges of our day is not courageous. Some policies are death-dealing. At different points in American history each party has endorsed extremely oppressive and unjust policies that have devastated the lives of vulnerable people. However, very rarely does either party get close to aligning with the kind of justice and shalom depicted in our sacred texts or with the kind of life Jesus lived.

I am not pointing out partisan battles and how they shape our political imagination for the purpose of calling the church to equivocate on everything, as if all politicians are equally bad or good. The goal of a disciple amid a partisan and polarized society is not to pretend that policies don't affect one's neighbors differently in very significant ways. The problem is that we are discerning what is good and righteous by allowing the powers and political parties that run society to dictate our sociopolitical agenda, instead of cultivating an imagination birthed out of the revolution of our Messiah and the new world God is bringing from heaven to earth.

Rather than adopting a mainstream way of thinking or building our convictions from predetermined partisan presuppositions, we need Jesus-shaped imaginations that have been delivered from their captivity. Jesus-shaped imaginations provide a robust and multidimensional way of knowing in Christ. There are elements that ought to shape the kind of world we hunger for as Christians. A Jesus-shaped imagination must, through Scripture, wrestle with God like Jacob. We must know the stories of Scripture and see their culmination in the life and teachings of Jesus. A Jesus-shaped imagination that is delivered from captivity yields to the Holy Spirit to guide and teach us as we face contemporary problems, and makes the resurrected presence of Jesus available to us. It is an imagination that flows from participating in a local congregation seeking to organize its collective life, in both its gathering and scattering in society, in awareness of the reigning presence of Christ. Such imagining will inevitably cultivate dangerous eschatological (God's future for us) dreams of God's delivered world, a world that has come and is still yet to come.[3]

This new society of God was ignited by Jesus, the true revolutionary, who subverted our sin and death-corroded ways of living that stand against God's desire for us. When we join this revolutionary way of Jesus that flows like a river, we see that it runs through history from below. We learn what freedom and justice really mean. Eventually our taste buds for the world as it is begin to change because we have tasted and seen God's deliverance firsthand. If we have indeed glimpsed God's just and righteous society and are yielding to the Spirit in our discipleship, then we have an opportunity to join the tradition of dreaming in Christ. Our dreams are threatening to those who hoard riches and slaughter innocent people. Christians ought to be the first people to know that there is an option for humanity other than dominating one another, and we also ought to be the ones risking our lives embodying the counter-community that is possible right now, from below, even as global corporations and paid-off politicians seek to recodify their power as permanent.

As Rev. Dr. William Barber suggests, we need a moral imagination and message for our society.[4] It is not acceptable for half the church to concede moral language to status quo religionists. It is not enough to draw on the abstract modernist language of rights. Instead, we must allow the Spirit to whisper restorative ideas into our ears before we speak of right and wrong. We must learn to speak truthfully and with integrity. We can and must name sinful and evil practices as such. Christians have a unique language to diagnose our world. Sin, when it is not reduced to superficial religiosity and inner piety, can comprehensively unveil our fallen structures and powers, relationships, practices, and identities. And we should not only describe the world as it is; we should be inspiring others with the world God has dreamed up for us, and what ultimately will be. Moral imagination and prophetic imagination go hand in hand. A prophetic word encourages us to remember that oppressive empires will not last forever. It offers everyone an opportunity to repent from domination and to live into God's new world that is emerging from the margins of society. The question is, Can you imagine God's deliverance?

An important aspect of this book is an invitation for the church to experience the delivering presence of God, and to join in with that holy vocation in our pursuit of justice. The word *deliverance* is inevitably a loaded word for some people. It may initially be a word you feel drawn to or repelled by, depending on its usage in your context. In this book, I use *deliverance*, *liberation*, *salvation*, and even *redemption* almost interchangeably. However, in my own experience, the word *deliverance* has often been the thicker, more holistic term compared to the others. Most of us hear the word *salvation* in the domesticated way it has been used in the Western church, which conflates it with "going to heaven when you die." The actual Bible doesn't reduce the word to that meaning. "Salvation" is an otherworldly category for most. Salvation and one's afterlife have been pressed together into one concept in many traditions, especially for evangelicals. If you want to understand what the Bible means by *salvation*, just read how the psalmists cry out to God in the midst of their earthly troubles and how God *saves* them. *Salvation* in the United States usually means something spiritual, individual, and heaven-focused. This watering down of language rips salvation away from God's holistic justice that can be spiritual at times but is also earthly and concerned with our material needs here and now.

I also use *liberation* quite frequently. This term tends to evoke an intimate relationship with God's justice. My only hesitation with solely using *liberation* is that it is frequently used exclusively to talk about God's intervention on behalf of oppressed and poor people in sociopolitical ways. That is an important dimension of God's activity but not all of it. It is rarely used in a way that is holistic enough to capture the full scope of human need, which should include the spiritual dimensions of reality along with the social, political, psychological, and economic. Social sin does exist, but so does personal sin. I'm not so modernist that I am ready to deny the existence of death-dealing spiritual forces that keep us captive to a life of exploitation, supremacist pursuits, and the harming of others and our earth. The word *liberation* is helpful (and I use it frequently) and it can imply a holistic journey toward God's freedom, but its typical usage has been narrower than that, lacking the fullness of all that God is doing to set us free.

To speak of God's deliverance, for me, invokes the broad scope of our earthly predicament. *Deliverance* helps us remember that God is the solution to the captivity to evil, injustice, and death that humanity experiences. God is active, present, and intervening in the midst of the crushing poverty that people are experiencing, even right now. God is present through the cycles of violence from which refugees are fleeing and that produce over thirty thousand American deaths from gun violence each year. God has not abandoned people locked up in oppressive cages but rather shows up for the most vulnerable of our human siblings who have been treated in inhumane ways. God is with the oppressed, the poor, the young people caught in vortexes of deprivation, and those with mental and physical disabilities who are stigmatized and vulnerable. God's delivering presence is a force that we can join. Through the power of the Holy Spirit, our revolutionary Messiah came and lived, and has overcome the cross and the powers that deteriorate our human condition. Jesus has broken into our house of captivity tying up "the strong man" and stealing us away into God's kingdom (see Mark 3:27). We are delivered from ourselves, from the exploitation of others, and from the unjust structures and institutions that deny the dignity of all human people. Our revolutionary Messiah is overcoming sin, death, and the evil that keep us captive. Deliverance is what we need from the sin, death, and evil that wreak havoc on humanity and the rest of creation. It's a term that reminds us to pray, "Your kingdom come on earth as it is in heaven," and to ask God to "deliver us" from the evil (one).

American conceptions of freedom are a different animal than God's deliverance. American freedom is concerned with rights that provide the liberty (personal autonomy) of choice for oneself. It is about not allowing someone else to "tread" on our right to do whatever we desire. For example, American understandings of freedom suggest that a person ought to have the right to obtain limitless weapons with mass killing precision and power despite it harming the overall well-being of others. The fact that someone may choose something that is harmful to oneself or others matters very little in this kind of freedom. The irony, of course, is that present gun rights reflect so clearly how our sense of freedom is selfish and individualistic. This freedom isn't about the wellbeing of all people (or creation for that matter) because it won't even account for how it is diminishing the actual freedom of another person. When we look at the broader patterns of our lives, we can see that so many of our desires and hopes for our lives are deeply socialized by the societies and communities that have most profoundly shaped us. Our belief that freedom means the ability to do whatever we want, or the agency to accomplish whatever we desire, is flawed; it refuses to account for our responsibility to the flourishing of all humanity as a beloved community. It also ignores how deeply our desires are already captive to much greater forces. We should not conflate American rights with God's righteousness, nor should we confuse American freedom for God's deliverance.

God's freedom does not hand us over to our base desires; rather, it delivers us from the mangled ways that corrode our lives—from our false sense of autonomy, from our unsustainable practices and abuse of the earth and its resources, and from our inclination to forget the presence of God through whom we exist and live. God's delivering presence ushers us toward the unfolding of shalom within creation. The Prophets in Scripture remind us of a time when the lion and the lamb will lie down together, when the people will flourish on their land, when justice and peace will embrace. It is a time of harmony and interdependence, when all of God's creation lives in goodness, mutuality, and flourishing because things have been set right by our Creator. Without a scriptural theology of shalom we will fail to understand the church's vocation of justice, peacemaking, and restoration.

Clearly, the earth is not flourishing in shalom right now. Neighborhoods across the United States where majority white and wealthy people live are engineered to insulate and protect them from encountering the historic and contemporary consequences of centuries of racial oppression that exploit and disadvantage people. Two million people are locked up in prison, out of sight, mind, and empathy from mainstream

America. Our bloated prison industrial complex is the largest in the world, and it is fed by a pipeline that begins in under-resourced neighborhoods and schools that were intentionally neglected and set up to fail. Black and brown children are jammed into overcrowded and understaffed schools where they receive "zero tolerance" punitive discipline and are taught to "know their place" in society through such practices. Their neighborhoods are groaning from unemployment and sup-pressed wages, inadequate and unaffordable housing, a lack of quality healthcare, and a surplus of debt-inducing medical bills. They are trapped in impoverished ghettos designed by white supremacist policies that began during the Jim Crow era.

This book asks the church to discover a faithful way to live out its vocation within our world, a world devastated by the legacy and contemporary practice of white supremacy and Christian supremacy. It is my hope that this book will lead us toward faithful resistance of injustice in the way of Jesus while remembering the history that shapes our present world. The implied challenge throughout this book is that we must be willing to embody the justice that we, as local churches, desire from the broader society, rather than asking more of society than the church is willing to live itself. This book is a call to reignite the revolutionary faith of Jesus that uncovers the vocation of justice for our own times. It asks us to be intro-spective about our contemporary practices and how they facil-itate justice work on the ground in our own neighborhoods.

Who Will Be a Witness? guides the church toward a non-violent revolutionary faith that bears witness to Jesus, seeking God's deliverance through a visible grassroots community that is mobilizing and organizing itself from below to share love, to seek justice, and to join God's delivering presence. This type of church subversively struggles for shalom and dares to dream of God's new society beyond a world dominated by white supremacy and scarred by the enduring legacy of Christian supremacy.

The earliest Christians understood how their public witness through good deeds in society was central to their faith, and that it was their faithful lives rather than their doctrinal statements that mattered most. It was not good enough to be a believer if you weren't also a doer. How you lived mattered. For example, in AD 256, Cyprian explained it like this, "Beloved . . . we are philosophers not in words but in deeds; we exhibit our wisdom not by our dress, but by truth; we know virtues by their practice rather than boasting of them; we do not speak great things but we live them."[5] This was not the type of faith that was otherworldly or that downplayed how Christians lived in the public square. The church knew that its public witness mattered.

In the sixteenth century, amid the rise of the Protestant Reformation, very different ways of understanding Christian faith clashed. Anabaptists and many communities emerging within the radical wing of the Reformation deeply believed that Christian faith and following Jesus were inseparably bound together. For example, Menno Simons in 1529 famously described his understanding of genuine "evangelical faith" as one that loved and served the most vulnerable of society just as Jesus did himself, doing so while persevering through suffering and persecution under violent Christian supremacy.

> True evangelical faith is of such a nature it cannot lie dormant, but manifests itself out in all kinds of righteousness and works of love; it dies unto the flesh and blood; it destroys all forbidden lusts and desires; it seeks and serves and fears God; it clothes the naked; it feeds the hungry; it comforts the sorrowful; it shelters the destitute; it aids and

consoles the sad; it returns good for evil; it serves those that harm it; it prays for those who persecute it; teaches, admonishes and reproves with the Word of the Lord; it seeks that which is lost; it binds up that which is wounded; it heals that which is diseased and it saves that which is sound; it has become all things to all men. The persecution, suffering and anguish which befalls it for the sake of the truth of the Lord is to it a glorious joy and consolation.[6]

As the antebellum United States ratcheted up its brutality and production of goods through the ongoing enslavement of African people, many black Christians subversively reinterpreted the diseased gospel that was preached, finding it to be nothing more than a counterfeit of the genuine faith of Christianity. The public life of white mainstream Christianity, in their eyes, was the furthest thing possible from the faithfulness seen in the life and teachings of Jesus. It had to be rejected if the public witness Jesus embodied was going to be claimed as their model for discipleship. Sojourner Truth, for example, described the hypocrisy of American Christianity practiced by the proponents of the "peculiar institution" of slavery in this way: "And what is that religion that sanctions, even by its silence, all that is embraced in the 'Peculiar Institution'? If there can be any thing more diametrically opposed to the religion of Jesus, than the working of this soul-killing system—which is as truly sanctioned by the religion of America as are her minsters and churches—we wish to be shown where it can be found."[7]

If Truth found this "soul-killing system" to be "diametrically opposed to the religion of Jesus," Frederick Douglass found it to be equally hypocritical and illegitimate because it was a violent and death-dealing religion, which looked to him nothing like Jesus.

What I have said respecting and against religion, I mean strictly to apply to the slaveholding religion of this land, and with no possible reference to Christianity proper; for, between the Christianity of this land, and the Christianity of Christ, I recognize the widest possible difference—so wide, that to receive the one as good, pure, and holy, is of necessity to reject the other as bad, corrupt, and wicked. To be the friend of the one, is of necessity to be the enemy of the other. I love the pure, peaceable, and impartial Christianity of Christ: I therefore hate the corrupt, slaveholding, women-whipping, cradle-plundering, partial and hypocritical Christianity of this land. Indeed, I can see no reason, but the most deceitful one, for calling the religion of this land Christianity.[8]

What the church needs now is a revolutionary break from its ties to the "hypocritical Christianity of this land," which will require God's deliverance and our repentance in a new direction. The mangled public witness of the church is unfolding while our world needs shalom. I hope to ignite, through this book, a revolutionary break from the Christianity of America's past by reminding the church of the revolutionary public witness of Jesus; by remembering our troubled history as a church that has led us to this present moment; by challenging Christian communities to be the church through worship and justice; by providing concrete entry points into local peacemaking, mobilization, and community organizing, practices of economic Jubilee; and most importantly through a recovery of the greatest commandment, to love God and one's neighbor as yourself. In doing so, we can find deliverance from our whitened and domesticated Jesus, from our legacy of oppression, from our socialized communities that have never known Jesus-shaped nonconformity, and from resentment and punitive inclinations that prevent us from being seized by God's love.

In chapter 1, we will confront the revolutionary clash and strategic resistance of Jesus as he enters Jerusalem and prophetically challenges the Jerusalem establishment for their exploitation of the poor masses, as described in Mark's gospel account. Similarly, chapter 2 will turn our attention to Barabbas, the biblical figure who is contrasted with Jesus in every single gospel account. We will consider why the gospel writers believed it was essential to include this character when telling the Jesus story, a reason that is different from the distorted descriptions of Barabbas we frequently spread in our Western tradition. In the end, this examination of the role of Barabbas in the Gospels will teach us something very important about the revolutionary yet peacemaking way of Jesus.

Chapters 3 and 4 focus on church history and human history and the ways the Western church has detoured from the way of Jesus, as well as the ways black Christians have prophetically spoken truth to power and provided a counter-witness to society. In particular, we will consider the history that led to the emergence of Christian supremacy over society, as well as how that Christian supremacy morphed into colonialism and white supremacy. Then we will grapple with American civil religion and the myth of American exceptionalism, and discuss how the black prophetic tradition provides a more truthful mirror in which the nation might see itself.

Because local congregations often have no idea where to begin in living out their desire to become a just community, I will describe some ways that local gatherings might move toward vocational faithfulness as the church. Therefore, chapters 5 and 6 will peer inside the organization and worship life of the church. In these chapters, we will reimagine the ways we structure our lives and how our belonging in Christ creates space for others. Likewise, there is a challenge concerning the church's worship practices and its relation to the God of deliverance and justice, since our communities ought to be discipling and forming people into our public witness as a just people in the way of Jesus.

Chapter 7 turns our attention to economic concerns, recognizing that poverty is a central but too often neglected concern for Christians. Jubilee economics rooted in Jesus' witness as described in the gospel of Luke are introduced and are particularly reframed in view of Zacchaeus's encounter with Jesus and other similar scriptural narratives.

In chapter 8, I frame the work of struggling for justice by reviving Jesus' language of peacemaking. This chapter is very practical and pragmatic, providing different approaches for working for justice that are both faithful and conducive to working as local congregations in the United States. In particular, nonviolent action theory, mobilizing theory, organizing theory, and some explorations of electoral politics are introduced and are intended to provide initial directions for congregations to consider as they go deeper. I provide theory and recommendations for choosing among these options in conversation with scholarship and my own experiences of pursuing justice through these methods.

Last but certainly not least, I end with a final chapter that reflects on the politics of love. Love for our neighbors ought to be the greatest motivator for why we do what we do. In particular, this chapter considers the political dimensions of the command and call to love. The chapter considers the love gap that is so common when considering particular people groups and demographics in our society. We will learn about love from Augustine, Howard Thurman, Martin Luther King Jr., Jonah, and of course Jesus as we consider the politics of love.

My hope is that the church will move beyond the spiritual platitudes and hypocritical religiosity that have become so common since Christendom began its reign and birthed white supremacy in our world. Now is the time for us to experience God's deliverance and to participate in God's justice. When Dr. King and his friends in Birmingham went out wearing their blue jeans, they signified to a watching world that they were going to be included among God's witnesses. It is time that churches everywhere discern and decide that they too are ready to put on their blue jeans. Let's put on our blue jeans for justice, because our world is groaning. Let's put on our blue jeans for peace, because we have all seen and experienced the cycles of violence that are destroying lives. Let's put on blue jeans for God's deliverance, because there is a better way to live that affirms God's desires and dreams for all God's children. This is an important part of our Christian vocation.

In the black church tradition of call-and-response during the preaching moment, the preacher will often call out, "Can I get a witness?" This provides an opportunity for the congregation to testify if the word resonates with their own experience of God's deliverance in their lives. This book takes that question but twists it. Since we are called to be the church not only when we gather together, but also as we scatter and go out, I am interested in our ongoing testimony by the lives we live all the time. My question is, *Who will be a witness?* It is an invitation to ignite Christian activism and put on our blue jeans in the public square in the way of Jesus, and proposes that we can do so by embodying the good news of Jesus through radical grassroots action as local congregations.

1

TROUBLE WON'T LAST ALWAYS

How long, O Lord, will oppressors prosper? How long will empires crush vulnerable people? How much longer will transnational corporations exploit the poor? How long must we wait, O God, until military powers no longer destroy civilians and create orphans to fend for themselves?" If the writer of Psalm 13 lived in North America today, their prayer might sound something like this.

It seems like mass incarceration, the military industrial complex, and policies that promote mass poverty and an enormous wealth gap are a permanent part of life. When we check in on world news we are overwhelmed by the suffering around the world, with ongoing reports of ecological devastation and disparities in health, education, and housing, as well as a lack of access to healthy food and livable wages for so many of God's beloved. These things seem like fixtures of our world. Sometimes people respond and claim that all these things are appalling, but that's just the way the world is, which suggests we ought to occupy our mind with other things. So is there no hope?

These questions haunt most of the world, even while those who are comfortable continue to maintain concentrated social, cultural, political, economic, and even religious power through the control of the policies and institutions that devastate poor people's lives. The United States of America, despite its myths claiming national innocence, exceptionalism, and divine favor, has played an enormous role in creating human suffering within and beyond its national boundaries. Nationalist propaganda implies that the United States as we know it will be permanent. That it is here to stay, and that it is not changing in any radical fashion. The social order and the current institutions that prop it up, we imagine, are fixed and unchangeable in the way that most people think about God. They tell us that the USA represents justice, equality, and freedom, while erasing the testimony of those who have experienced its structural violence, white supremacy, and poverty. Imperial permanence is the daydream of the elite and the haunting nightmare of those who are trampled upon by the wheels of empire.

However, the United States is not the first empire this world has seen, and the prison and military industrial complexes are not the first institutions that have destroyed lives on massive scales.[1] In fact, the gospel accounts in the New Testament testify that without anyone noticing, an anointed One was born under another empire, and that empire also believed that it was permanent, along with its institutions that propped up the social order. It claimed to be the promise of peace and security to the world as it conquered territory after territory. Under the expansive control of the Roman Empire, a poor Jew was born. Throughout his life he heard about nearby towns destroyed by Rome because of Jewish resistance. He witnessed poverty and exploitation throughout Galilee, and the cooperation of Roman powers and the Jerusalem establishment, which maintained the status quo. According to the gospel writer Mark, "the beginning of the good news" began under these circumstances (Mark 1:1). From Galilee (the ghetto of that ancient society, and away from Jerusalem's centralized power) came Jesus, a man who was baptized by John the Baptist and understood that he was the anointed One whose life gave God great pleasure. He did not come to find fans filled with religious sentimentality, but followers committed in solidarity to a revolutionary movement that bore witness to God's coming reign and new social order that was flipping everything upside down. There the first will be last and the last will be first.

Two thousand years later, the delivering power and presence of Jesus continues to "show up" and "make a way out of no way" for people cornered by the powers and institutions of our world. And the appropriate response to the presence of Jesus is discipleship. The call of Jesus is really quite simple, despite how complicated we have made it by obfuscating that basic Christian vocation. Follow after the way of Jesus. Certainly, there are some more challenging and difficult things to understand in our faith, but their significance pales in comparison to the simple call to follow Jesus in our everyday lives. In fact, the entire New Testament points us in that direction, to the call of discipleship to Jesus Christ. The gospel accounts frequently use the language of "following after" Jesus and of "discipleship," indicating that Jesus' legacy is an invitation to come and follow. The same idea is conveyed in other ways as well. We are told to imitate him, to walk in his footsteps, to

live as he lived, to participate, or share, in the life of Christ, to
die and rise with Christ, to be in Christ, and to have the same
mind that Christ had. We are also told to follow the way of
the Lamb, to hear and follow his voice, to let Christ live in and
through us so that it is no longer us who lives but Christ himself who is made visible in our bodies. And of course we are
told become like him. There are many admonitions to imitate
Jesus and God's characteristics and actions: to love because
he loved, to forgive because he forgave, to show mercy as we
have been shown mercy, to be perfect like God by loving our
enemies. It is clear that there is no Christian vocation more
vital than the call to become Jesus-shaped through discipleship
to the Jesus story and his living presence among us. If we are to
overcome the troubles of life when they come, we must firmly
plant ourselves on the rock of Jesus' teachings according to the
Sermon on the Mount and the four gospel accounts.[2]

It is no wonder then that the church passed down four different accounts of Jesus' life, teachings, ministry, death, and
resurrection. Each account represents the compiling of the
earliest stories and oral traditions about Jesus as they developed in diverse regions in the ancient Greco-Roman world.
As the church collected them together, it rejected attempts to
harmonize them all into one super gospel, but believed instead
that the four gospels altogether were like four legs supporting
a table. With each of their individual theological emphases,
the four accounts bring depth and width to the person of Jesus
and to our vocation of radical discipleship in his way. After a
slow and careful study of the four gospel accounts, that doesn't
impose our twenty-first-century experience onto the text, we
begin to see a revolutionary Messiah who reigned through a
different kind of kingdom, that ushered in God's deliverance
for the poor and oppressed and for anyone experiencing any

kind of life-devouring captivity. He spoke truth to power, subverted law and order when it didn't serve humanity, and was crucified through the cooperation of the powers of Rome and the Jerusalem elite. Yet despite the belief that the nation-state bears the final word over life and death, the early church insists that on the third day after being crucified, Jesus rose again. His disciples spread that world altering news across the known world, risking life and limb to do so.

Matthew's gospel emphasizes Jesus as a new and greater Moses and a teacher of the law as expressed through the Sermon on the Mount. Luke's gospel pays special attention to the way God's reign flips social hierarchies on their head so that the rich are sent away empty-handed and the poor and hungry are filled with good things, and the first are last and the last are first. In Luke's gospel, we see that the Samaritans, vulnerable women, and the exploited and socially stigmatized are prioritized around the Messiah's table. John's gospel tells us that God's Son came from heaven and dwelled among us in glory. His kingdom is not like kingdoms of this world (if so, they would battle and fight like everyone else), but instead God's love was freely shared as Jesus laid down his life for us. It demonstrates how we too ought to lay our lives down for one another as we follow the Lamb of God who takes away the sins of the world, as well as abide in the source of life and yield to the Spirit to guide us as we await Jesus' return. I'll say more about Mark's gospel in a moment.

Even though it is clear that Christian faith demands that we become Jesus' disciples and that we participate in the very life of Christ through the Spirit, sharing in his suffering and death so that we can share in his resurrection, many of us evade Jesus at every opportunity. We have developed a domesticated Christianity in which we are consumed with worshiping Jesus, to the exclusion of a life committed to following him. Our gatherings and celebrations of Jesus are increasingly elaborate productions, while we simultaneously seek to dodge basic discipleship—the gospel of Jesus is just too disruptive to our lives. Jesus is extremely subversive, and we enjoy our status quo lives just as they are. The teachings of Jesus are too radical and hit at the core of who we are, and we prefer our respectable congregational life as it is. The death and resurrection of Jesus have revolutionary implications. We are more comfortable with the belief that Christians in the United States are not meant to actually pursue God' kingdom on earth as it is in heaven or experience genuine backlash from the social order because of Christian allegiance to God's reign. Many American Christians are maintaining an unspoken pact: that as long as everyone else remains silent about the radical call of discipleship articulated in the gospel story, we too will not name the contradictions between our lives and the way of Jesus. As a result, "discipleship" now describes anything generically related to our spirituality that results in a safe and entirely uncontroversial faith.

Readers sometimes believe that the gospels of Mark and John are less radical than Luke and Matthew. This perception is false—in fact, one could argue that Mark and John, if accurately understood, are actually more radical. Luke is a nonviolent revolutionary's dream book because it makes so plain and obvious Jesus' commitments to poor, oppressed, and marginalized people. Mark has some of those stories as well, but there are a lot of themes people simply miss when reading Mark. Much of the edgy and provocative symbolism in Mark goes over the heads of North American readers. Talking about "pigs" and "legion" being cast into the sea in the first century, especially for Jewish listeners, would have evoked a different reaction than it does to our contemporary North American ears. Jesus' first audiences would have heard double meanings in many of the stories, just as Brer Rabbit stories or Negro spirituals frequently contained double meanings for enslaved Africans, meanings that frequently went over the heads of white society. Paying attention to the historical, cultural, and sociopolitical context of the first century, and how Greek, Roman, and Jewish cultures constantly overlap in New Testament texts, provides a window into these ancient stories about Jesus, and the profound understanding early church Christians had about their Messiah.

There is no quantitative measurement of a text's radicalness, but suffice it to say that it is much more revolutionary than most readers recognize. The best book to unveil this, in my perspective, is Ched Myers's *Binding the Strongman*, which uncovers some of the political and anti-imperial symbolism packed into Mark's account.[3] For a more accessible text, consider reading *Say To This Mountain* with others.[4] Mark's narration is fast-paced and action-packed, even in the English translation, and much more so in the original Greek language, which uses *and* or *immediately* so frequently that they haven't all been translated. This is a story that should be retold with voice inflection, plot suspense, and twists and surprises as one might tell a story to a child. Subtle changes occur partway through the story. In particular, careful readers will notice what some scholars call "the messianic secret," which appears in stories that depict Jesus as initially attempting to keep a wrap on his identity to some people. Some have suggested that this is Jesus' attempt at orchestrating the public perception of his movement. Later in the narrative, as Jesus prepares to go to Jerusalem, his vocation and identity is evident and public. I contend that this initial attempt at containing the news of Jesus' identity is actually Jesus' embodiment of a strategic grassroots revolutionary consciousness. Finally, in contrast to the hopeful tone the other three gospel accounts end with, Mark's gospel, assuming it ends at chapter 16, verse 8, as the oldest manuscripts indicate,[5] concludes in a manner that appears to communicate uncertainty, fear, or the feeling that it is unresolved. The story, then, is begging for completion and faithfulness through its readers' own lives.

Readers are supposed to complete Mark's gospel through their own lived discipleship in the way of Jesus. The fear and uncertainty at the end of Mark's gospel wasn't intended to produce despair. My understanding is that Mark's ending would have resonated with Christians in Rome in particular, and especially if they were communities that survived being targeted by Emperor Nero. They would have understood that suffering and persecution were very real possibilities. Following Jesus required stepping out in faith, understanding that there could be very real consequences for following Jesus and identifying as part of a Christian community. Those first readers would have known that it was important to be very careful, since the way of Jesus was inherently subversive. They would need to discern how to proceed in the public square strategically yet faithfully because God's delivering presence had broken into the world through Jesus Christ, and as a result nothing would ever be the same. Under the surveillance of Roman power, in the face of its claims of permanence and its propaganda proclaiming Caesar to be the one who brings good news to the world, providing stability and peace—right there, from below, Jesus preached good news, announcing a kingdom other than Rome. This grassroots messianic reign was where God's deliverance would reach the lives of those desperate for God's new world to come.

MARK 11:1-7, STRATEGIC PREPARATION FOR HIS MESSIANIC DEMONSTRATION

In Mark's narrative, the escalating conflicts with the Jewish and Roman establishment climax as Jesus approaches Jerusalem in the eleventh chapter. Mark tells his readers that as Jesus approached Jerusalem near the Mount of Olives, he sent two of his disciples ahead of the group into a nearby village, instructing them to find a colt that was tied up and to bring it to him so that he could use it to enter the city. A reader should wonder why Jesus wants them to bring a colt? And why does he seem to have a plan already set that just needs to be executed? One way that Mark illuminates the person and ministry of Jesus is precisely through his strategic messianic theatrics. Jesus could have simply walked into the city with his crowd of admirers, but instead, Mark depicts Jesus intentionally orchestrating a plan that required some strategic preparation. And as we will see in a moment, getting a colt rather than a horse was important for the reign of God embodied in his movement. This was all sociopolitical theater being staged. Mark's depiction of Jesus is organized; he has come to Jerusalem as Passover is approaching and he has a plan that he intends to execute. In Mark's telling of the good news, Jesus is a master strategist, carefully executing his messianic demonstration, which begins with obtaining a colt.

Many Christians prefer to think of Jesus as coming to Jerusalem apolitically, solely to die for our sins. Few Sunday schools tell the story in the way that Mark does, unveiling Jesus as a perceptive strategist who is engineering particular responses from people through theatric protest. Nonetheless, that is precisely what we find. Jesus' strategic preparation places a challenge at the feet of the church.

Too often the church leaves the work of sociopolitical strategy to those with greedy motivations, those in search of more money, more power, more influence, more fame. In the gospel of Matthew, ironically, Jesus actually calls his followers to be "wise as serpents" yet "innocent as doves" (Matthew 10:16). We are called to the work of scheming and plotting for good, for God's delivering presence on the earth, for justice, righteousness, and peace in our world. And we do this while refusing to use the evil means that the powerful employ to accomplish their goals. We remain as innocent as doves by employing strategies of peacemaking and nonviolence, by overcoming evil with good, through radical love and prophetic intervention, and through vulnerable noncooperation with anything that clashes with the reign of the Messiah. We are invited to scheme and plot for God and to engage in strategic preparation in the way of Jesus.

We began this book by considering Dr. King's faithful witness which led him to put on his blue jeans and get arrested and jailed in Birmingham in an attempt to keep the movement going. But very few people realize that Project C was the brain child of Wyatt C. Walker, a creative strategist who planned to confront the pressure points of Birmingham, especially the business district. We know how the story ends, with the children filling the streets, arrested by the masses, attacked by dogs, and sprayed with water hoses that ripped off their clothes. The evening news footage of these events horrified the nation and led to further civil rights legislation. But those events didn't happen randomly or coincidentally. They were the result of preparation, planning, and strategy. The goal was to dramatize the structural oppression through creative political theatrics. Often when justice on the large scale occurs, it is because people put their minds together and planned and plotted. Action that leads to victories like these requires intentionality.

Jesus' orchestrating the colt to ride on was itself central to Jesus' intentionally creative demonstration, which is why Mark takes so much narrative plot space to describe the disciples being instructed about obtaining this specific animal.

MARK 11:8-10, STRATEGIC REVOLUTIONARY SYMBOLISM

Mark tells us that after the disciples faithfully followed through with Jesus' strategically orchestrated plan to secure a colt, people threw their cloaks on the animal, which Jesus began to ride. Crowds began to form and spread their cloaks and branches on the road for Jesus to travel upon, responding as if he were royalty beginning a new reign. The political theatrics Jesus designed clearly evoked something deep and profound within the people, who responded to him with cries of "Hosanna!" and "Blessed is the coming kingdom of our ancestor David" (Mark 11:10). Formally, *hosanna* was used for praise, but it literally meant "Save us!" and both meanings are probably being expressed simultaneously at this moment. The people believe that God, using Jesus as their liberator, will restore the kingdom of David. They look to Jesus as their revolutionary savior, the one in whom they have placed all their hopes for deliverance from the oppression, exploitation, and degradation that they experience every day. They believe that a new age for Israel will begin in Jesus, that he will inaugurate restoration and ignite independence from their occupying oppressors. What was it that sparked such radical expectations and hopes from the crowd?

If we are to understand the response of the people, we must recognize Jesus' actions in this moment as the execution of strategic revolutionary symbolism. There are two primary images Jesus is evoking for his Jewish audience that would spark this kind of response. First Jesus is symbolically embodying Zechariah 9:9-10:

> *Rejoice greatly, O daughter Zion!*
> *Shout aloud, O daughter Jerusalem!*
> *Lo, your king comes to you;*
> *triumphant and victorious is he,*
> *humble and riding on a donkey,*
> *on a colt, the foal of a donkey.*
> *He will cut off the chariot from Ephraim*
> *and the war-horse from Jerusalem;*
> *and the battle bow shall be cut off,*
> *and he shall command peace to the nations;*
> *his dominion shall be from sea to sea,*
> *and from the River to the ends of the earth.*

The crowd on the road were Jews who would have understood this messianic text and the meaning of Jesus' dramatized sociopolitical demonstration. Their response indicates that they were filled with faith that God was about to do a new thing, that divine deliverance was unfolding before their eyes. They believed divine intervention was about to be ignited through human faithfulness. The Creator and Sustainer of all things was about to take action in history through this anointed king, giving them ample reason to shout, "Hosanna! Hosanna!"

There is a second very powerful reason for their response as well. The Jews, more than a hundred years prior, had successfully revolted against Syrian oppression. During that revolt, Judas and the Maccabees rode triumphantly into Jerusalem in similar fashion, with palm branches layered on the road before them. By the time of Jesus, the Maccabees were legendary. Because of them, the possibility that God might actually intervene in their affairs through a messianic figure was etched into the minds of the people. In the next chapter we will consider in more depth the movements of revolution and resistance that persisted from the time of the Maccabees all the way up until the Jewish-Roman War around AD 70. The Gospels were written within this historical backdrop.

Jesus' choice to enter Jerusalem in this particular way was loaded with radical symbolism from both Scripture and history. The crowd's response of praise and turning to Jesus for deliverance from their hardships was not coincidental; they had just experienced very strategic revolutionary symbolism. This response evoked in the hearts and minds of the people was exactly the kind of response one would expect, given Jesus' action. Their hopes for deliverance from their oppressors and the restoration of David's kingdom were not out of nowhere; the evoking of their revolutionary hopes was the intended goal of Jesus' symbolic action.

Strategic revolutionary symbolism occurs when a particular social action, political embodiment, or prophetic witness awakens people to the awareness that another social order is possible. Often, empires and those with concentrated power project the impression that they will never cease, and that things will always be as they are. In such conditions, the best option for survival is to align as best as possible with those structural realities. Hope for anything else is often beyond one's imaginative possibilities. We are not able to envision God's dream of a just world for us, but this kind of strategic revolutionary symbolism can begin to foster hope. In the case of Jesus' messianic demonstration, this strategic revolutionary symbolism broke open a subversive hope in God's Messiah and in a new age that was dawning. And so here came Jesus riding on a colt.

As Jesus symbolically fulfilled Scripture and evoked historical consciousness, the people awakened to the Messiah's reign. Despite the risks, many of them began to place their bets that divine intervention was breaking through in the person of Jesus. As Jesus rode, each branch or cloak that was laid down before him represented the desire to break free from captivity to the status quo. Each praise lifted up by a member of the crowd represented the recognition that Caesar or the Jewish establishment was not lord over their lives. Their praise and cries of salvation were directed to the only worthy recipient. Their embodied worship was a revolutionary act of awakening and expectation. They had previously attributed to their current social order the divine attribute of eternal permanence, an idolatrous view. With their awakening to Jesus as the Messiah, they could begin to imagine new possibilities of God's deliverance and for pursuing true justice and righteousness in this world.

Don't miss that the two symbolic images evoked by Jesus' action clash with each other. The Maccabean revolt was a violent overthrow of the system. Zechariah 9:9-10 is a peacemaking liberator that ends "chariots", the "war horse", and the "battle bow" which grounded military power, and instead he brings peace to the nations. They both bring victory and end oppression, but the means are different. Here we find Jesus awakening the people through these powerful symbols of liberation, but ultimately he rides in on a humble colt rather than a military horse. This is God's deliverance, where divine power expressed through human weakness rather than military strength is on display.

A great example of strategic revolutionary symbolism in more recent history occurred in the Salt March that Mahatma Gandhi led against the British in the early twentieth century.

The British Empire had taken complete control over salt in India, so they controlled the production of salt and taxed it as well. In March 1930, Gandhi and seventy companions began the salt campaign, which was a 240-mile walk to the sea at Dandi. Gandhi and his companions stopped at town after town, announcing the campaign, rallying local villagers, and inspiring people to engage in *satyagraha*, a word which translates as "truth-force" and that Gandhi used to describe the force of nonviolent resistance. Thousands and thousands of people caught the vision and joined the mass movement heading for the shore. On April 6, the group arrived at the beach, where Gandhi engaged in a very simple act; he extracted a handful of salt from the ocean. This action was strategic revolutionary symbolism. When Gandhi defied the unjust laws of the British empire by holding up the salt he had taken from the sea, his action had a liberating effect for the consciousness of the people watching. Like dominoes, Indians everywhere began disobeying British claims over salt, boiling seawater and making their own salt in defiance. While this act alone did not end British rule, it did revolutionize the mindset of many people. Freedom became a real possibility. We should never underestimate the power strategic revolutionary symbolism can have in delivering people from passive submission to oppression when enacted through a prophetic witness courageously in public.

MARK 11:11, STRATEGIC DISCERNMENT

Mark tells us that Jesus entered Jerusalem and headed straight for the temple. Those with him must have been thinking that everything was about to go down, that this was the place and time when the Messiah would liberate their homeland. Divine time had taken them to this very moment, it seemed, when the Messiah's reign would go public and be made manifest for the world to see. People's expectations were at a peak, and the crowd's anticipation was bubbling over. From the start of the gospel of Mark until this point, listeners and readers of the story have experienced Jesus engaging in escalating conflict in preparation for this revolutionary climax. Jesus versus the elite Jerusalem Temple establishment was a clash that was inevitable. But unlike Matthew and Luke, which portray Jesus beginning his demonstration the moment he arrives at the temple, Mark tells us that Jesus entered the temple, looked around while scouting out the situation, and then left. It's hard to imagine a more anticlimactic moment.

Mark's narration tells us that rather than taking revolutionary action at the temple right away, Jesus engages in a reconnaissance mission first. He takes notes on the situation, and then discerned that it was too late in the day to initiate what he had planned. This would have been especially puzzling for onlookers because the crowd was with Jesus, ready for action. For those watching, this had to be a terribly disappointing and underwhelming end to what had begun as a revolutionary day.

However, knowing the right time to act is an important feature of Jesus' discernment in Mark's gospel. As mentioned earlier, in Mark we see Jesus frequently trying to keep his identity a secret, because he didn't want to broadcast his messianic intentions for everyone quite yet. Some Christians make distinctions between *chronos* time and *kairos* time in the New Testament, with *chronos* time as more chronological and *kairos* time as the right season or moment for something to occur. Jesus, in this narrative, is strategically discerning his kairos timing. A common proverb in the black Christian community says God is "never on schedule, but always right on time." And those engaging in strategic discernment understand that just because everyone is hyped, does not mean it is the right time to act.

The church needs to pray and seek God to discern our strategic kairos moment for action. We want to strike when the iron is hot, which must always align with when God's delivering presence is active and moving. We want to go with the currents of the Spirit's activity rather than against it. We also want to use wisdom. Engaging in strategic discernment involves using our minds and being conscious of factors that could thwart our ultimate goals. In this case, Jesus' decision was simple; he wouldn't have had the dramatic impact that he wanted in his demonstration had he acted impulsively. Despite the anticlimactic nature of the moment, Jesus and his disciples quickly slipped out of the city and headed back to Bethany for the night.

Dr. King also famously made an unpopular and anticlimactic decision during his work with the southern freedom movement, when he discerned that the consequences of moving forward might work against their ultimate goals. In 1965, Dr. King and the Southern Christian Leadership Conference came to Selma, Alabama, a decision that was already problematic since Alabama was the territory of the Student Nonviolent Coordinating Committee, or SNCC, where this younger and frequently more radical group of young people had already been engaged in grassroots organizing work, registering people to vote and recruiting them to defy white supremacist intimidation. Nonetheless, Dr. King and the SCLC came to Selma. The nonviolent demonstrations there drew national attention very quickly because Sheriff Jim Clark and others from Selma seemed incapable of responding to black people with anything other than blunt and unveiled physical violence. In February, during a smaller evening march, police and troopers

ambushed the crowd, shooting and killing Army veteran Jim-
mie Lee Jackson. Jackson's death came just five days after the
assassination of Malcolm X, who had recently visited Selma.

Movement leaders decided that Jackson's casket would be
walked from Selma to Montgomery, Alabama's capital, as a
symbolic act. While that symbolic action was never carried
out, a march was organized shortly after the funeral. About
five hundred marchers arrived at Selma's Brown Chapel and
began walking two by two, heading to Montgomery. When
they arrived at the Edmund Pettus Bridge, they found it
blocked by waves of white officers and troopers. They proceeded anyway. Then they were warned they had two minutes
to turn around. The marchers persisted, and all hell broke
loose. One trooper yelled, "Get 'em! Get the niggers!"[6] Troopers and officers lunged at the nonviolent and unarmed marchers, setting off tear gas and cracking skulls with their billy
clubs. Many marchers, finding themselves trapped and unable
to make their way through the armed officers, thought they
might die. Eventually, the marchers were able to escape and
return to the church, while those who had been seriously hurt
were taken to Good Samaritan Hospital. This repressive act
of violence against these nonviolent black marchers would be
remembered as Bloody Sunday.[7]

Thousands of people who saw the news footage of the
Bloody Sunday violence came to Selma to support the movement. But the movement leaders received an injunction forbidding them from holding another march. Dr. King and others
felt that they needed to confront the violence with courage,
especially since thousands had joined their struggle, so they
proceeded anyway. Once again, when marchers arrived at
the Edmund Pettus Bridge, they met state troopers waiting
for them. Dr. King had been out of town for the first march,

but he was present and leading the march from the front this time. Seeing the troopers, he stopped, knelt down, and prayed. When he rose to his feet, the marchers behind him were antsy. Many had, ironically, come ready to nonviolently confront the violent "law and order" that kept that city under its thumb. Dr. King, however, discerned that going against the court injunction, rather than waiting to get it reversed and have a legal ruling on their side, would be a short-term win but long-term mistake, and could cripple their ultimate goals. He made the anticlimactic and very unpopular decision to turn the thousands of marchers around and head back to the church. This decision was likely the impetus for the final fracture between SCLC and SNCC, one that would never fully heal.[8]

As Dr. King predicted, they did get the court's approval to demonstrate, so on March 21, 1965, for the third time, nonviolent protesters gathered to march all the way from Selma to Montgomery. This time, the crowd of marchers was very large and included those who came in response to the invitations of Dr. King and others, and federal marshals and troopers escorted them instead of blocking their way. By the time the crowd reached Montgomery, after days of walking and camping, it had grown to over twenty-five thousand people. In Montgomery, Dr. King delivered his famous speech, calling out the words of the Civil War–era hymn, "How long? Not long, because mine eyes have seen the glory of the coming of the Lord, trampling out the vintage where the grapes of wrath are stored. He has loosed the fateful lightning of his terrible swift sword. His truth is marching on. He has sounded forth the trumpets that never call retreat. He is lifting up the hearts of men before His judgment seat. Oh, be swift, my soul, to answer Him. Be jubilant, my feet. Our God is marching on."[9]

MARK 11:12-19, STRATEGIC PROPHETIC DISRUPTION

Mark tells us that while Jesus is leaving Bethany and on his way back to the temple he is hungry. He sees a fig tree in the distance. As Jesus approaches it, he discovers that the plant has produced no fruit. We are told that the reason for the lack of fruit is because it was not the season for figs. Fair enough. But then Jesus does something that to North American sensibilities seems odd and harsh. He curses the tree for having no fruit, so now no one will ever eat from it again. Yes, he curses a fig tree for having no fruit, even though it isn't its season to produce fruit. At first glance, this moment seems like it has nothing to do with the rest of this story. Why would Jesus get upset with a fig tree for not producing fruit when it isn't the right season? That should be a clue to readers that his judgment on the fig tree is symbolic for something more significant. We must continue the story to see how it parallels the fig tree's fate. So Jesus condemns the tree; and then the disciples and Jesus move on and reenter Jerusalem.

Now it is finally time for Jesus to escalate things through a prophetic demonstration. The time has come, and he has the perfect audience for his dramatic political theater. The people's hopes and expectations are upon him. They believe that Jesus will be their liberator. They are hoping that Jesus will restore Israel and that the Jews will finally get national independence. Rome has been a devastatingly powerful empire, and the Jews throughout the Galilean countryside have been experiencing excruciating poverty.

In Scripture, God repeatedly judges oppressive empires. Whether it was Egypt, Babylon, or Assyria, divine judgment against harming the vulnerable was consistent. God judges concentrated power that exploits the oppressed and crushes the poor. With that in view, there is hope that God's Messiah will target the forces and seats of power that have a foot on the necks of the people.

When Jesus finally enters the temple he does not direct his righteous indignation directly toward Rome. Instead, it is the economic, political, and religious practices of the temple that Jesus has come to judge. God has always stood against oppression and exploitation, against imperial domination and concentrated power that crushes the poor, the widow, and the foreigner, and the Jerusalem establishment had become complicit in that very thing. The temple leadership and high priestly families benefited from the temple tax, from their collaboration with Rome, from the sacrifices of the Jews who traveled from all over to worship God. The pillars of power resided in Jerusalem. Jesus does not need to confront an external Babylon when the ways of Babylon (concentrated power and exploitation) are occurring right in the temple by the hands of the Jerusalem power brokers. Jesus holds a mirror up to the rulers and authorities, to the temple bankers, to those profiting off expensively priced animals, and those benefiting from the exploitation of the poor Jewish masses.

Jesus engages in a strategic prophetic disruption of the temple. The evil practices are unveiled for what they are, and Jesus brings God's judgment. For the moment, all business as usual is halted through Jesus' prophetic disruption. The Jerusalem elite certainly would have thought that Jesus' behavior was irresponsible and uncivil. In general, when the status quo is working for one's favor they are inclined to think that disrupting the central institutions of society is always inappropriate and "disrespectful." The intensity with which Jesus damages property and intervenes to disrupt the commercial flow of money would have been described as outrageous and criminal by the authorities. This strategic prophetic disruption by Jesus had three targets. Jesus disrupted the temple overall, shutting down the flow of currency which turned the "house of prayer" into an exploitative marketplace. But even more targeted, his disruption overturned the tables of the moneychangers and the seats of those who sold doves.

Ancient Jews in that Greco-Roman society saw Roman money as dirty and ungodly, so the temple used Jewish/Tyrian currency. The temple created a holier alternative for travelers seeking to offer sacrifice to God. First, understand that worshipers couldn't sacrifice an old or unhealthy animal, because the sacrifice would be inspected to see if it was worthy to be given to God. If the temple priests, who had the final word, decided that it was not worthy, the worshipers would need to purchase a temple animal. However, if the money brought to pay for a sacrificial animal was a Roman coin, it would need to be exchanged for Tyrian coinage. After worshipers converted their currency into temple coins and made their purchase, they would finally have an animal to sacrifice. Between the temple exchange rate and the purchase of the sacrifice, they could easily be exploited twice.

This reminds me of trips to Chuck E. Cheese with my kids. I get to this place designed to entertain kids with food, games, and prizes. But my money is not going to work there; I need to exchange it for Chuck E. Cheese currency. Of course, the amount of money you pay so you can get the exchange seems ridiculous, but it is for the kids, so you just go along with it. You give the kids the Chuck E. Cheese money and they run off and spend it all on games where they receive tickets in return (yes, another currency). This double currency exchange just throws you off because it is hard to calculate its worth at this point. After eating and an hour of play, the kids are tapped dry of coins. So you gather them together and head to the gift store in the corner, where they can turn in their tickets for their prize. As you peruse the options on display you realize quickly there is no perfect sacrificial lamb to pick. To get the most bang for your buck, you convince the kiddos to limit their choice to the best item they can get from the store in exchange for all their tickets. And so, after spending fifty bucks in coins, they each walk out of the store holding an eraser and a tootsie roll. They are smiling and happy, but you leave feeling as if you have just been pickpocketed. It is a terrific scam they run with that giant mouse. Well, these temple worshipers might have felt something like that but worse after moving through the temple system while desiring to do nothing but offer a sacrifice to God. Too often it was a well-oiled machine of concentrated exploitation that squeezed the last bits of money from poor people. Exploitation came through tithes, coin exchanges, and sacrifice, on top of the overall debt these struggling people were entrapped by because of the merciless practices of these wealthy elite families in Jerusalem that denied them their Jubilee.

Do not miss it: the problem wasn't merely that there was buying and selling in God's house. It was that the flow of currency in the temple was going against its vocation and purpose. The temple was supposed to be a place of prayer and worship to God, and it was supposed to form the people of God to be a people of justice. They were supposed to make provisions for the poor, care for the widows and orphans, care for the strangers in the land. Bringing shalom to all people was the vocation of the people of God. But now the economic flow of wealth was creating the haves and the have nots. The Jerusalem power brokers were getting wealthy from the temple offerings. History and archeological evidence indicates that many of these Jerusalem elite families lived in extravagant wealth while the masses of people were malnourished and in deep poverty. The temple, which was meant to be a house of worship for all nations, had become a hideout and refuge for those who used their concentrated power to exploit the poor.

When Jesus said they had turned the temple into a "den of robbers," he is invoking Jeremiah. In Jeremiah 7, centuries before Jesus, there was a prophetic judgment against the temple. The leaders thought they could do no wrong because they were the temple leaders, and they thought they would reign forever. In contrast, the prophetic word to them is that God is coming and will judge them for their mistreatment of the poor and the most vulnerable in society. And so Jesus' strategic prophetic disruption is in fact the culmination and embodiment of that same prophetic judgment from Jeremiah. God in Jesus Christ has come to the temple and stands against all forms of oppression and exploitation. This judgment holds true regardless of whether it is aimed at an external empire or within the very life and institutions of God's people.

Jesus' prophetic disruption and divine intervention in the temple immediately placed people into a moment of dilemma. In a dilemma situation, people are forced to respond one way or the other. There is no distanced apathetic ignoring of God's intervening through prophetic disruption. One must decide how one will respond. Obviously, repentance is the right choice. But those in power rarely are willing to leave their old way of life sustained by the exploitation of others so they can follow Jesus. In that scenario, the dilemma for those who reject repentance becomes whether they will allow the disrupter to continue to demonstrate and denounce their complicity in the establishment, which of course means the person will continue to unveil the injustice for what it really is. Allowing such prophetic witness to go on erodes the foundation of the institution's power and respect. The other option is for those who wield the power to try to put an end to the thing causing them trouble. These temple leaders choose the latter and immediately begin looking for ways to crush this messianic movement by taking out its leader.

There are always consequences for truly engaging in prophetic disruption of this old order. This is because the old order believes it will live forever, and its mangled ethics lead it to do anything at all costs to continue on. This is no surprise to Jesus, though. The empire always strikes back. There is always a backlash to eliminate the threat to power. Jesus understood this well before beginning his revolutionary action. And he expects that his followers would also count the costs and accept the consequences of clashing with the powers of society.

Jesus and the disciples leave after a full day of disruption and a temple takeover of the teaching ministry. Once again, they slip out of the city. The next morning they pass by the fig tree they saw the day before, but now it has withered away. Jesus explains to them that if they have faith, even *this* mountain, referring to the Temple Mount (which would be in view from where they stand), can be thrown into the sea if they believe.[10] That statement and the symbolism of the fig tree leave us with a dangerously subversive pronouncement by Jesus. That is, like the fig tree that was not producing fruit, the temple and its representatives are not producing true fruit. It has lost its holy vocation. It has veered off from its mission. It has missed the mark of its purpose. And now it has been condemned. Ched Myers explains that "the fig tree was a symbol of peace, security, and prosperity in Israel. The fruitful fig tree was a metaphor for God's blessings, while a withering tree symbolized judgment."[11] Therefore just as the fig tree had begun to wither away, so Jesus proclaimed the end to the concentrated power controlled by the temple elite, which will also "dry up." Babylon from without or from within will come to an end, and will not last forever. But do not twist Jesus' judgment. This is not a supersessionist turn; Jewish people will continue to walk in covenant with God, but anytime and anywhere "dens of robbers" rear their ugly head, God stands decisively against them. This was a condemnation of the Jerusalem establishment in power, not a condemnation of all Jews.

God's consistency on this matter throughout Scripture extends divine judgment of the temple in this one moment and presses it outward toward all imperial and institutional "dens of robbers." Every practice of oppression and harm, every institutionalized coercion and exploitation, every hierarchy and form of human domination that exists is caught in the currents of this judgment. The old order won't last always, because Jesus' reign and God's deliverance has begun.

CONCLUSION

In the minds of many American citizens, the United States is God's chosen empire. It is a divine demonstration of justice and liberty. It is exceptional and a beacon of light to the world. And many believe it will last forever. While many have come to this land as a place of refuge and opportunity, it has just as equally been a nightmare for millions of others. For several centuries, Native Americans have been forcibly removed, displaced, attacked, killed, and erased from public memory. Similarly, people of African descent have been forcibly brought here, enslaved, beaten, oppressed, segregated, terrorized, exploited, disinvested, and criminalized. The reality that black and Native American historical memory teaches is that too often it looks like the wicked do triumph, while the blood of the innocent is spilled over and over again in the land.

Yet despite it looking as if things will never change, do not lose hope. My faith and hope are placed in the Messiah who has come and will one day fully establish his reign. I believe in the God who has chosen the weak to shame the strong, and has chosen the things that are considered nothing to shame the things that are considered something (see 1 Corinthians 1:18-31). I believe in a God who has revealed Godself in a radical revolutionary crucified Christ. And in that paradoxical truth I know that God works along the axis of vulnerability and that even though things look gray and grim now, God's deliverance is coming.

So bet on God's delivering presence by joining the Messiah's revolutionary movement. Trust that although it may be dark and late in the midnight hour, God is going to turn it around. Bet on God's justice and righteousness. Bet on the fact that these empires and powers are temporary rather than eternal. Believe that justice will "roll down like waters, and righteousness like an ever-flowing stream" (Amos 5:24). Bet on the messianic reign. Right now, we are struggling. We are struggling against gun violence that kills thousands of people every year unnecessarily. We are struggling against systems designed to incarcerate millions of our people, we are struggling against powerful economic forces that deny families livable wages and leave them in poverty and despair. We are struggling so that people can have housing; so that immigrants without documentation can get sanctuary, and ultimately belonging; so that children growing up in poverty can have access to education and the necessary resources to thrive; so that girls and women can live without the threat of sexual harassment and abuse. What I am saying is that we take this struggle up in the way of the Lamb, because the slain Lamb, at a second glance, is the victorious Lion of Judah (Revelation 5:1-14).

Never forget that rulers, authorities, and thrones in high places are puppets to evil forces that seek to kill, steal, and destroy, but in the final analysis they are nothing but fig trees that will one day wither away and die. So do not be discouraged. Turn your eyes toward our Messiah and say "Hosanna! Hosanna!" Because though we may face hardships and trials, empires, centers of power, and coercive institutions are not permanent. As you follow in the strategic and revolutionary way of Jesus while struggling against the mountains of injustice and exploitation, hear the echoing wisdom of my ancestors, who knew that "trouble don't last always."

2

LIBERATING BARABBAS

AND THE THINGS THAT MAKE FOR PEACE

Next to Jesus, Barabbas might be the most misunderstood person in the Bible. Readers of Scripture frequently sever both Barabbas and Jesus from their first-century sociopolitical context, which distorts their meaning and challenge for the church today. Mainstream Christianity continues to convert Jesus into a status quo religious mascot who provides no hope to people suffering from oppression or seeking God's liberating intervention. This Jesus has been westernized, whitened, and domesticated, particularly when compared to the first-century poor Palestinian Jew who preached good news to the poor and came to "let the oppressed go free" while living under Roman occupation (Luke 4:18-19).

For many people raised in mainstream American Christian communities, the idea of a liberative Jesus not only is strange but also feels misguided. For some, such an idea has nothing to do with Christianity. In American evangelicalism, salvation is often personal and individualistic, is spiritual with few social implications, and is primarily focused on its adherents escaping hell and going to heaven. However, the mainstream American Christian portrait of Jesus is often inconsistent with the Jesus of Matthew, Mark, Luke, and John. The American church must carefully reexamine Jesus in the biblical accounts, which provide the most authoritative witness to the person and character of our resurrected Messiah.

For this chapter I will reexamine one dimension of Jesus' story through a reconsideration of the person named Barabbas in Scripture. This chapter will demonstrate that the gospel portrait of Barabbas is not included merely to serve as a metaphor for atonement theology in which a rebellious people release a sinful murderer in place of a sinless savior. Much more than that, the gospel's highlighting of Barabbas in the Jesus story provides actual sociopolitical analysis. A fresh look at Barabbas, I contend, also reveals Jesus as a nonviolent liberator responding to the earthly conditions of poor and oppressed people. Participating in the delivering presence of this living Messiah leads disciples of Jesus into empathetic joining and intimate presence with the oppressed, while committed to struggling for liberation and the things that make for peace in the way of Jesus.

Mainstream Christianity holds mental projections of Barabbas that are unscriptural yet taken for granted. Speaking to congregations or young people in the classroom, I have asked whether they have ever looked carefully at Barabbas in Scripture. Without fail, most people say no. Apparently, Barabbas is not a popular biblical figure to engage in contemplative reflection or on which to do a close reading. People will sooner study the prayer of Jabez than examine and strengthen their faith and life in Christ by making sense of why Barabbas is present in Jesus' story. This lack of careful consideration, however, has not halted stereotypes and ideological manipulations of Barabbas in mainstream thought.

Widespread sentiments and ideas persist about Barabbas that dehumanize him or turn him into an evangelical foil to Jesus' innocence. I also once perceived Barabbas through the ableist stereotype of a "psycho" serial killer who went town by town, randomly killing innocent people. In Sunday school class he was presented as the epitome of sinful and fallen humanity, rebelling against God, harming himself and others. Most striking, though, was the perception that his murders were random. No logical rhyme or reason was provided for why he was so violent and dangerous. Nothing provoked his action.

Another popular stereotype depicts Barabbas as a brutish barbarian. An online search of Barabbas will result in many images that come straight from movies. Many of these images dehumanize Barabbas as an animalistic brute. Sometimes he is cockeyed, other times he is drooling from the mouth. Frequently his facial features form a stereotype of a crazed man, lacking social cues and civility. One particular movie clip depicts Barabbas laughing uncontrollably while bound in chains, suggesting again that his atypical mental state led him to this destination. Taken collectively, the messaging is clear; Barabbas is an evil and dangerous animalistic brute, a madman lacking logical thinking. Scripture might not be the primary source for these Barabbas portraits, but they are powerful controlling images nonetheless.

In mainstream American evangelical theology, Barabbas usually has a more sophisticated role, yet this approach still ignores the sociopolitical focus provided in Scripture. Evangelicals often understand Barabbas as Jesus' foil, which is correct. It is the way the two are related to each other that needs reexamination. In this framing, the primary subject that matters most is Jesus' innocence (referring to his sinless life), as opposed to Barabbas's sinfulness as a murderer (referring to his guilty status under God's law). The dominant atonement theology of mainstream evangelicalism is not Christus Victor (Christ the Victor), in which Christ is demonstrated to be victorious over sin, death, Satan, the rulers and authorities, and the evil forces of this world that keep humanity in captivity.[1] Many evangelicals prefer the penal substitutionary atonement model, emphasizing that Jesus took the place of punishment under God's law that humanity deserved. This theological approach is often understood to have its primary origins in Anselm's satisfaction theory which was further changed and developed by John Calvin's atonement theory.[2]

The kind of atonement theology adopted matters, in this case because the penal substitution model provides the framework for interpretation that directs how Barabbas is understood for many evangelicals. Barabbas, in this model, represents all of sinful and guilty humanity that deserves the divine penalty of death, but instead Jesus takes his (and our) place on the cross as a substitution.[3] This atonement model does not demand one ignore the sociopolitical cues in the text, but it tends to have that result. Jesus' taking our place on the cross is interpreted as an individual transaction, with Jesus providing spiritual salvation from God's wrath with no liberative consequences for sociopolitical conditions. Ultimately, Jesus' substitution is often understood in this theory to provide Christians with salvation from hell and an escape to a spiritual heaven. In this model, Jesus' salvation has little to do with social concerns like the human condition under oppression and violence on earth. Barabbas, in this theological framework, is a sophisticated way to dramatize Jesus' substitutionary atonement for sinful and guilty humanity.

I suggest that Barabbas needs reconsideration. As noted, popular stereotypes portray him as an animalistic brute, a "psycho" serial killer, and a dangerous murderer randomly taking life without reason. American evangelical theology is often more sophisticated. Often drawing from an individualistic and otherworldly framework coupled with commitments to a penal substitutionary atonement model, this theological system uses Barabbas to bolster itself. However, in the process, the sociopolitical focus surrounding Barabbas (and Jesus) that is actually recorded in the Bible continues to be ignored. The result is that Barabbas's presence in Scripture continues to be distorted, domesticated, and misdirected away from what Scripture suggests to us. In doing so, Jesus also continues to be distorted, domesticated, and misdirected away from how the biblical narrative reveals his liberative significance.

Getting familiar with some historical background helps illuminate often missed features of the Jesus narratives. Such familiarization prepares readers to reconsider Barabbas according to biblical accounts. A reconsideration of Barabbas also helps to better understand Jesus. After those steps, this chapter will conclude by articulating how empathizing with Barabbas aids us in living Jesus-shaped empathetic solidarity through intimate joining and liberative struggle with oppressed communities facing oppression, poverty, and death-dealing violence.

REVOLUTION WAS IN THE AIR

Revolution was in the air well before, and well after, Jesus and Barabbas walked the earth. Getting a glimpse of this history will help contextualize the life and words of these two men. Barabbas and Jesus responded to the death-dealing threats that overshadowed their people's lives every day. Likewise, when these gospel accounts of Jesus were recorded, imperial dangers continued to exist. When scholars consider the dating of the Gospels, a big concern is whether they were written before, during, or after the Jewish-Roman War. The war was the culmination of Jewish resistance that persisted for generations. In reality, the anti-imperial spirit traces all the way back to the exodus story in Hebrew Scripture, followed by life under Babylon, Assyria, and Persia. For our purposes, it will suffice to take snapshots beginning with the Maccabees.

By the time of Jesus, the Maccabees were larger-than-life legends. In 164 BC, while under the rule of Syria, the Maccabees led a surprisingly successful revolt. As an act of religious and sociopolitical resistance to overreaching foreign powers, the Jews cast out their oppressors. It began while taking a stand against an imposition on their religious practices and a takeover of the temple. Not all Jews were willing to accept this imposition, and a revolution was born. However, once the freedom struggle started unrolling, complete political independence became the new goal. Their victory ushered in the Hasmonean dynasty and created a new Jewish holiday; Hanukkah. This dynasty would continue ruling for about a hundred years, formally ending in 63 BC. After the dynasty ended, their revolution and reign would continue to shape Jewish radical political imagination and subversive dreams of a messianic revolt. The Maccabees fostered Jewish loyalty to the Torah, a willingness to accept martyrdom ("take up your cross"), uncompromising resistance when foreign powers crossed a line, and violent revolutionary action, believing God would intervene on their behalf. It would be mistaken to understand such sociopolitical action as merely secular revolution like the revolts derived from the Enlightenment in the West. Not so. They sought to participate in God's liberation as demonstrated through the Maccabees as well as the exodus. Salvation for them had a thicker and more holistic meaning than most Western theologies (especially compared to evangelicalism).[4]

In 63 BC, the Roman Empire took over, causing the end of the Hasmonean dynasty. The empire appointed puppet kings in their place, but they were a hollow shell compared to true independence under God's rule. There would be numerous clashes with the Romans moving forward. Sporadic revolts and acts of Jewish resistance would reoccur in different regions. The mass poverty and economic exploitation that people experienced resulted in the emergence of the *lestai* brigands, or bandits. Facing impoverishment, these revolutionaries strategically robbed the wealthy of their riches as defiant acts throughout the first century. Hyper-individualism might lead some to think of stealing only in terms of personal immorality. However, when an oppressive society and the weight of its unjust institutions are stacked against you, and when "law and order" is organized around your community's exploitation and slow death, then these responses are often enacted as defiant acts of resistance to a society that puts its foot on your throat and calls it benevolence. Such was the case for these bandits living under empire and experiencing devastating poverty.

There were many acts of resistance around Jesus' lifetime as well. In fact, Galilee was fertile soil for revolutionaries to be born. Around AD 6, Judas of Galilee led an infamous revolt against Rome. In that struggle, he was encouraging Jews not to participate in the census and not to pay taxes to the empire. While the gospel of Luke tries hard not to overtly sound anti-imperial, if you read between the lines of Jesus' birth story, one can see the sociopolitical occupation and exploitation of the people in full manifestation as Mary and Joseph head to Bethlehem for the census. Historically, we know of other acts of Jewish resistance during the time of Jesus. There were multiple acts of Jewish resistance, as well as imperial backlash, under the governing watch of Pilate between AD 26 and 36. Revolts often turned into bloody massacres. In AD 48, twenty thousand Jews were murdered under Cumanus during a revolt. New resistance groups would continue to emerge throughout the first century. In the middle of that century, the Sicarii, or "dagger men," emerged. They became a serious Jewish resistance movement seeking liberation.

The Jewish sect that is most associated with seeking liberation from Roman oppression is the Zealots. Despite the name recognition of this group, scholars debate whether the Zealots actually existed during the time of Jesus. It is argued that the usage of the term *zealot* is anachronistic in the gospel accounts. For our purposes, it matters very little if the formal group called the Zealots had formed during the time of Jesus, since it is clear the revolutionary spirit that would eventually lead to the formation of the Zealots was already in place during Jesus' time. When the gospel writers use the term *zealot* to describe a revolutionary-minded disciple of Jesus, we get the point even if that term was not yet functioning in that way until the gospel accounts were written a few decades later.

That aside, revolutionary zeal culminated in the forming of the Zealots, who, alongside other groups like the Sicarii, fought against Rome in the Jewish-Roman War beginning in AD 66.

Were they freedom fighters? Yes, but they were also acting by faith that God would deliver Israel from their enemies as God had done in the past. They were zealous for God and ready to cooperate with God for Israel's liberation. Unfortunately, the Jews were completely put down and slaughtered in Jerusalem by the Roman forces. By AD 70 it was all over. They were also defeated because of internal fighting and battling between competing revolutionary Jewish sects. It was a bloody and horrifying loss. The temple was completely destroyed. About six thousand Jews were crucified as a public spectacle to show everyone else what happens when people resist Rome.[5]

While the Jewish-Roman War occurred after Jesus' lifetime, it is important to note that the gospel narratives record Jesus as predicting its coming. Jesus suggests that it happens because the people do not choose his way. Revolution was in the air long before Jesus or Barabbas lived; it repeatedly occurred while they lived; and those movements would coalesce into a much larger war with Rome after their lifetimes. The importance of this sociopolitical backdrop is vital to understanding the gospel accounts. Understanding this historical context helps readers make sense of what the gospel writers want us to know about who Barabbas was (as well as Jesus).

LIBERATING BARABBAS

Despite the mainstream stereotypical images that suggest Barabbas was a foaming-at-the-mouth cockeyed serial killer, or the evangelical temptation to force his meaning to fit this man exclusively into a penal substitution model of atonement, Scripture has a different emphasis. The scriptural record will be our primary authority for reflecting on the meaning of Barabbas. The task for us is to take seriously how Barabbas is described by the gospel writers. Keep track of this concern moving forward: Is there a specific characteristic or description of Barabbas that is central to the biblical accounts? Next, does our knowledge of the historical background enhance our reading and interpretation? What might the audience have heard and understood when these scriptural passages were first written? Soon we will discover that Barabbas, as described in the Bible, was a revolutionary and liberating figure.

Every gospel writer has something to say about Barabbas. This is not an insignificant observation. There are only a handful of biblical units that appear in all four gospels of Matthew, Mark, Luke, and John. Yet at the end of the gospel accounts, Barabbas shows up every single time. Barabbas is important. Contrast it to Jesus' birth. Christmas, which recognizes Jesus' birth, is easily the biggest celebration in the United States. Only two gospel writers write about the birth of Jesus. Even then, they do so differently, with varying purposes. Barabbas, on the other hand, consistently emerges right before Jesus is crucified.

The gospel of Mark, thought by most scholars to be the oldest gospel account, is definitive about Barabbas's revolutionary involvement.[6] In Mark 14, Jesus holds the Last Supper with his disciples, and goes to Gethsemane, where he is betrayed. He is condemned by the Jerusalem establishment and then condemned by Pilate. It is in the context of Pilate questioning and condemning Jesus that Barabbas makes his first appearance in the story. The gospel of Mark writes, "Now a man called Barabbas was in prison with the rebels who had committed murder during the insurrection" (Mark 15:7).[7]

Barabbas, translated as "Son of the Father," was arrested as an insurrectionist. This means that he resisted the imperial forces that were crushing his community. Barabbas, however, was not a lone ranger in this work; he was participating in a broader insurrection. His acts of murder should be understood only in light of this insurrection. He was not killing people randomly but was participating in Jewish revolt. Ultimately, in Mark 15:11-15, we are told that Pilate provides a customary option of release for Jesus, but the leaders convince the crowds to choose Barabbas for release. He was a political prisoner of a well-known insurrection, according to the story, and is now being released. Barabbas is an insurrectionist and freedom fighter who was not opposed to utilizing religious violence to gain victory. Gospel of Mark scholar Ched Meyers explains Barabbas's place in this account:

> Mark describes Barabbas in a manner that had concrete historical signification: as a Sicarius terrorist. . . . There was constant insurrectionary activity in Jerusalem during this period. What Mark calls "murder" . . . would have been characteristic of the modus operandi of the Sicarii . . . , or "dagger men," who were infamous for their stealth in political assassination. Thus Mark's narrative concern here is to dramatize the choice. Jesus and Barabbas each represent fundamentally different kinds of revolutionary practice, violent and nonviolent, both of which have led to a common fate: prison and impending execution.[8]

In the gospel of Luke, Barabbas appears during Pilate's examination of Jesus. Pilate is concerned with particular charges brought against Jesus. We will explore these charges later, but for now it suffices to say that Jesus is found innocent of the charges. Luke portrays Pilate as the most sympathetic. Right as Pilate is about to have Jesus beaten and released, the people respond:

> Then they all shouted out together, "Away with this fellow! Release Barabbas for us!" (This was a man who had been put in prison for an insurrection that had taken place in the city, and for murder.) (Luke 23:18-19)[9]

Barabbas is only mentioned one more time in Luke's account. It is a repeat of the sociopolitical identity and activity of Barabbas, who is now being freed by Pilate: "He released the man they asked for, the one who had been put in prison for insurrection and murder, and he handed Jesus over as they wished" (v. 25).[10]

We will consider Matthew's narration of Barabbas later, but right now we turn to John's account. Some might be tempted to interpret the gospel of John as hovering above temporal and earthly concerns. This is because it has an explicitly theological portrait compared to the more subtle theological narratives of the synoptic gospels; nonetheless, the apolitical stereotype is a poor reading. Even the Johannine account turns the focus to Barabbas's political act of resistance rather than dramatize his sinful and guilty status before God. Right before Barabbas's introduction, we find Pilate engaging the Jerusalem establishment leaders. He mocks them by encouraging them to execute justice for themselves, when he knows good and well that Rome does not permit them to execute their own law and justice. They must admit their helplessness in the situation: "We are not permitted to put anyone to death" (John 18:31).[11] Then comes an exchange between Jesus and Pilate. John, of all the gospel writers, portrays Jesus as the most defiant with Pilate. The primary concern for Pilate is whether Jesus considers himself a king. Jesus does not answer the question. By the end of their exchange, Pilate is now asking Jesus about the nature of truth. This initiates Pilate's referencing the custom of releasing someone for Passover. He mockingly says, "Do you want me to release for you the King of the Jews?" The people respond resolutely: "They shouted in reply, 'Not this man, but Barabbas!' Now Barabbas was a bandit" (v. 40).[12]

Some translations say that Barabbas had taken part "in an insurrection." That is an excellent dynamic equivalent of ideas, although the NRSV provides a more literal translation with "bandit" from *lestai*. But given how the word was used at the time, *lestai* does connote "insurrectionist."[13] John includes no mention of Barabbas other than this one description. One might have expected an explication of Jesus as a spotless lamb in relation to Barabbas's sinfulness. We have none of that. For the gospel of John, Barabbas's sociopolitical act of resistance is what matters for the Jesus story.

It is fair now to begin deconstructing false depictions of Barabbas. He is not a killer out of one's worst nightmare, he is not an animalistic brute, a random and stereotypically crazed serial murderer, nor is he thoughtless and merely acting out of base instincts. Nor is Barabbas merely a foil to Jesus' sinless life (although that is certainly closer than the previous options); instead he was a Jew who sought to engage in insurrection as a religious freedom fighter, believing his resistance aligned with how God had acted on Israel's behalf in the past. We must think of Barabbas more like Nat Turner or Thomas Müntzer and less like the Joker or the Zodiac Killer.[14] We should interpret him as frustrated and angry that oppressors occupied his land, mocked his God, and exploited his people. He dreamed of a restored Israel standing tall next to its neighbors. He wanted shalom to be established and was willing to risk his life in its pursuit. This sociopolitical portrait of Barabbas has been narrated repeatedly in the Gospels. To dilute, domesticate, or misdirect this simple and clearly stated aspect of Barabbas is not only problematic; it also affects our understanding about an essential dimension of who Jesus was and is today.

Ironically, Jesus' disciples also responded in fashion similar to that of Barabbas. Jesus routinely said revolutionary things, pronouncing good news for the poor and oppressed. Moreover, the disciples eventually recognize Jesus to be the Messiah. Our twenty-first-century sensibilities miss Jesus' first-century sociopolitical relevance, which emboldened the disciples toward revolutionary struggle. Just remember the response of Jesus' disciples when he is arrested. All four gospel writers portray the disciples as ready for insurrection. During Jesus' arrest the disciples ask, "Lord, should we strike with the sword?" (Luke 22:49).[15] According to Matthew 26:47-56; Mark 14:43-52; and Luke 22:47-53, an unnamed disciple cuts off the ear of a servant of the chief priest. The gospel of John, however, snitches on Peter as the one who tries to kick off the rebellion (John 18:10). It is clear that the disciples have their own revolutionary aspirations. These radical commitments are the result of witnessing the teachings and ministry enacted in Jesus' life.

One can finally make sense of the charges leveled against Jesus in Luke's account. As mentioned earlier, most evangelical theologies are focused on Jesus' innocence, which is language found in the gospel of Luke. However, when many evangelicals refer to Jesus' innocence, they usually mean Jesus' sinless divine life. A careful reading of the charges placed against Jesus in the gospel of Luke demonstrates that the concern is not whether Jesus lived a sinless and perfect life but whether he is guilty of the political charges made against him. In Luke 22:52, as Jesus is about to be arrested, it states, "Then Jesus said to the chief priests, the officers of the temple police, and the elders who had come for him, 'Have you come out with swords and clubs as if I were a bandit?'"[16] The NIV translates this as "Am I leading a rebellion, that you have come with swords and clubs?" The parading of armed power to arrest Jesus is something that would be expected for a political revolutionary. It is interesting that Jesus does not exactly answer his own question. Jesus is not involved in a revolution in the traditional sense, but has inaugurated the reign of God, a new social order on earth, which is revolutionary and threatens the foundations of the old order.

The charges leveled against Jesus while before Pilate are sociopolitical acts against the empire. Here is the first charge: "We found this man subverting our nation, forbidding us to pay the tribute tax to Caesar and claiming that he himself is Christ, a king" (Luke 23:2 NET). This was false on the surface but true on a deeper level. Pilate asks for himself, "Are you the king of the Jews?" However, he continues to see Jesus as innocent of this charge. "But they persisted in saying, 'He incites the people by teaching throughout all Judea. It started in Galilee and ended up here!'" (vv. 3, 5 NET). Jesus is then sent to Herod, where he is mocked and then sent back to Pilate. Again, for Pilate, the issue is whether he is innocent or guilty of the charge put before him. Therefore, Pilate says, "You brought me this man as one who was misleading the people. When I examined him before you, I did not find this man guilty of anything you accused him of doing" (v. 14 NET). The concern is not whether Jesus had a sinless life (whether true or not), Luke's focus is on his innocence in relation to the sociopolitical charges brought against him. Is Jesus a threat to the present social order?

JESUS BARABBAS OR JESUS THE CHRIST?

Matthew's account of Barabbas will help us pull these various arguments together to consider the often ignored sociopolitical meaning of Jesus. In Matthew 26, Jesus is betrayed by Judas, and then approached by a crowd carrying swords and clubs. Here, according to Matthew, "one of those with Jesus put his hand on his sword, drew it, and struck the slave of the high priest" (v. 51). Jesus, however, does not recognize this revolutionary approach as compatible with the reign of God he is inaugurating. In John's account, Jesus explains to Pilate, "If my kingdom were from this world, my followers would be fighting to keep me from being handed over to the Jews" (John 18:36).[17] In Matthew 26:52, Jesus says to his disciples, "Put your sword back into its place; for all who take the sword will perish by the sword."[18] Violent revolution is incompatible with the way of Jesus and leads to destruction. At other times, Jesus directly suggests that the destruction from the Jewish-Roman War will fall upon Jerusalem for the path they have chosen.

Once again, Jesus asks them why they have come so heavily armed to arrest him, "as though I were a bandit?" (Matthew 26:55). Jesus is taken to the Jewish establishment leaders, where charges are leveled against him. Matthew's emphasis is less explicitly concerned with the anti-imperial implications of Jesus as seen in Luke, but it is still attuned to sociopolitical concerns. The central focus is whether Jesus is God's anointed Messiah of Israel. They pressure Jesus, saying, "I put you under oath before the living God, tell us if you are the Messiah, the Son of God" (v. 63).[19] Jesus does not answer the question but instead quotes from Daniel 7:13 and Psalm 110:1, implying that he is. It is on the charge of claiming to be the Messiah and King that they seek his execution.

During Jesus' interrogation before Pilate, Barabbas is introduced in Matthew for the first time. Matthew provides a longer unit with Barabbas but is completely focused on his relation to Jesus. We are told immediately that Barabbas is "a notorious prisoner." Yet Matthew narrates Barabbas's presence more provocatively than ending there. Among the oldest manuscripts of Matthew, we are told that Barabbas is "called

Jesus Barabbas." However, later scribes omit "Jesus" as part of Barabbas's name in the gospel of Matthew. Now some contemporary translations have left out "Jesus" as part of Barabbas's name, like the King James Version; in contrast, the NRSV, NET and the latest NIV translation include it. Omitting "Jesus" from Barabbas's name probably was an attempt to honor Jesus. Unfortunately, omitting Jesus from Barabbas's name leaves out some of the rhetorical punch:

> Now at the festival the governor was accustomed to release a prisoner for the crowd, anyone whom they wanted. At that time they had a notorious prisoner, called Jesus Barabbas. So after they had gathered, Pilate said to them, "Whom do you want me to release for you, Jesus Barabbas or Jesus who is called the Messiah?" . . . Now the chief priests and the elders persuaded the crowds to ask for Barabbas and to have Jesus killed. The governor again said to them, "Which of the two do you want me to release for you?" And they said, "Barabbas." Pilate said to them, "Then what should I do with Jesus who is called the Messiah?" All of them said, "Let him be crucified!" . . . So he released Barabbas for them; and after flogging Jesus, he handed him over to be crucified. (Matthew 27:15-17, 20-22, 26)[20]

The contrast between Jesus Barabbas and Jesus the Messiah leaves us with a choice between two revolutionaries, offering two paths to liberation. Barabbas already had a proven record of insurrection. Like the disciples, he was tired of his people being humiliated, he was tired of the excruciating poverty, and he was tired of witnessing Roman domination over his people. And Barabbas had already put his own life on the line before. He was "notorious" for his revolutionary activity. It was Passover weekend and he fit the Maccabean mold more than Jesus, who seems to have folded before the powers right when the revolutionary moment had come.

Of course, Jesus had not been a status quo religionist. Jesus courageously came to Jerusalem and defiantly clashed with the establishment rulers and authorities. In fact, he called them a "den of thieves" for their participation in the concentrated exploitation of the people. Jesus hungered for a just and righteous world. We know he preached a radical message to the poor, condemned the wealthy, and invited people to new life organized around himself. Preaching the kingdom of God was subversive. However, his "revolutionary" reign did not justify religious violence. His path meant enduring suffering as the faithful consequence that comes with accepting God's intervening liberation. The visible manifestation of Jesus' way is demonstrated in the reality that he would sooner be crucified than crucify his enemies. No matter how radical Jesus was, one can imagine why not everyone would be convinced that God's victory would unfold through a crucified Christ.

Jesus' message was revolutionary good news for the poor. Jesus, in Luke, offers his messianic manifesto in Luke 4:18-19:

> The Spirit of the Lord is upon me,
> because he has anointed me
>   to bring good news to the poor.
> He has sent me to proclaim release to the captives
> and recovery of sight to the blind,
>   to let the oppressed go free,
> to proclaim the year of the Lord's favor.

Throughout Luke-Acts we are told stories about several wealthy people. Some voluntarily lay down their riches, while others are unwilling to redistribute it with others on behalf of the poor: examples include the rich young ruler, Zacchaeus, the rich man and Lazarus, the rich fool who hoarded resources, Barnabas, and Ananias and Sapphira. In the gospel narratives, Jesus is shown to privilege in his upside-down kingdom the least, the last, and the lost. It is surprising how ethnic outsiders and Samaritans, vulnerable women, lepers, and the poor hungry masses are prioritized in Jesus' new order manifesting on the earth. Other books have tackled this subject more thoroughly, but for now we can say that the politics of Jesus were revolutionary.[21]

We ought not miss the liberative and revolutionary relevance of Jesus and Barabbas. Each offers something concrete for the here and now, and both are Jews with a holistic understanding of liberation that would never split the spiritual apart from the social. A common mistake at this juncture would be to suggest that Barabbas was for an earthly kingdom, while Jesus had an exclusively spiritual kingdom in mind. That is scriptural malpractice, and the Bible never suggests anything close to that. In fact, Jesus' teachings and ministry do not make sense within a "spiritual only" framework. Jesus explicitly teaches his disciples to pray that the kingdom come "on earth" as it is in heaven. Denominational or ecclesial doctrine ought not override Jesus' own teaching. Both Jesus and Barabbas have implications for how we organize our lives on earth.

We get a hint of this holistic meaning of liberation when we take the name of Jesus literally. Jesus is Joshua, or Yeshua, "the one who saves." Both Jesus the Christ and Jesus Barabbas are given names that identify them as the one who saves. This is not a thin, watered-down salvation only good for individuals, a salvation having merely spiritual implications, or a salvation only able to spare us from hell so we can escape to heaven. This is salvation in the tradition of God's intervening in the life of Israel. This salvation is thicker and holistic, touching every area of our lives. This is divine deliverance that saves us from anything that holds us captive. When both of them are identified as Jesus, we are confronted with a choice between what kind of liberator we will trust and follow in our own lives. Who can save us? Will we have faith in God's Messiah when violence seems to make the world go round? Or will we take up the way of Barabbas which makes sense to us? Violence, the logic goes, only listens to more forceful violence. Who can save you? Who will you follow? Who will be your liberator? I believe you have to feel the lure of violent resistance before you really understand the liberating way of Jesus.

That is why Jesus should not be contrasted to Barabbas carelessly. They are not opposed to each other in all things. Jesus empathizes with every Barabbas of the world. His own disciples had the spirit of Barabbas in them, because they cared about the oppression of the people and wanted to join in God's liberating intervention. Very little separated Jesus' disciples from Barabbas. Jesus intimately understands Barabbas and empathetically journeys in solidarity with his oppressed community. Jesus disagrees that Barabbas's method of violence is a fruitful path to liberation and peace, but he also identified with, healed, and spoke up for the most vulnerable of society through his joined presence among them and sought deliverance from whatever kept the people bound.

Jesus' response to those who chose violence as the means for liberation, instead of shalom-shaped deliverance on earth, was not condemnation but lament. Jesus empathized with the revolutionaries and desired they become peacemakers in his way in society. The coming loss of life and the destruction of Jerusalem from the Jewish-Roman War pained Jesus tremendously to the point of deep empathetic lament:

> Now when Jesus approached and saw the city, he wept over it, saying, "If you had only known on this day, even

you, the things that make for peace! But now they are hidden from your eyes. For the days will come upon you when your enemies will build an embankment against you and surround you and close in on you from every side. They will demolish you—you and your children within your walls—and they will not leave within you one stone on top of another, because you did not recognize the time of your visitation from God." (Luke 19:41-44 NET)

The temptation for those who want to justify violence is to spiritualize or avoid Jesus' radical message so that it has no earthly demand on our lives. On the other hand, the temptation of principled and doctrinal pacifists is to apathetically condemn oppressed people's revolutionary methods from the sidelines of comfort. The distance from the oppressed, the condemnation of the oppressed, and the apathy to the lived social conditions of the oppressed are all out of alignment with the way of Jesus. That is not participating in God's choosing of the vulnerable, weak, and oppressed of our world as sites of divine vocation and deliverance (1 Corinthians 1:18-31). Only when we empathize with every Barabbas in our midst through actual joining of life, sharing intimately in suffering, and taking up our cross in the struggle for God's dream of a new reign can we grasp the things that make for peace that Jesus calls us to live.

The things that make for peace will never be found on the sidelines, and they won't be found through condemning how others deal with oppression that does not affect you, but they do demand empathetic solidarity and liberative struggle that intimately joins people living on the underside of the empire. There we find both Barabbas and Jesus caught in the whirlwinds of the establishment and under the punitive control of the empire. Moreover, each desires liberation and ultimate shalom.

CONCLUSION

Barabbas has been (intentionally?) mischaracterized and misunderstood in many Christian communities. He has been dehumanized, used as an ideological tool to fit into elaborate theological systems, and the result is that Scripture's portrayal of him is ignored. The four gospels are consistent; Barabbas was a political prisoner held for his participation in a Jewish insurrection against oppressors. Barabbas sought liberation and freedom. His understanding was not unique, since God's liberation is embedded into the story found in the Hebrew Scriptures of Israel's journey with God. Ignoring the long history of Jewish resistance inevitably leaves readers missing key aspects of the Jesus story as well (of which we have only scratched the surface). However, not only have we missed the revolutionary role of Barabbas, but in renarrating his story for other purposes, the church developed one more trick to disregard the revolutionary vocation of Jesus. Once again, the church is able to continue on as the church of the status quo, of the establishment, of the empire, without recognizing the obvious contradictions with the life and teachings of Jesus.

Barabbas's presence in the gospel story leaves us wrestling with the sociopolitical implications of Jesus' messiahship. If he is the anointed One, and if he claimed that the new society was "here," "near," and "among them" while injustice and oppression persisted, what does that mean for his disciples? It has been argued here that Jesus rejected the method of violent revolution as God's liberation, but he did not reject the oppressed and their desire for liberation. The entire New Testament repeatedly invites us to follow Jesus, to walk in his footsteps, to become his disciples, to share in his life, death, and resurrection, and to obey his teachings. The big secret that has been kept from most of the church is not only that this is what being a Christian is, but that the way of Jesus reveals the revolutionary "things that make for peace." Jesus is liberation and is the way of liberation. And his way includes empathetic solidarity that intimately joins oppressed and vulnerable people in liberative struggle against that which comes to steal, kill, and destroy life. We are all invited to participate in the liberative things that make for peace.

The things that make for peace are not self-evident or taken-for-granted church doctrines. The things that make for peace are the exercise of faith in God's liberation and peacemaking on earth, even amid a social order organized around the strategic and systemic use of state violence. The things that make for peace include the practice of empathetic solidarity that intimately joins the crucified of the world through presence. The things that make for peace confront and clash with the establishment and the dens of exploitation and are willing to accept the consequences for such faithful resistance. The things that make for peace lead us to visibly embody the radical story of Jesus before our neighbors, manifesting God's reign on the underside of the empire. And strangely, it is a revolutionary named Barabbas who helps us see the things that make for peace once more. When we liberate Barabbas from our own mental frameworks, we see Jesus anew and are graced with the opportunity of experiencing God's deliverance from status quo religion. When we liberate Barabbas, the doors of the church are opened as we are invited to encounter afresh the revolutionary Messiah, who is able to save, deliver, and liberate all of us from every captivity and stronghold and continues to invite each of us to join the Jesus-shaped struggle toward God's shalom.

3

THE SUPREMACIST CAPTIVITY OF THE CHURCH

Christianity supremacy birthed white supremacy into our world and corrupted our discipleship to Jesus. Two unforgettable experiences uncovered for me how mangled Christian formation is in America. These experiences pulled the curtain back on the church's ongoing captivity to supremacist socialization, which often means holding racialized and nationalistic commitments above clinging to the life and teachings of Jesus.

CHAPEL WITH JOHN DEAR

I was a sophomore in the fall of 2001. My second year of college was my most social year. I successfully navigated the culture shock of being a black male at a predominately white Christian institution. Yes, I learned how to survive, but more so, I learned how to cultivate authentic relationships with folks across boundaries of race, class, and culture. My sense of our shared humanity and faith felt strongest in the fall of 2001.

One unifying experience that fall was processing the September 11, 2001, terrorist attacks that targeted sites of political, economic, and military power in the United States. I remember being in my dorm with roommates and other friends, watching the news. One of the Twin Towers was blazing. Then the other was struck by another plane. The whole thing was surreal. "How could this happen?" people asked. The images of the damage in New York City seared into our minds. In the way that collective tragedy can, this experience facilitated a shared bond for many people. Though that was not the experience of everyone, and especially not for those who were Muslim or were perceived to be.

After 9/11, narratives about enemies in the Middle East rose to the surface. The George W. Bush administration told us myths about weapons of mass destruction to justify going to war against an "axis of evil." Saddam Hussein's name rented space in our minds and dwelled there as we learned about groups like the Taliban. At that time, I had very little grasp of global history, but I knew that war seemed inevitable. Military powers attack when they feel threatened. We were a military superpower like nothing the world had ever seen before. I could do the math. And so American "unity" easily moved to America's need for punitive justice and for restabilizing its dominance.

Things were no different on my Christian campus among most of the student body. A general mix of American pride and a spirit of revenge resided in the minds of many peers. Few would have used the word *revenge*, but most believed that America needed to "get" whoever had done this. American justice demanded retribution. It required a strong military response. When our enemies were annihilated, then we could take our rightful place again as God's chosen nation in the world, modeling and sharing freedom and democracy to the nations. And to war we went.

The first experience that helped me see the corruption in our Christian formation took place in a post-9/11 context. It was a year or two after the Twin Towers were destroyed and thousands were killed. Our campus administrators had invited John Dear, who at the time was a Jesuit priest, to come speak to us for a chapel. At the time I did not know who he was. As far as I was concerned, going to chapel that day was going to be like every other Tuesday morning, when many speakers brought a word to us. I remember John Dear speaking and reflecting on passages from Jesus' Sermon on the Mount. "Blessed are the peacemakers" and "turn the other cheek" and "love your enemies" all made their way into the talk. The gist was that Jesus called us to a different way of responding to violence in our world.

I didn't grow up in a peace church tradition, and I was both intrigued and suspicious of this different emphasis on Christianity's meaning for our lives. My particular (black) home church did not have a distinctive theology to help us navigate questions of peace and violence in our lives. In general, nonviolence was certainly preferable. Yet it was an unstated assumption that our world was violent and that sometimes we had to protect and defend ourselves to survive. Sometimes that required taking the life of others. John Dear was definitely emphasizing peace much more than my own Christian ethics. At the same time, because the college I attended had some Anabaptist influences, these ideas were not brand new by this point. In my biblical studies classes I had many Anabaptist and nonviolence-oriented professors who raised questions about whether scriptural texts, especially the gospels of Jesus, had ethical demands on our lives that led to peace. In college, I slowly wrestled with questions of peace and violence in my own way. But John Dear's emphasis that the life and teachings of Jesus courageously and directly challenge us toward the way of peace was more disruptive.

In that chapel service, Dear seamlessly moved from reflection on Jesus' teachings to considering the world of violence we lived in. He talked about our country's military role in Latin America, about protesting American nuclear weapons, and most memorably, about the current wars of our nation. He brought dissonance to us through an awareness of the spirit of revenge that was in the air and of how easily Christians were breathing it in and out. It was at this point that he really caught my attention. I have memories of him going on about George Bush, the Iraq War, militarism, and the Christian ethic of peace and nonviolence. At that moment, I began to lean forward to hear him out. I wanted to make sure I heard him clearly, so I could weigh whether what he was saying was faithful to the gospel. My home church growing up did not have an explicit theology of peace or violence, but I was gifted with a community that invited us to make Jesus the center of our faith and joy. The crucified and resurrected One had a privileged place in my life because of that formation. What struck me most about John Dear's words was the fact that he was emphasizing Jesus' direct teachings and example in everything he said. These kinds of conversations usually prioritize Israel's conquest in the Old Testament or provide a more "realistic" path forward than the gospel of Jesus. Monarchy and war, drawing on fancy systems of theology that circumvent the gospel story (and ignore the passages of peace in the Old Testament), always trump what Jesus said. I leaned forward to hear Dear's message because he seemed to take Jesus so seriously.

Right as I was leaning in, completely captivated by this chapel speaker, I noticed something else happening. In the darkened auditorium, lots of movement was occurring around me. In fact, right as I was leaning in, attempting to discern the truthfulness of this talk, I looked around and realized that many of my peers were bailing out. Hundreds of students were engaged in a massive exodus from chapel in protest to the message. Literally hundreds of students were offended and angry and were embodying their disagreement through a walkout. Our Christian college valued a generous and gracious orthodoxy and had always invited speakers from a wide variety of denominational, theological, and political views. Never before, at least while I was attending, had a mass of students disrupted a chapel service by leaving in the middle. You can be sure students are living out some sacred convictions when they leave a chapel service before having the opportunity to swipe their card to get their chapel credit for attending.

I realize that John Dear's message was controversial. Some students had family members who were in the military. A small percentage of students probably were more directly affected by 9/11 itself. These would not be hypothetical concerns for everyone. That alone, though, does not explain their response. My older brother was in the military during some of my early years of college and I had not even fathomed the need to walk out on the chapel speaker. To me, it was a strange response. I understood that many believed differently than John Dear, but I did not understand why such a dramatic response was needed at that moment. Could we not sit through chapel for thirty minutes with someone speaking to us, regardless of whether we agreed with them? Was this really the ultimate test of one's Christian faith? Was this moment the point at which one must take their stand? Was challenging us to love our enemies and put away vengeance, to be peacemakers and practice nonviolence, really so offensive that it could not be considered or tolerated? I had to grapple with Dear's hard challenge because it was rooted in the life of Jesus, to whom I had committed my life. Jesus was my deliverer. Wherever he goes, I go. I felt I had no choice but to grapple with our speaker's chapel talk. Was Jesus calling us to a different ethic of enemy love and peacemaking, especially when it is hard and difficult? Was it true for both interpersonal conflict and global conflict?

After that chapel I began trying to make sense of why many of my peers responded as they did. My interpretation at the time, which has not altered much, was that many of my peers were socialized deeply into the American way and received their identity, vocation, and political imagination from within the nation-state and mainstream culture. To be fair, we all do to varying degrees. However, it seemed as if their Christian and baptismal identity were subsumed by their Americanness. In that moment of protest, their ultimate allegiance appeared to be their national identity as Americans. Christianity and national identity seemed deeply intertwined and integrated into one another. That is why a critique of America's global behavior, and its violence toward our neighbors near and far, was a deep violation of their sense of who they were. The logics of the American way, the political imagination it forms, were deeply set. When the rubber hit the road, many of my peers clung to their American identity over and above wrestling with the teachings of Jesus.

It was after that chapel that I began to ask deeper theological questions relating to Christian formation and the American empire. How should the church relate to our nation? In what way does faith that articulates a "God and country" allegiance distort and misdirect us away from faithfully following the resurrected and living Messiah today? My sophomore fall semester began by providing me with a deep sense of shared belonging and faith. My experience during and after this chapel service, however, was of a growing sense of alienation from many of my peers, which stemmed in part from what seemed to be the particular kind of formation we received in the church and from how the United States had socialized our imagination and convictions.

CULTURE SHOCK CHAPEL

I had a second experience that further illuminated the mangled and corrupted identity and imagination of white American Christianity. Ironically, it also happened during a college chapel. This experience provided a window into the racialized formation of so many white Christians. It also helped me think through why mainstream Christians often could not grasp a different way forward in the face of centuries of racial injustice in this country. This chapel, however, occurred under very different circumstances from the first. In fact, the different setting of the chapel itself functioned like a teacher and a classroom. It is also not hard to make sense of the second chapel service in view of the first. Teachable moments of this nature are not normally planned into a syllabus but instead happen organically in everyday situations.

Like many historically white Christian colleges, there was a desire to foster more racial diversity into the campus community. Such attempts are usually done awkwardly because too often, few people within the institution are committed to identifying how white normativity shapes the contours of its programs and initiatives on campus. Similar to non-Christian colleges and universities, little hubs of survival for underrepresented students exist inside an institution originally designed for white students. These community spaces nurture those on the edges of, or beyond, institutional belonging.

Culture Shock chapel was one of the programs on my campus that fostered belonging for students of color. Back then, the school offered chapel twice a week. So holy. Students were required to rack up a certain number of chapel credits every semester. Tuesdays were the main chapels. Thursdays, however, were usually designated for alternative chapels. Thursday morning chapels provided an opportunity to choose from a plethora of options. Student leaders of color on campus, mostly black and brown, organized and ran a chapel called Culture Shock. Many nonwhite students regularly gathered for worship with Culture Shock. Black gospel was usually the dominant worship music style, which contrasted with the preferred white "contemporary Christian music" and Eurocentric hymns that dominated most other chapels.

Black students, in particular, played a significant role in leadership, but this space enticed folks to gather for worship across many racial, ethnic, and cultural boundaries. There were always some white students present as well. This diverse multiracial space, where black leadership was centralized, created a unique community space within the larger institution which often failed to live up to its own priorities of diversity and inclusion.

On one occasion, we had a guest speaker at Culture Shock. I do not remember the man's name. He was a black man in his thirties or early forties. His message, however, struck a chord with me, and left a lasting impression.

Our speaker began by talking about God taking sides with the oppressed and standing against injustice. He reminded us that God stood with the Israelites in Egypt and liberated them. He narrated their journey in Scripture, and how the Israelites eventually became a monarchy that sometimes violated its own poor and vulnerable residents. So God sent prophets, the speaker explained. They were his mouthpieces to the people, reminding them to do justice, and to let it flow like a river. For our speaker, this story culminated in Jesus, who lived in solidarity with oppressed people in his own day. On the basis of this biblical thread, revealing God's commitment to justice and liberation for the oppressed, he challenged us to align with those same commitments.

Next, he turned the conversation from biblical Israel and the Jesus story and toward the legacy of the United States. Our speaker shared how America's foundations were born out of chattel slavery. That white supremacy defined the character of the nation. How our society moved from slavery to Jim Crow to our present moment, but that it never repented of white supremacy. One thing that struck me about his talk was that it was not a cute racial reconciliation talk or a multicultural church talk during which white and black people were invited to hold hands and sing "We Shall Overcome." He described a hermeneutic that centralized oppressed people in relation to Israel throughout Scripture, and God's response and commitment of liberation for them, then drew parallels with the American way seen over the past four hundred years. For him, the United States, including the Republican and Democratic

Parties, was racist, and white Christians were deeply complicit at every stage.

I was raised in a black church. I was not a stranger to talking about racism through the lens of Christian faith. Yet there was something very different about what he had to say. His talk made arguments about the central character of the scriptural story and God's activity. And his analysis and condemnation of our white supremacist society was bolder and more thorough than anything to which I was accustomed. It was in this chapel talk that I was first introduced to the embodiment of what Walter Brueggemann wrote about in *The Prophetic Imagination*. I knew that our speaker was engaging in a prophetic act that was unveiling the world before us.

Once again, I began to lean in. This was not an ordinary chapel talk. It was courageously truthful speech. The scriptural, historical, and social challenge gripped me. Every word out of our speaker's mouth was challenging and profound. Insights from the black radical tradition and wisdom from Israel's prophetic tradition locked arms in that moment. I could have stayed and listened all day.

And just as I was leaning in, some of my white peers began bailing out once again. This talk was apparently just too much. They had not come to chapel to hear *white* used in such a pejorative way. They had come to worship Jesus. White supremacy. White privilege. White Jesus. White complicity. White Christianity. They had signed up for none of this. White fragility kicked in and they had to make a hard choice. On one hand, this speaker was making a biblical argument climaxing in the life of Jesus. His scriptural arguments demonstrated God's commitments on behalf of the little ones crushed by the Egyptians, Babylonians, and Romans of our world. On the other hand, he dared talk openly and truthfully about the white supremacist legacy of this country, and he implicated Christians in it. Those historical facts are not convenient, and they do not feel good if one has learned to avoid thinking about what has gone on over the past several centuries to make the contemporary church and nation possible.

Unfortunately, many (though not all) of my white peers who were gathered for chapel that day got up and left. This time it was less disruptive than the other chapel protest. Not that many white students were present to begin with, so their departure did not have the same degree of disruption. Instead of protesting through mass exodus, this was more of a silent yet noticeable trickling of white students from that majority black and brown space. Those who left were still very visible, nonetheless.

I won't lie, their departing bothered me a lot. I struggled with the fact that they were incapable of just sitting through our speaker's chapel talk. Our chapel was titled "Culture Shock." With a title like that, one should not be caught off guard by the possibility of being exposed to different ways of seeing, believing, and living. I had thought that if white students literally chose to attend Culture Shock, among a variety of options, they would be more open to considering how racism and their lives are interrelated. I was wrong on that front.

I also thought, even more so, that our faith called us to stick with hard conversations in search of greater truth and deeper faithfulness. In this chapel service, I certainly was not as challenged as my white peers. But the truth of the matter was, as a student I had sat through all kinds of nonsense, especially out of the mouths of some white students. And now this black man was providing a challenging message rooted in Scripture, the book that many evangelicals claim is the highest authority in their lives. His talk was profoundly Christocentric and Christ-otelic, both centered in Christ and finding its fulfillment in Christ. I had probably hoped that our shared faith which calls us to follow after Jesus could hold us together through difficult and "culture shocking" truths, despite our fragile humanity.

Nope. Instead of chasing after Jesus, as folks used to say, some students clung to their white identity. When the rubber hit the road, their whiteness, and white comfort, and desire to protect a sense of white innocence became preeminent. This was a troubling observation. Their disagreeing with the talk was not necessarily what bothered me, although much of it was just historical facts. It was that they decided they were not going to wrestle internally with what was being said and remain in the conversation. They could have stayed after the chapel service and asked good questions. They could have sought to understand why a black Christian man thought and spoke the way our speaker did. Instead, by bailing out, they performed a racially socialized response that reflected their formation by white imagination and practice. By remaining insulated from racial history and the ways that black oppressed communities sometimes read scriptural stories differently, they clung to power, advantage, comfort, and a white social imagination.

Once again, this experience raised all kinds of theological questions for me. Why and how does white identity work in relation to Christianity? In what way has Christian identity been consumed by a white supremacist imagination? If white supremacy and Western Christianity have fused together, what is required to begin severing them from each other? And since most of my white peers wouldn't normally talk about identifying as "white," how do we disciple people beyond whiteness when they don't even see that they have been born captive to these social forces in the first place? How can the church be the answer to Christian supremacy and white supremacy in the United States when it is also an instigator and product of this mangled history?

To get a better handle on the captivity of the church to supremacist identities, mindsets, and ways of living, we need to know our past. The past is never just in the past. It lives on with us. It returns and remains with us in a variety of ways. It is most dangerous when it binds its victims without them knowing it. When we ignore the inertia of what has come before us, we are unable to resist history from puppeting us. We dance and jump on command without realizing why. We need opportunities to see the ways that the history of Christendom and colonialism have mangled our political imagination. If we can begin to see the supremacist mindsets woven into American Christianity, we can begin pulling on the threads and unraveling the idolatry that defines the church's ongoing sociopolitical vocation. This is a necessary step toward repentance so we can faithfully collaborate with the delivering presence of God in our world. Church history is entangled with the rise and decline of Western Christendom, the violent conquests and pillaging of the colonial era, as well as with more recent forms of Christian nationalism and modern racism, which partner with exploitative policies and practices in our globalized society. It is a devastating part of Western Christianity's history. One cannot understand the Western (and especially white) church's captivity to ways of domination without realizing that Western Christendom is the parent of white supremacy.

One form of top-down supremacist society mutated into another form of top-down supremacist society. For many centuries throughout church history, Eastern Christians were the majority. At the earliest stages of the church, Asian and

African Christians left a remarkably powerful imprint on the global church, guiding its customs while defining and clarifying its beliefs. This history is mostly forgotten in the West. Even many Christians of Asian and African descent are severed from the knowledge that the center of Christianity was originally not in the West. However, the social and political power of Western Christianity was on the rise for centuries. By the time it became the Christian majority in the world, it had forgotten from whence it came. Western civilization was conflated with Christianity. It eventually appeared as if Christianity were indigenous to Europe; to be a Christian meant you were European. This process was racialized during colonial conquest and birthed white supremacy. In the United States, Anglo-Saxon Protestant identity morphed into the skeleton that grounded what it meant to be properly white. In other contexts like Spain, Great Britain, or Germany, Western Christian identity also morphed, but always contextually, making the phenomenon of white supremacy global in scope but specific and particular according to the land it inhabited.

The historical impact of Christian supremacist and white supremacist political practice and ways of conceiving the church's vocation still lives with us today. Rather than name every instance of Christian supremacist and white supremacist ways of imagining and being in our contemporary world, I will help us glimpse where we have come from. Our unknown past allows these hidden forces to keep us captive without much resistance.

The rest of this chapter will introduce us to the rise of Christendom and what some call a Constantinian shift, as well as to the emergence of colonialism and what I am calling a Columbusian shift. For those invested in this history, I am not claiming a "fall" of the church in an over-simplistic way, but intentionally prefer the word *shift*. I think the language of shift is more accurate in describing how the social and political vocation and witness of the mainstream church in the West was derailed. This project would itself be derailed if it attempted to detail the long, complex, and nuanced history of the Western church, so instead we will get glimpses of these two shifts by focusing on the legacies of Constantine and Columbus. Other resources cover this history in more detail. I don't believe Constantine and Columbus are, as individuals, primarily responsible for the shifts of the church's vocation (the church as a whole must be accountable for its own behavior and political engagement). I do, however, think both of these men are great symbols of these shifts, and they certainly aided and facilitated new trajectories for the church, further and further from the way of Jesus.

CHRISTENDOM AND CONSTANTINIAN CHRISTIANITY

A community committed to following the anti-lording-over-others way of Jesus eventually morphed into a powerful institution that practiced top-down supremacy over its society (Matthew 20:20-28). The age of Western Christendom has fractured and declined since those days, but the church still wields enormous social and political power in many places around the world. Maybe more significant for our contemporary concerns is that even where Western Christianity no longer controls the laws and culture of society as it used to, there remains a desire and political imagination among many of its adherents to return to those so-called "good ole days." We can call this a Christendom mindset and imagination for society. The political power to coercively and comprehensively impose perceived Christian "law and order" on society is deteriorating, but the political logic and desire remain intact. Many, if they had the means to enforce a top-down Christian society in the United States, for example, would do so. For those with a Christendom mindset, the establishment of Christian supremacy is their political hope for society, imagining it to be how God's reign will be realized on the earth.

We must grapple with how Christendom, by which I mean *Christian supremacy over society*, emerged and how it lives on in our sense of vocation as the church. Some describe a Christendom impulse with the language of Constantinian Christianity. To different degrees, Constantinianism sees either Constantine or the church falling or shifting from its Jesus-shaped vocation during the fourth century. A more nuanced reading of history must acknowledge events beginning before Constantine and continuing many centuries after him during which the shift climaxed. The main thing to consider is the long Christian tradition of thinking historically about the witness of the church in its sociopolitical context. We too must wrestle with what it means to think in a Jesus-shaped way about the church's history. Such faithful historical thinking does not mean we take up the task of defending the church at every turn as our Christian duty. Rather, we must measure the witness of the church against scriptural wisdom fulfilled by the rule of Christ. It is then and only then that we are positioned to confess the church's seemingly strange wisdom expressed through weakness, which is often misunderstood by the broader society, or to prophetically critique the church for encompassing within its own life the ancient practice of hoarding political, economic, and military power over others. The world has seen this way of life before. The hypocrisy of claiming to follow the way of Jesus while dominating others is particularly self-incriminating.

CONSTANTINE, THE CHURCH, AND THE RISE OF CHRISTENDOM

For the earliest Christians, Jesus' life and teachings, as the climax of the Hebrew Scriptures and messianic hope, were central for shaping belief and practice. These Christians imperfectly lived as a voluntary, minority, countercultural community. Those seeking full entry in the church went through a significant and sometimes long and rigorous multistage catechesism prior to baptism. This process formed people into the ethical way of Jesus and provided them a scriptural imagination and essential Christian beliefs. Discipleship oriented one's identity and sense of belonging in community, as well as one's ethical life and social commitments, and it taught disciples how to think and make sense of their society from a distinctly Christian vantage point. The early church expected that Christian conversion ought to shape one's behavior, belief, and belonging in society.[1]

For the first three centuries of the church, Christians were a quickly growing yet minority religious movement throughout the eastern and western parts of the Roman Empire. Although in most cases the church remained a minority for centuries, occasionally some towns had a majority of people baptized and belonging to the church. As early as the third century, there were some social elites who were attracted to the church. Cyprian, an important African church leader, is an example of this. In Christian community, they found relief from the social expectations of their class, and they lived in solidarity with the largely lower-class Christian gatherings. Even then, social dominance over the empire's political life was not conceivable. Whether because of experiencing persecution directly or hearing stories of Christian persecution, members of the church imagined themselves as resident aliens. Domination was not a faithful option in society. The way of the Lamb was a different kind of calling.

One wave of persecution of Christians happened under the emperor Diocletian and was more widespread and severe than previous persecutions. As an emperor, Diocletian created a four-member imperial team to manage the vast Roman Empire. The arrangement made sense from the perspective of delegating responsibilities, but these were all ambitious men thirsting for more power, and they had militaries at their disposal. That was a recipe for disaster, and produced war and struggles for power. *Game of Thrones* has nothing on actual history.

When Constantine's father, one of the emperors, died, Constantine was chosen by the people to replace him. In AD 312, Constantine defeated Maxentius to become the sole ruler over the western portion of the empire. In another decade, Constantine would defeat Licinius as well, obtaining the throne as sole ruler over the Roman Empire.

Even before fighting and taking over the political power of the empire, Constantine already looked favorably on the church, so once given the chance in 312, he began formally ending Christian persecution and instituting a variety of social advantages for the church. Why would he do that? Some evidence suggests that Constantine initially made sense of Christianity by enfolding it within his already existing pagan social imagination. Emperors were responsible for the success of the entire empire and sought to align with divine power to win battles over their enemies. It seems that the God of the Christians appeared to be victorious. Some also argue that Christianity's exponential growth amid paganism's decline made Christianity an obvious candidate to provide religious unity across the empire. It was politically expedient to use Christianity as the empire's new civil religion to foster a new cohesion. In my view, Constantine initially adopted the Christian God through a genuine pagan-style conversion.

What exactly did Constantine do for the church? For starters, he created laws that favored Christianity over paganism and Judaism. He provided money, resources, and even large basilicas to the church; and potentially most importantly, although often neglected, he began elevating the bishops in place of the Roman Senate, which gave the church much more political power and demoted the Senate's political power and prestige.[2] Tax exemptions and exemptions from war were given to clergy. Constantine's record on violence is complicated. In some ways, he curbed some of the sacrificial customs and ended gladiatorial violence, but he also continued violent conquest and killed many of his political enemies. After defeating Maxentius, he rolled into town with Maxentius's head on a spike as a public spectacle of his military victory. He also had his own wife and son executed.

Constantine took a lot of interest in the doctrinal disputes of the church. He convened and even interjected his views during the Council of Nicaea, taking sides in heated debates and schisms. Many believe he didn't fully understand the nuanced positions at that time. For the first time, imperial decree would help decide which beliefs were orthodox or not, and the consequences of such political interference were significant, resulting in the banishment of some Christian leaders whose beliefs didn't align with the theology of the bishops whom Constantine backed. Constantine also interfered with and persecuted African Christians, now known as the Donatists. They were rigorists who believed that those who betrayed the gospel by yielding to the pressures of persecution could no longer administer the sacraments. Whether or not one agrees with this perspective, they represented an indigenous

African Christian tradition that Constantine coercively and violently targeted. One might wonder if this is how Christian disputes should be settled. The legacy of Constantine is complicated, not least because he still engaged in pagan customs through most of his life. He was not all bad, but at the end of the day he was an emperor committed to imperial pursuits that were not consistent with the way of Jesus.

Given that a few decades before Constantine took power, segments of the church were undergoing its most severe persecution, it is astonishing how the church moved from the margins and toward the center of society so quickly. For the first time under Constantine's reign, conversion to Christianity became an advantage for people who wanted to move up the social ladder. Mennonite theologians have long argued that it took courage to be Christian before Constantine, but after Constantine it took courage to remain pagan. Even John Wesley argued that it was not persecution, but the impact of Constantine's advantaging of the church, that greatly wounded "genuine Christianity":

> Persecution never did, never could give any lasting wound to genuine Christianity. But the greatest it ever received, the grand blow which was struck at the very root of that humble, gentle, patient love, which is the fulfilling of the Christian law, the whole essence of true religion, was struck in the fourth century by Constantine the Great, when he called himself a Christian, and poured in a flood of riches, honours, and powers upon the Christians, more especially upon the clergy.[3]

A century after Constantine's reign, Emperor Theodosius would legislate Christianity as the official religion of the empire. The way one imagined Christianity in relation to society was morphing. The church moved from the margins to the center, and ultimately began dominating the society from the top down. There was no instant Constantinian fall as some might suggest, but rather an ongoing centuries-long derailment and shifting from a fallible yet distinctive counter-witness of voluntary communities of disciples to the eventual practice of coerced state-religion and sometimes mass conversions, and eventually a world in which every member of Western civilization was assumed to be Christian by birth. The law of the land would eventually entangle Christian baptism and state citizenship. But this trajectory was centuries in the making. Whether the bishops under Constantine, or the broader faith community, it was the church that went along with the decisions that mangled its social and political imagination and witness.

When everyone and everything is labeled Christian, regardless of people's commitment to conform their imagination and way of life under the preeminence of Christ, this inevitably leads to watering down the meaning of the word *Christian*. In this case, the ecclesial vocation that was crucial to being Christian was replaced by a status that came with one's membership in a society dominated by Christianity.

One dimension affected by the church's acceptance of Constantine's decision to advantage the church was an increased division of ethical expectations for clergy versus laity. Clergy were to strive for a higher and more rigorous way of life than the laity. The laity would increasingly be expected to conform to the expectations of the state rather than those aligned with the life and teachings of Jesus. Killing one's enemies, for example, was consistently taught against by early church leaders. After Constantine and in the rise of Christendom, this became a justified and necessary action for everyday Christians, part of their responsibility as good citizens. The clergy became distinguished in ethics. "Normal" Christians could bloody their hands; only clergy could not. It is not hard to see how conservatives and progressives today still operate out of the same logic, with clergy symbolically wielding claims of moral and ethical superiority to which everyday laity are not called to follow.

Within a Christendom mindset, the church's vocation of discipleship and formation into a counter-witness to the sins of domination, exploitation, and violence became impossible, and no longer even the goal. Over time, one's citizenship and allegiance to the empire (or nation-state) easily displaced the priority of participating in the way of Jesus' radical new society.

It is no surprise that as Christendom emerged, so did monastic communities. Not without their own shortcomings and failures, monastic orders were made up of people who couldn't take up the more costly and faithful way of Jesus in a watered-down Christian supremacist context. It was not clear how to follow Jesus when Christianity was fusing with the empire, and the gap between Jesus' call of discipleship and the ethical life of Christians grew increasingly wide. While there are troubling tales of some monks engaging in disturbing behavior, their broader story is one of voluntary poverty and asceticism, shared resources, deep devotion, and spiritual practices under a common rule and common life. However, their common life together and the rigorous and disciplined practices they undertook did not provide a prophetic critique for the broader church. Monastic orders practiced separation through isolation from society, which is hardly the way of Jesus. Therefore monasticism was positioned as an option for "super-Christians," which meant there continued to be a watered-down version for "regular" Christians who didn't want a costly way of life. In the end, monasticism reinforced the existence of different tiers of Christians. Most Christians today still operate with the idea that some people are called to be super-Christians, while the rest must get on with life just like everyone else.

Western Christendom's rise was centuries long, and it peaked at the turn of the millennium. By this point, Christianity and Western civilization were completely conflated with one another. It was during and after the climax of Christendom that Christians engaged in crusades against those they labeled "infidels," Muslim people who had taken over parts of previously Jewish and Christian regions in the East. Within this new Christendom mindset, enemies of the state were necessarily enemies of the church. The language of "heathen" or "infidels," along with anti-Jewish theological frameworks (which have an older origin), defined who were considered enemies of Western civilization, internally and externally. The once persecuted church was practicing top-down political persecution of religious minorities internally, while crusading against its political enemies externally. The church was captive to a mangled political imagination and witness.

Constantine did not single-handedly cause all of this. Western Christendom's marginalization of Jesus' life and teachings, I contend, was more the fault of the church than of Constantine himself. The church did not have to go in that direction. Ironically, it seemed that Constantine was quite aware of the ethical demands of Christian life back in the fourth century, as evidenced by his avoidance of formal conversion to Christianity for most of his life. For ancient Christianity, true conversion required becoming a catechumen who would submit to the church and its teachings and ethical instruction until affirmed as ready for baptism. Constantine did not submit to the church's authority for most of his life. It was not until his deathbed that he decided to be baptized and commit to no longer live and act contrary to the way of Jesus. Ironically, by not getting baptized earlier, Constantine may have demonstrated a greater sensitivity to the sacredness of baptism and the ethical vocation of Christian life than many baptized Christians do today.

The church must take responsibility for its own behavior, even if shifts were encouraged by Constantine's policies of Christian favoritism. Some people excuse the church for its idolatrous compromises because of its surviving previous persecution, which Constantine ended. Which of us, they argue, if living at that moment, would not see Constantine as God's deliverance manifested to the church? Who could pass up the chance to grab imperial power over society and govern in view of godly wisdom and for the common good? I understand the lure to grab for power at that moment. The question still remains whether using political top-down power for the church's advantage over society is itself contrary to the way of Jesus. It's not hard to see Jesus' renunciation of Satan's offer for political power (the kingdoms of the world), economic and material power (turn stone to bread), and religious power (miracle at the temple) as central to Christian discipleship and characteristic of earlier Christian (and Jewish) communities. The temptations Jesus faced are not only the same temptations that the people of God faced in an ancient world, but the whole world's ongoing temptations. And in Jesus we are delivered from the evil that tempts us away from God's reign. The suffering and life of service expressed in Jesus, in response to the top-down and coercive power of this age, appears multiple times in Matthew, Mark, Luke, and John. We too are invited to live life in the reign of God as we renounce imperial ways. Constantine did not force the church and its leaders to take the path they did, but he certainly represents the kind of political action the church and its leaders would increasingly follow in various ways for the next millennium and a half.

More recently, Constantine has been praised as an example to follow. Theologian Peter Leithart still identifies Constantine as "a model for Christian political practice."[4] Only Jesus ought to hold that preeminent role. There was a time when Jesus (and those who faithfully and creatively followed his way in their own context), rather than Constantine, would have been lifted up to serve as the primary model for social action for the church, as the one who would definitively shape our political imagination. In the United States today, "Christian politics" is frequently oriented toward "God and country" fusions, with coercive top-down legislation of perceived Christian morality, while neglecting justice for the poor and the common good of all people. Too often, the church serves as a puppet and mascot for the empire's interests rather than as a prophetic voice that conceives of the gap between our social order and God's future world.

Christendom is a Christian supremacist society. It is a "Christian" supremacist social order, as a partnership between the church and state, attained through top-down legislation and encouraged through cultural hegemony. There are a variety of configurations of Christendom over the centuries. Sometimes an emperor had the most power, sometimes it was a pope. In the Reformation era, sometimes princes favored a particular Protestant teaching and provided military might and protection for it to grow, while other times a Christian council governed society. The point is that even during the Protestant Reformation, Christendom fragmented, but it did not go away. Under Christendom, Christian supremacy encompasses a society from the top down through law and custom.

Today, a more formal Christendom social arrangement no longer exists in most of the West. Christian supremacy continues to lose its grip and influence over society as the years pass. Of course, a Christian majority in the United States, with our complicated electoral college system, representative form of government, and inequitable distribution of wealth, still results in enormous direct and hegemonic power for many Christians in the United States. More significantly, the imagination and mindset of Christendom still lingers within the hopes and imagination of most mainstream Christians. Many self-professed Christians want to regain that old power. For them this would "make America great again." Some possess nostalgic memory of a past full of "good ole days" for the church. They see Christendom not as a departure from the life and teachings of Jesus, but rather as the fulfillment of divine will. Others want a more progressive vision to mimic conservative Christian political power. I think we must problematize all attempts at Christian supremacy and must liberate the ways that we pursue a more just society as Christians without Christendom instincts. The legacy of Christendom, despite some of the helpful innovations that developed along the way, has been tragic because it continues to disfigure our Christian imagination and our Jesus-shaped witness in the public square.

COLONIALISM AND COLUMBUSIAN CHRISTIANITY

White supremacy was birthed in the womb of late medieval Christendom. To grasp how colonialism reshaped the interaction of people groups all around the globe and our ongoing ways of perceiving, categorizing, and creating racist policies for different people groups, we must tell the story of how the church directly promoted the conquest of non-European people in different continents. The figure who often stands at the heart of this narrative is Christopher Columbus. Slowly, the truth about his violence and oppression of Indigenous people is becoming more publically known. He perpetrated the violent conquest, pillaging, slavery, and rape of Indigenous people. However, he did not single-handedly cause Western Europe's colonial conquest.

For our purposes, I propose we consider *Columbusian Christianity* as a symbol of the Christianity that Columbus embodies and exemplifies. This colonial and Columbusian Christianity directly produced global white supremacy. But before we move ahead of ourselves, we need to pick up where our Western Christendom story left off, at the turn of the first millennium.

LATE MEDIEVAL CHRISTENDOM AS WHITE SUPREMACIST WOMB

In 1095, Pope Urban II began the first crusade against Muslims in the East in an attempt to preserve Christian control over Jerusalem. The impact of those Christian-Muslim wars still reverberates in our society today. To get Christian soldiers to fight, the pope guaranteed an eternal reward in the afterlife for those who took up the sword against the enemies of Western Christendom. At the same time, Pope Urban II invented a new papal bull (a formal church doctrine) called *Terra Nullius*, which meant "empty land." Any land occupied by non-Christians was deemed "empty land" and could be seized through war by Christians (read: Europeans). The result of three centuries of crusading against Muslims in the East was that the church intensified its self-identity as a Christian civilization at war with infidels and heathens.

Moving forward, the West would numerically have more Christians than the East. And the power of Rome in the west started to eclipse the power of Constantinople in the east. The binary of a Christian/heathen framework that developed in medieval Christendom would be redirected from Muslims and toward other people groups around the world as well. This terra nullius doctrine of "discovery" of heathen lands developed further to imply that the land itself, if not settled and cultivated according to Western civilization's standards, would also be deemed terra nullius and given a divine stamp of approval for Western conquest.

The origins of the African slave trade are related to this history, but in a nuanced way. Slavery was a global practice before Western European colonial conquest. It is intellectually dishonest to bypass the fact that people all over the earth, including Western Europeans and Africans, were already practicing slavery. However, the racialized and perpetual character of Christian European chattel enslavement which developed out of Christendom societies is peculiar to this story. And the Christian custom, which originally believed that a Christian could not hold another Christian in slavery, eventually changed in some of the colonies. The first Africans enslaved by the Christian West were kidnapped by the Portuguese in 1441. In some societies, a proto-racial anti-black perspective already existed, and that, coupled with anti-Muslim views, made many North Africans targets of enslavement and exploitation.

Then, in 1455, Pope Nicholas V issued a new papal bull entitled *Romanus Pontifex*, which ignited the era of Western European conquest, pillaging, and colonial settler-ism as we know it. With this papal bull, Portugal was given formal permission by the church "to invade, search out, capture, vanquish, and subdue all Saracens and pagans whatsoever, and other enemies of Christ wheresoever placed, and the kingdoms, dukedoms, principalities, dominions, possessions, and all movable and immovable goods whatsoever held and possessed by them and to reduce their persons to perpetual slavery, and to apply and appropriate to himself and his successors the kingdoms, dukedoms, counties, principalities, dominions, possessions, and goods, and to convert them to his and their use and profit."[5] What is noteworthy is that the papal bull came after, rather than before, the Portuguese slave trade had begun. The church was getting its hands dirty doing the heavy theological lifting, improvising its teachings on behalf of Christian domination over other people's bodies and lands. The outcome was that the church provided divine approval for expanding efforts of conquest, which would eventually include South America. As we'll see, colonialism was shaped by Christianity and Christianity was shaped by colonialism.

Now we are ready to situate Christopher Columbus within the story of the Western church engaged in colonialism. I will describe how Columbus is symbolic of an emerging white supremacy born out of Western Christendom that has continued to mutate and shift further from its Jesus-shaped track.

COLUMBUS AND THE WHITE SUPREMACIST CAPTIVITY OF THE CHURCH

As most already know, Christopher Columbus came across many Caribbean islands, as well as the coast of South America and Central America, beginning in 1492. He erroneously thought he had reached the Indies via a new route. His claim to "discovery" was not because he thought he had found a new land, but rather because the land fit the description of terra nullius, which church doctrine had prescribed centuries before. The ways that Columbus's mindset and imagination had been socialized to see and interact with different non-Christian people groups were evident from the moment he reached the Bahamas in 1492.

Rather than approach the inhabitants with curiosity and an interest in mutual learning and a sharing of cultural knowledge and gifts, Columbus instantly thought about conquest and domination over the unknown people he encountered. He wrote his initial thoughts in his journal, saying, "We could subjugate them all and make them do whatever we want." This could have been a moment of expanded belonging based on recognition of their shared humanity, especially in light of the Christian teaching from Hebrew Scripture that states that all humanity was created in the image of God. Instead, Columbus only thought about the potential to strip these lands of resources. People could be enslaved as property and resources could be pillaged, and both could be taken back to Spain to exchange for wealth. And so Columbus returned with fifteen hundred armed men on seventeen ships and began capturing, enslaving, and shipping Arawak men, women, and children back to Spain. If those atrocities were not enough, the armed men Columbus brought with him engaged in horrendous and brutal violence toward the Indigenous people. Native people were mutilated, raped, and killed. Attempts at resistance resulted in mass genocide, with subsequent mass suicides of survivors. Bartolomé de las Casas, a priest who accompanied Columbus, described what he witnessed during the conquest of the Bahamas:

> They forced their way into native settlements, slaughtering everyone they found there, including small children, old men, pregnant women, and even women who had just given birth. They hacked them to pieces, slicing open their bellies with their swords as though they were so many sheep

herded into a pen. They even laid wagers on whether they could manage to slice a man in two at a stroke, or cut an individual's head from his body, or disembowel him with a single blow of their axes. They grabbed suckling infants by the feet and, ripping them from their mother's breasts, dashed them headlong against the rocks. Others, laughing and joking all the while, threw them over their shoulders into a river, shouting: "Wriggle, you little perisher." They slaughtered anyone and everyone in their path, on occasion running through a mother and her baby with a single thrust of their swords. They spared no one, erecting especially wide gibbets on which they could string their victims up with their feet just off the ground and then burn them alive thirteen at a time, in honour of our Savior and the twelve Apostles, or tie dry straw to their bodies and set fire to it. Some they chose to keep alive and simply cut their wrists, leaving their hands dangling, saying to them: "Take this letter"—meaning that their sorry condition would act as a warning to those hiding in the hills. The way they normally dealt with the native leaders and nobles was to tie them to a kind of griddle consisting of sticks resting on pitchforks driven into the ground and then grill them over a slow fire, with the result that they howled in agony and despair as they died a lingering death.[6]

The Columbusian Christian pattern of colonial conquest, stealing resources, enslaving people, and horrific violence, was joined by more and more Western Christianized societies, continuing for centuries. In the soon to be United States, one of the most common patterns that emerged was the slaughter and death and forcible removal of Indigenous communities from their ancestral lands, followed by the forcible removal and enslavement of African people to these same lands. Land and labor were pillaged to attain wealth, build the empire, and exert sociopolitical dominance. All of this was sanctioned by church teachings. The core of Christian ethics had to change to accommodate and bolster these new practices.

The enslavement of African people in the English colonies in North America did not begin until 1619. Enslaved Africans had already been brought to Florida by the Spanish in 1565, but that was not yet a part of the new American experiment. Africans were forced by Western powers into slavery much earlier in other parts of the world. Initially in the United States, Africans were forced into working alongside other laborers as indentured servants, which provided the hope that they might eventually be freed like their European counterparts. However, within one generation, the American colonies codified blackness as the permanent marker for chattel slavery. Likewise, they changed English common law, making slavery for Africans perpetual, including for an enslaved mother's children, and their children, and so forth.

Some of the most intensified anti-black oppression developed under the claims of white supremacy, as millions more black people were forcibly brought to the colonies. The practice of racialized slavery, of violently stolen African people, along with the genocide and forcible removal of Native Americans, provided the foundation for the existence and rise of the United States of America. In its earliest practice in the American colonies, slavery was a morally complicated practice. Initially, slave masters and planters did not want their slaves to convert to Christianity, because Christians were not allowed to enslave another Christian. Conversion would undermine their labor and economic profits. It was also believed that Christianity made the enslaved Africans uppity and hard to control.

Eventually, Anglican missionaries, wanting to promote evangelization in the colonies, developed teachings and pamphlets for these slave masters that would help change their moral imagination. The missionaries taught that there was no conflict in keeping converted black Christians as slaves, and that Christianity did not make enslaved people rebellious as once assumed. Christianity and slavery, they contended, were completely compatible. The only problem was that slave owners were not correctly teaching Christianity to their slaves. The missionaries demonstrated the need to change the Christian formation and catechism process for enslaved Africans and to impose the practice of "absolute obedience." By executing severe punishment of every minor infraction, they explained, full submission could be expected from enslaved Christians. That practice, coupled with Christian teachings on submission of slaves to masters, was argued to be congruent with Paul's words "Slaves, obey your masters." This is just one of the examples of how Christianity shaped the nature of slavery and how, simultaneously, slavery shaped the character of Christianity in this land. This trajectory of white supremacist domination under the banner of a Christian society is best revealed through Frederick Douglass, a former enslaved man who, after getting free, unveiled the hypocrisy in what he witnessed:

> What I have said respecting and against religion, I mean strictly to apply to the slaveholding religion of this land, and with no possible reference to Christianity proper; for, between the Christianity of this land, and the Christianity of Christ, I recognize the widest possible difference—so wide, that to receive the one as good, pure, and holy, is of necessity to reject the other as bad, corrupt, and wicked. To be the friend of the one, is of necessity to be the enemy of the other. I love the pure, peaceable, and impartial Christianity of Christ: I therefore hate the corrupt, slaveholding, women-whipping, cradle-plundering, partial and hypocritical Christianity of this land. Indeed, I can see no reason, but the most deceitful one, for calling the religion of this

land Christianity. I look upon it as the climax of all misno-
mers, the boldest of all frauds, and the grossest of all libels.[7]

By the time Douglass wrote these words in the nineteenth
century, the practice of Western Christian supremacy over
society had fully given birth to white supremacy, and the
two functioned as two hands within the same body. In fact,
for most people, more often than not they would have been
indistinguishable from each other. Their mangled and white
supremacist theology justified organizing all of civilization
according to the logics of white supremacy because it was
divinely ordained by God. The dangerous aspect of white
supremacy is that it is completely capable of continuing on
without Christianity as its host. While white Christians continue to demonstrate the most severe commitments to Christian supremacist political imaginations—whether in the form
of participation in the Ku Klux Klan or the support of an overwhelming majority of white Christians, both evangelical and
mainline, for Donald Trump's racist policies—nonbelieving
and atheist white people are also inclined to adhere to various
white supremacist myths and ideologies that bolster racialized
inequality and oppression in the United States. But to focus on
that would be to shift the blame. The church has been at the
center and the forefront of this global scandal.

This chapter has described, through various glimpses, the
rise of Christendom and colonialism as a story of Christian
supremacy over Western Europe, which morphed during the
late medieval era into the violent conquest resulting in the
plundering of people, land, and resources. Furthermore, it
has described the vandalizing of the name of Jesus and the
derailed path the church took away from a Jesus-shaped way
of life. I have done so by demonstrating the ways that the

church justified these practices with a mangled Christendom imagination of its vocation and politics, permitted by church teaching. White supremacy developed during critical moments of encounter involving various ethnic populations across the globe. White supremacy was the ideology that justified European conquest and exploitation throughout the world to achieve dominance and control over God's creation (which is idolatry). White supremacist ideas mandated the reorganizing of our societies according to an imagined racial hierarchy, and a claim of divine exceptionalism of European bodies and cultures over nonwhite bodies and cultures.

White supremacy, whether enacted by Christians or non-Christians, is the practice of organizing all of life around the lie of racial hierarchy so that white people, and in the United States especially white men, dominate and control society. White supremacy is a mangled social and political imagination from which people concoct policies, rules, and customs to create their vision for "law and order" in society. Until we grapple with how Christian supremacy morphed into white supremacy and then took on a life of its own, this racial inertia will continue to keep the church and broader society captive from God's dream of humanity and all creation flourishing together.

CONCLUSION: HOW DOES THE INERTIA OF CHRISTIAN AND WHITE SUPREMACIST IMAGINATIONS LIVE ON TODAY?

We see the racial inertia of Western Christendom still haunting us today when white Christians, whether evangelical or mainline, support and vote for a president who promised to ban Muslims, to build a wall to keep out Mexicans, and to support tougher "law and order" policies despite black people's concerns about police brutality and mass incarceration. This racial inertia lives on through complete allegiance to unrepentant politicians, even after they are known to have violated and sexually assaulted women. It is supporting politicians who say, in response to white supremacist rallies, that there are very fine people on both sides. My concern, however, is actually less with these politicians and more with self-professed Christians' deteriorated Christian ethics and moral compass. For example, when Donald Trump claimed to be a practicing Christian while disregarding the way of Jesus in such blatant ways, such hypocrisy might even make Constantine blush, which is why Constantine remained unbaptized most of his life. He knew to avoid baptism until his deathbed because he understood the seriousness of it. The American church has derailed from its Jesus-shaped vocation, and its political witness is distorted and domesticated. Christianity today is still haunted by our past, and we must be accountable for our decisions and allegiances and for how they measure up against the rule of Christ.

Today, we are haunted by our past when self-professed Christians push for tax codes that benefit those who are already filthy rich, instead of centralizing the concerns of the poor and working-class people who do not have decent jobs with livable wages, healthcare, and adequate housing. We are haunted by our past when adequate funding for black and brown public schools continues to be denied while state-of-the-art prison facilities are scattered across the nation. It is visible when those who claim to follow Jesus have turned their eyes and ears away from the suffering and cries of the people most affected by racist and inequitable policies. Dr. King once said, "A nation that continues year after year to spend more money on military defense than on programs of social uplift is approaching spiritual death."[8] We are climbing closer and closer to spending a trillion dollars on our military industrial complex while diminishing our commitment to a social infrastructure that could create the opportunity for every person in our society to flourish in their neighborhoods. We are haunted by the global climate crisis and the tone-deaf ears many churches have toward ecological injustice and devastation for the poorest and most vulnerable populations around the world. We are haunted by our past because our claims of American exceptionalism pull us into nostalgia and denial, perpetuating a dishonest narrative about this country that erases the actual experiences of black and Native people, along with the varying forms of discrimination experienced by Latinx, Asian, African, and Muslim people in our society. Many Christians encourage homophobia and patriarchy, but I am confident that Jesus would respond to folks in our day as he did to the eunuchs and vulnerable women that he loved in his day. We are still deeply haunted by our past.

What we need now, for those who consider themselves followers of Jesus, is God's deliverance from the bondage of Christian supremacy and white supremacy through radical discipleship to Jesus and through yielding to the liberating presence of the Holy Spirit. This is available to us through Christian discipleship and ecclesial counterintuitive solidarity with those who have been crushed by ongoing forms of supremacist policies and institutions. We are invited by Christ to join in empathetic solidarity and mutuality with the crucified of our world, reimagining the world from that standpoint. Christians must do so because we are taught that Christ joined the thousands of crucified victims in the first century, an act which Paul explained was the revelation of God's power and wisdom. Deliverance from supremacist captivity requires that Christians complicit with status quo society empty themselves like Christ into anti-dominating ways of life in community with the poor, while reconceiving our society in conversation with the Jesus story and the intuitions and wisdom of oppressed people.

We experience Jesus' delivering presence from the bondage of Christendom and colonialism when we follow his lead and struggle for justice and peace from the bottom up. We can engage in grassroots mobilization and organizing in a way that multiplies and disperses power back into our neighborhoods rather than concentrates it in top-down hierarchies, which are so frequently abused by those who govern society.

We can find deliverance from captivity to Constantinian Christianity and Columbusian Christianity when the powers and systems of oppression are unveiled for what they truly are through prophetic truth-telling. As Jesus courageously challenged the establishment of his day, we too must form people capable of speaking truth to power, where the control and domination over society resides. Rather than becoming a puppet to the evil forces and powers that manipulate institutions and do harm to others, we can be a prophetic witness allowing God's unveiling truth to permeate our consciousness about the way we live.

Jesus provided a radical model for political action that ought not be circumvented for the example of Constantine or Columbus. Jesus points us toward something beyond partisanship, a conceptualization of God's just and righteous society. We ought to hunger and thirst for God's reign. We participate in God's salvation on the earth when we refuse to give divine sanction to the status quo and the way things are, and instead prophetically imagine God's dream for a new humanity and new society. We can begin living into that world right now, believing that God's liberation from death-dealing forces is able to break into our world, even amid this old order's persistence. It requires that we believe that another world, and another way of relating to one another, is possible. It requires that we lean into the kind of love, the kind of justice, the kind of empathy, the kind of shared belonging with others that is available in and through Christ.

While it is true that there is a legacy of large portions of the church going off its rails, departing from the way of Jesus, it is also true that there is no better time than now for the church to find its way back to loving our neighbors, centralizing the most vulnerable, and participating in God's deliverance. This is the vocation of the church on the ground as it forms communities that strive for shalom from the underside of supremacist reasoning, and that know how to form disciples who are capable of imagining God's deliverance for us.

4

"TALKING BACK, TALKING BLACK"

UNVEILING AMERICA'S SINS AND ITS MYTH OF EXCEPTIONALISM

I have no love for America, as such; I have no patriotism; I have no country.
—Frederick Douglass, speech, American Anti-Slavery Society, 1847

During the end of my fall semester in my first year of college, I witnessed the strange power of "God and country" ideology, and how it easily shaped white Christian culture without any sense of irony. Like many colleges, we had several traditions on campus. One happened during finals week. Since everyone was stressed from staying up late while studying for exams (and some were anxious because they had not studied), students coped by releasing all that pent-up anxiety through their participation in a campus ritual known as "the midnight scream." When the clock struck twelve, students would open their windows in their dorm rooms, and do exactly what you are imagining; they screamed and yelled for at least thirty seconds. Not everyone on campus participated in this, but enough people did that you could hear screaming from all over campus.

Many peers on my floor participated in this tradition every night during finals. Given the pressure of my first semester, I too desired to release some stress through the midnight scream. On one memorable occasion, many of the guys from the floor huddled in my room. When midnight struck, we lowered the windows, and with a burst of youthful energy, and a bit of masculine pride, we yelled, screamed, and roared our loudest. Giving your vocal chords a workout is energizing, especially when done with others. You feed off those around you. In my book *Trouble I've Seen*, I explained that I was the only black guy on my floor freshman year. None of that mattered in this moment. It was a genuinely innocent ritual that brought many of us together. Our hearts were pumping, our lungs opened up, and we returned our stress back to the universe. After the midnight scream is complete, some people call the night quits, thinking that sleep after a long evening of study is the best thing they can do to prepare for their exam. Others would press on, putting in a few more hours of work. And then there were the few who, in a moment of desperation, planned to go the distance with the dreaded all-nighter. The midnight scream functioned like a break from a football huddle. Once the midnight scream was over everyone would go their separate ways, naturally transitioning to the next phase of their night, in whatever form it would take.

However, on this distinct night, there was no organic break. When our midnight scream wrapped up, some of the guys on my floor had something more in them. And so, seemingly out of nowhere, one of the guys started chanting "USA! USA! USA!" With each incantation of USA, more people from our floor joined in. This may not seem noteworthy to some. Certainly, it may seem too mundane to describe this moment in a book. Yet I share this moment because of the disorientation I experienced in response to it. I remember almost immediately joining in with the chant. People talk about groupthink, and that adequately described my initial response. My mind and body were performing in concert with those around me. However, my participation did not last long. I quickly stopped, feeling like the moment had taken a strange and inexplicable turn. I did not think there was anything wrong with chanting "USA." But I was confused about where this spontaneous urge to chant USA came from to begin with. There seemed to be no precipitating cause or instigator. It was like it was lingering beneath the surface and was ready to emerge at any moment. As I reflect, I have never had a parallel experience within my black community or black church when inexplicable patriotic chanting occurred without explanation. If you gathered together a bunch of black veterans who are usually quite proud of their military service, I'm still not convinced that they would break into unprovoked patriotic chanting without demonstrable cause. On my Christian campus, among my white peers, I stood and watched my floormates chant USA repeatedly, and I was genuinely confused.

Why did this chanting just organically erupt out of thin air? Why was uncontextualized patriotism unlikely for most of my black community? These questions briefly gripped my thinking as an eighteen-year-old student. I am sure I did not think too long about it, but my mind did repeatedly resurface that memory during other situations that triggered similar confusion. It was much later that I came to believe that a "God and country" ideology was a vital part of the theological frameworks of most white mainstream Christians, although certainly to different degrees for different communities. The sacredness of America's exceptionalism and greatness is a deeply engrained ideology for so many white American churches in the United States. Nationalist myths keep mainstream Christians captive to their tales, consequently deterring the church from participating in the anti-imperial delivering presence of God made especially evident in the life of Jesus, who was crushed by Roman powers and the establishment in Jerusalem.

If the church wants deliverance from our nationalist ideology, we need to unveil the United States's sins. We cannot act righteously if we define social sin as national greatness. Human sinfulness is a matter of fact according to Christian teaching. It runs through every person, community, and institution, and this includes nations and the people that govern them. And some societies have caused greater harm to our world than others. Evil forces hidden from our eyes keep us captive to death-dealing ways of relating with others and organizing our collective lives.

I believe that the black American prophetic tradition provides an opportunity for the United States to hold a mirror up to its own face. Our nation must see itself, rather than only the branded image and stories of exceptionalism it has concocted. More controversially (at least among scholars), I contend that any effort to salvage American civil religion without undergoing a radical revolution of values, Jesus-shaped repentance, and social rebirth and transformation will dodge, one more time, the invitation of God's deliverance that is available in this land.

THE MYTH OF AMERICAN INNOCENCE AND THE UNITED STATES OF AMNESIA

In March 2008, ABC News, after reviewing dozens of videos of Jeremiah Wright preaching, released a clip from one of his years-old sermons at Trinity United Church of Christ in Chicago. The clip shocked many white Americans because of Wright's judgmental stance toward the United States. The release of the video sparked a national frenzy because Wright was Barack Obama's pastor, and he preached the sermon while the Obamas were members. At the time of ABC's broadcast, Barack Obama was still a candidate running for president. The media went wild, sharing the thirty-second clip over and over again. I still remember seeing it on the news and online. The most memorable line was Rev. Wright's declaration, "Not God bless America, but God damn America!"

Almost like a marching band, mainstream America fell in line with condemnation of the pastor's words. Fox News not only shared that footage, but also took the opportunity to condemn "black theology" and theologian James Cone. I was saddened to see self-identified black theologian Anthony Bradley on Fox News, being manipulated into joining their propaganda and denigrating black theology and the prophetic wing of the black church in front of the network's predominately white audience. White-controlled mainstream media across the board pushed a message of concern and even disgust. The political pressure got bad enough that Barack Obama delivered a speech to explain himself. He tried to frame Wright as a product of his times while disavowing Wright's strongest rhetoric. But the pressure did not let up, and eventually the

Obamas fully severed ties with Wright, who had been their pastor for decades, and denounced his words and behavior.

Amid the twenty-four-hour news cycle circus, few took the time to watch the entire sermon, or even to watch enough to place his words into context. It was much easier to condemn and dismiss the pastor and sermon wholesale than to take a moment to listen to why a black pastor of a large black congregation on the South Side of Chicago might say what he said. Had they taken a posture of listening before speaking, as the book of James encourages, they would have had an opportunity to encounter one voice within a long great tradition. What Jeremiah Wright was doing was not something unique to him. He had joined a great chorus of black men and women who spoke a truth to the American empire that was difficult to hear. We must interpret his sermon, and specifically his word choice, in light of the black prophetic tradition.

The black prophetic tradition emerges out of black lived experience, coupled with a moral imagination and a commitment to prophetic truth-telling inspired by the Hebrew prophets in Scripture. Black lived experience recalls unceasing anti-black oppression in the form of centuries of slavery, another hundred years of Jim Crow, followed by the more recent decades of ongoing ghettos, underfunded schools, plundered resources, suppressed wages, and the development of the largest incarceration system in the world that targets our neighborhoods. The Hebrew prophets frequently called Israel to repent of its idolatry and the practice of injustice. Then, and only then, would God's peace and flourishing break forth in their land. The message was to "let justice roll down like waters," to "let the oppressed go free," and to "do justice, love mercy, and walk humbly before God." Israel was accountable for how they treated the poor and exploited, widows and orphans, foreigners and the oppressed. The prophets called them to be righteous in how the most vulnerable were treated in their land. Black experience, coupled with the Hebrew prophets, created a powerful truth-telling tradition. The prophetic wing of the black church, in particular, has played an ongoing role in the struggle for freedom. One cannot understand black abolitionists during slavery or civil rights leaders in the twentieth-century freedom struggle without being attentive to this tradition.

When Wright delivered his sermon, he connected the witness of God's condemnation of oppression and divine judgment in the Bible with the violence and injustice that consumes American life in our contemporary world. He spoke truth to power, telling a more truthful account of the United States, one that rejected the myth of American exceptionalism. Instead, he focused on actual history. Some might argue that some of his comments were conspiracy myths. It is true that some of what he said likely cannot be proved, but that was a tiny fragment of his sermon. At least 95 percent of what he said was historical fact that isn't arguable. To quibble over the remaining 5 percent is to intentionally major in the minors, detouring around the main arguments which are historically undeniable. Let's take a look at the portion of the sermon that led up to his famous quote, "God damn America." Listen to the black prophetic critique that sought to hold a mirror up to the nation so it could see itself beyond its claims of innocence and peer into the depths of its atrocities against people made in the image of God:

> And the United States of America government, when it came to treating her citizens of Indian descent fairly, she failed. She put them on reservations. When it came to treating her citizens of Japanese descent fairly, she failed. She put them in internment prison camps. When it came to treating her

citizens of African descent fairly, America failed. She put them in chains, the government put them on slave quarters, put them on auction blocks, put them in cotton fields, put them in inferior schools, put them in substandard housing, put them in scientific experiments, put them in the lowest paying jobs, put them outside the equal protection of the law, kept them out of their racist bastions of higher education and locked them into positions of hopelessness and helplessness. The government gives them the drugs, builds bigger prisons, passes a three-strike law, and then wants us to sing "God Bless America." No, no, no, not God bless America. God damn America—that's in the Bible—for killing innocent people. God damn America, for treating our citizens as less than human. God damn America, as long as she tries to act like she is God, and she is supreme. The United States government has failed the vast majority of her citizens of African descent.[1]

When the church is willing to receive and grapple with the centuries-long suffering of black people, and the current ways in which our nation continues to cripple, exploit, and denigrate black communities, it will be able to hear Rev. Jeremiah Wright's words. So long as the story of America's greatness remains the dominant script, so long as white American Christians continue to search out a "black friend" who will cosign the myth of American exceptionalism while giving white supremacy a pass, then the mainstream church will continue to choose hardheartedness toward black people rather than love and compassion that leads to repentance and justice. The narrative of American exceptionalism is a hard drug to break free from.

CONVERSING WITH AMERICAN COVENANT

If one was raised to believe that the United States is good, just, innocent, and most importantly, God's chosen nation, then internalizing the scope of its sins will be difficult. There are multiple ways to respond to what has happened, and to what is occurring now. For those steeped in the story of America's exceptionalism and greatness, one strategy of coping is to try to split the difference so that one can be truthful about the national nightmare while still believing in the American dream. This approach ultimately suggests that there is no need for the United States to be born again, it just needs time to mature into what it was always destined to be. The core of the American experiment is good and righteous, the argument suggests, and just needs to be nudged along on its way to becoming a "more perfect union" as we struggle to affirm its highest ideals of democracy, equality, and freedom.

I disagree with this effort to salvage the story of American empire, knowing that as I do so, I am taking a controversial stance that will clash with many of my allies. While I do not expect it, I believe what the United States needs is not reform, or tweaking, but a revolution of values, Jesus-shaped repentance, and social rebirth. That is where our deliverance is found. So long as we deny the need for full holistic deliverance through rebirth and transformation, we allow the myth of white supremacy and American exceptionalism to live on. To make this argument I will dialogue with the thoughtful work of sociologist Philip Gorski in *American Covenant*.[2] Gorski's book provides a strong, thoughtful, and scholarly articulation of a pro–civil religion argument, making him an important dialogue partner for thinking about the subject with a nuanced take, even if ultimately I depart from his proposal.

In *American Covenant: A History of Civil Religion from the Puritans to the Present*, Philip Gorski describes three competing ideologies that he compares and contrasts in a desire to make a case for a viable path forward for our polarized

American society. Behind the arguments and proposals he lays out throughout the book resides an anxiety about the current dilemma of our society and the cultural and political gridlock we are experiencing. And those problems are not fabricated. Gorski sees our society torn apart by radical ideologies. In his view, we are gridlocked by political dysfunction that renders us incapable of governing our society well, and we are plagued by culture wars that have deteriorated our best traditions. Religious nationalism and radical secularism are the most damaging in crippling the American project.

As Gorski explains, "The religious nationalist wishes to fuse religion and politics, to make citizenship in the one the mark of citizenship in the other, to purge all those who lack the mark, and to expand the borders of the kingdom as much as possible, by violent means if necessary."[3] In contrast, radical secularism, he contends, is "an equally noxious blend of cultural elitism and militant atheism that envisions the United States as part of an Enlightenment project threatened by the ignorant rubes who still cling to traditional religion."[4] Throughout the book, Gorski problematizes the historicity, rationale, and vision of these competing political visions. They are equally dangerous in his view, and he cuts no slack in either direction. It is worth stating now that I have very little critique to make of his problematizing of religious nationalism or radical secularism. As a Christian intellectual, I find religious nationalism to betray the posture and heart of Jesus' life and teachings. It is closely related to what I have called Christendom and Christian supremacy in this book. Instead of coercively grabbing for power, Jesus rejected "lording it over others" as the path forward for his followers. Likewise, radical secularism's starting point suggests that people of faith ought not allow their religion to shape public life. While I am sympathetic to the view that Christians in this land have too often practiced Christian supremacy, I also do believe that Jesus continues to provide a model for faithful political action that does not require top-down coercive religion, one that is seen in the black church's twentieth-century freedom struggle. People of faith can play an important role in struggling for a just society where everyone is able to flourish without dominating others.

Of course, Gorski is not only concerned with taking religious nationalism and radical secularism off the table; most importantly, he has his own proposal for how we can move forward amid the plurality and differences that exist in our society. His proposal for how to move forward is where I want to initiate a dialogue. In an argument that remains fairly close to sociologist Robert Bellah's scholarship on civil religion,[5] *American Covenant* proposes American civil religion as a viable American tradition capable of negotiating the space needed to create critical and constructive dialogue for our diverse population. For Gorski, civil religion has its roots in both prophetic religion and civic republicanism. And this option "provides a framework for connecting past and future, and for conjoining sacred and secular."[6] Thinking about his book in view of these three options (religious nationalism, radical secularism, and his call for the use of civil religion) sets up the organization and central thesis of the book. And to be fair, if the only concern was finding a path forward between religious nationalism and radical secularism, then his proposal would be compelling.

Of course, anytime an author presents three options, in which there exist two "extremist" positions and then arises a single reasonable option in the middle, readers should slow down and ask some critical questions. We must wonder what other options exist beyond the ones being provided for us and what other concerns could be erased from the dialogue. Rejecting the ideology of religious nationalism or radical secularism does not mean the only other option is adherence to some American project already underway. Nor does it require that the path forward require holding to Gorski's vision of civil religion, even if it is a more benign national project than what black people have experienced in the past.

While reading the book, two concerns kept resurfacing for me. First, I wanted to keep track of how black lived experience and struggle for freedom fit into Gorski's vision for civil religion. Secondly, I was concerned about whether Gorski's proposal is honest about the American project's impact on Native American experience in this land. Everyone has different metrics for evaluating a proposal they encounter and the power of a particular claim; these two were at the forefront of my mind while reading Gorski's book. In view of black experience and struggle, Gorski draws on Frederick Douglass and Martin Luther King Jr. significantly, but I'm curious how he would have talked about Nat Turner, Henry McNeal Turner, or Angela Davis, for example, and whether they would be defined as out-of-bounds for constructing American democracy. My point is that a long line of black people have prophetically claimed America to be a lie. My concern is whether the non-negotiated starting point of Gorski's project is that one must believe, at some level, in the significance of America and its creed as sacred. That seems to be the unstated implication throughout the book. In contrast, even Dr. King, if we move beyond some of his early rhetoric, deeply problematized America's origins and modern way of life. In his "Beyond Vietnam" speech one year before his death, Dr. King called America "the greatest purveyor of violence in the world."[7] Furthermore, Dr. King came to believe that America needed rebirth, not just reform and tweaks. Consider his "Where Do We Go From Here?" speech in 1967, in which he said:

> [Jesus] said, in other words, "Your whole structure must be changed." A nation that will keep people in slavery for 244 years will "thingify" them—make them things. Therefore they will exploit them, and poor people generally, economically. And a nation that will exploit economically will have to have foreign investments and everything else, and will have to use its military might to protect them. All of these problems are tied together. What I am saying today is that we must go from this convention and say, "America, you must be born again!"[8]

When Dr. King says that America must be born again, he moves beyond the civic prophetic republicanism that Gorski describes, which imagines ongoing tinkering with the system toward greater and greater inclusion and equality. Instead, Dr. King calls for a revolution of the very values and core practices of our country.[9]

Finally, I must ask the same question about how Gorski's proposal fits with Native American experience. In all honesty, I could not give Gorski's book to any Native American friend as a proposal to take seriously, or at least not without deep embarrassment and blushing, which is a problem. Honest grappling with Native American experience since the American experiment began is severely lacking in Gorski's proposal. But that is no surprise for a proposal seeking to salvage the United States' foundational identity. The American project literally devastated the way of life and ancestral lands of Native peoples. Their world was turned upside down and inside out. Nothing would ever be the same. It sounds nice to speak of the American project as a nuanced and complex (classic)

republican freedom in contrast to libertarian liberalism without that as part of the conversation. However, the American
project was also, and continues to be, death-dealing for Indigenous peoples. A story that is inclusive of, and informed by,
Native American experience is not taken up. Sadly, central to
Gorski's proposal is an adoption of a partly supersessionist
reading of Scripture that envisions Europeans as a replace-
ment for Israel in covenant with God. That is where the idea
of "American covenant" arises. This, however, is the very
theology that fueled the sense of chosenness that animated
Manifest Destiny and the conquest of the land to begin with.
Gorski's proposal for readopting a kinder covenantal theology for our civil religion without grappling with how any
national identity of chosenness and exceptionalism can easily
lead to the practice of exploitation and social domination is
a flaw.

Gorski's *American Covenant* helped me think through
some of our contemporary challenges in fresh ways, and
certainly aids in a growing conversation about making space
in the public square for people of faith and atheists to pursue the common good with integrity. Yet in my final analysis,
American Covenant fails to grapple with the extent to which
the American republic is still a white supremacist and settler
colonial capitalist project that needs to undergo a revolution
of values, repentance, and social rebirth. If God's deliverance
is sought, which is not the norm for empires, it must do so
while hearing the sacred stories and experiences, including the
pain and suffering, of the most vulnerable in our midst. The
way of Jesus invites the church to be in proximity to the least
of these and to receive their truthful word. To begin that path,
let us turn our ears to the black prophetic tradition as it speaks
back to empire.

TALKING BLACK AND THE BLACK PROPHETIC TRADITION

When Jeremiah Wright said not "God bless America" but instead "God damn America," mainstream America nearly lost its mind. Yet for a lot of black Christians, as well as scholars of history or black intellectual thought, Wright's words were not that unique. While not all black congregations participate in a radical tradition of social witness, such faith leaders and communities have existed going all the way back to their birth under slavery. The prophetic tradition animated the courageous words of black ancestors struggling for freedom while they spoke truth to this nation. While the majority have taken for granted the American creed that the United States has been mostly on the side of goodness and equality, black prophetic utterances have called for repentance and rebirth before God's judgment. The United States branded itself as God's chosen nation, but black people, and especially many black Christians, talked back with a different account. It was black lived experience, harmonizing with Hebrew prophetic Scriptures, that allowed black people to be a mouthpiece of divine condemnation against the horrors done to God's children. This talking back to empire through talking through black lived experience must be heard if the church is to find deliverance from the story of American exceptionalism.

David Walker was born in 1796. He was born free because his mother was a free woman living in Wilmington, North Carolina, although his father was enslaved. He eventually moved to Boston and became a prominent abolitionist. He is best remembered for his *Appeal* written in 1829 to enslaved black people. Walker was unsettled by the horrors of slavery, had the rare opportunity to learn how to read and write, and had deep faith in Jesus. He also believed that most who professed faith in Christ did not actually take Jesus seriously. According to Walker, "Pure and undefiled religion, such as was preached by Jesus Christ and his apostles, is hard to be found in all the earth."[10] However, I want to turn our attention to Walker's courageous talk-back to the nation. He directly challenged their belief that God ordained the United States to be what it was and provided a divine condemnation and warning that God Almighty would bring an end to the country if repentance and reform do not come. He wrote,

> Perhaps they will laugh at, or make light of this; but I tell you Americans! That unless you speedily alter your course, *you* and *your Country are gone!!!!!!* For God Almighty will tear up the very face of the earth!!!! Will not that very remarkable passage of scripture be fulfilled on Christian Americans? Hear it Americans!! "He that is unjust, let him be unjust still:—and he which is filthy, let him be filthy still; and he that is righteous, let him be righteous still; and he that is holy, let him be holy still." I hope that the Americans may hear, but I am afraid that they have done us so much injury, and are so firm in the belief that our Creator made us to be an inheritance to them forever, that their hearts will be hardened, so that their destruction may be sure.— This language, perhaps is too harsh for the American's delicate ears. But Oh Americans! Americans!! I warn you in the name of the Lord, (whether you will hear, or forbear,) to repent and reform, or you are ruined!!!!!![11]

Walker was not the only one who talked back. The most famous of abolitionists had even more severe words for this country which celebrated itself as a beacon of freedom. In 1852, Frederick Douglass was invited to give a talk for Independence Day. While he was grateful to have escaped slavery, he did not forget the suffering and shackles of his brothers and sisters. As an abolitionist, he spoke and wrote on behalf of freedom for the enslaved, and this invitation to speak seemed like no better time to prophetically tell the truth to America in view of its most hypocritical holiday. How could America celebrate itself as a land of the free when it persisted in enslaving black people, even as other nations had ended the practice? He named the nation's lies and sins throughout the speech. Without mincing words, Douglass prophetically condemned America for its "great sin and shame":

> I shall see this day and its popular characteristics from the slave's point of view. Standing here, identified with the American bondman, making his wrongs mine, I do not hesitate to declare, with all my soul, that the character and conduct of this nation never looked blacker to me than on this Fourth of July. Whether we turn to the declarations of the past, or to the professions of the present, the conduct of the nation seems equally hideous and revolting. America is false to the past, false to the present, and solemnly binds herself to be false to the future. Standing with God and the crushed and bleeding slave on this occasion, I will, in the name of humanity, which is outraged, in the name of liberty, which is fettered, in the name of the Constitution and the Bible, which are disregarded and trampled upon, dare to call in question and to denounce, with all the emphasis I can command, everything that serves to perpetuate slavery—the great sin and shame of America! "I will not equivocate; I will not excuse"; I will use the severest language I can command, and yet not one word shall escape me that any man, whose judgment is not blinded by prejudice, or who is not at heart a slaveholder, shall not confess to be right and just.[12]

Douglass believed that "America is false to the past, false to the present, and solemnly binds herself to be false to the future." While he did articulate a hope in the ideals of the Constitution, for Douglass, America itself was not rooted in those words. The greatness of the United States was patently false. And again, in line with the black prophetic tradition, he named America's sin and hypocrisy. If you have never read his full speech, you should put this book down and read it in its entirety.

A contemporary of Douglass, William Wells Brown, also exposed America's hypocrisies in 1847 while lecturing for the Female Anti-Slavery Society of Salem at Lyceum Hall. Multiple times in his speech he unveiled the hypocrisy of living under America's banner, which for him meant slavery and oppression:

> If I wish to stand up and say, "I am a man," I must leave the land that gave me birth. If I wish to ask protection as a man, I must leave the American stars and stripes. Wherever the stars and stripes are seen flying upon American soil, I can receive no protection; I am a slave, a chattel, a thing. . . . This is deplorable. And yet the American slave can find a spot where he may be a man—but it is not under the American flag.[13]

There are countless black prophetic voices that spoke courageously to their nation. Another notable one was Henry Highland Garnet. Garnet is often best remembered for his fiery speech "Let Your Motto Be Resistance!" in which he called for resistance through an uprising. Trained as a minister, he prophetically decried the church's failure to speak up and stand up for enslaved people. He explained that "slavery had stretched its dark wings of death over the land, the church stood silently by—the priests prophesied falsely, and the people loved to have it so."[14] Garnet clearly saw himself in the tradition of David Walker, and had his own speech published alongside a republication of the "Appeal" a few decades after it was written. Garnet's rhetoric combined a black prophetic tradition with a call for radical resistance. His most famous words from the speech come at the end. After challenging enslaved people not to submit any longer to oppression, he urged: "Let your motto be resistance! *resistance*! resistance! No oppressed people have ever secured their liberty without resistance. What kind of resistance you had better make, you must decide by the circumstances that surround you, and according to the suggestion of expediency. Brethren, adieu! Trust in the living God. Labor for the peace of the human race, and remember that you are four millions!"[15] The black prophetic tradition and the practice of radical resistance came together courageously in his speech.

Transitioning from this black prophetic tradition under slavery to under Jim Crow reveals an ongoing habit of talking back to America through talking black. Henry McNeal Turner, an African Methodist Episcopal (AME) minister and then bishop, exemplifies this living tradition and its capacity for adapting to new circumstances and speaking truthfully about the United States. He is also remembered for his theological imagination, which undermined the white supremacy and anti-black idols that construed god as a white man. Instead, he believed that black people could not and should not submit to a white god but instead should believe that "God is a Negro." Let us consider how living while black informed him of the incongruences of his country:

> I know we are Americans to all intents and purposes. We were born here, raised here, fought, bled, and died here, and have a thousand times more right here than hundreds of thousands of those who help to snub, proscribe and per-secute us, and that is one of the reasons I almost despise the land of my birth. I have been commissioned twice as a chaplain in the United States army, and have seen colored

men die by the thousands on the field of battle in defense
of the country, yet their comrades in time of peace, who
survived the war blast, I have also seen ignored on account
of their color to such an extent that they could not procure
a dinner on the public highway without going into some
dirty old kitchen and sitting among the pots, while the riff-
raff from the ends of the earth were treated as princes.[16]

In another speech before the Georgia state legislature in
1868, Turner held a mirror up to the nation right in the face of
those seated in power. He explained, "The black man cannot
protect a country, if the country doesn't protect him; and if,
tomorrow, a war should arise, I would not raise a musket to
defend a country where my manhood is denied." Furthermore,
Turner deeply believed that God sided with the oppressed and
against those who practice injustice. His critique was theologically grounded, rooting him at the center of the prophetic tradition. An example of this comes from the same speech before
the Georgia state legislature:

> You may expel us, gentlemen, by your votes, today; but
> while you do it, remember that there is a just God in
> Heaven, whose All-Seeing Eye beholds alike the acts of the
> oppressor and the oppressed, and who, despite the machi-
> nations of the wicked, never fails to vindicate the cause of
> Justice, and the sanctity of His own handiwork.[17]

After slavery formally ended (though continued by other
adapted practices), new forms of terrorism took rise. Lynching was the most public and trauma-inducing practice that
arose after legal chattel slavery ended, taking about five
thousand black people's lives and terrorizing many more who
were left behind in the aftermath of the torture and murder.
Ida B. Wells was clearly the most courageous prophetic voice
against the evils of lynching. After close friends of hers were

lynched and their execution justified, she began to crusade against it by doing significant investigative journalism and speaking nationally and internationally against this American sin. The ways that her faith shaped her work are not always recognized, because her faith was not central in many of her speeches, which focused more directly on specific lynching accounts and the devastating statistics of this racial violence. But Ida B. Wells was a participant in the black prophetic tradition and was shaped deeply by her Christian faith. For Wells, lynching directly conflicted with the way of Jesus and stained the United States with its sins. As lynching grew nationally, her prophetic courage grew proportionally to confront those evils: "Time was when lynching appeared to be sectional, but now it is national—a blight upon our nation, mocking our laws and disgracing our Christianity."[18] There was a white backlash for courageously exposing American lynching and for describing with detail the gruesome violence against black men's bodies at that time. Wells's prophetic witness resulted in her getting chased out of her hometown, having her business destroyed, and having a bounty placed on her head. This did not quiet her voice one bit.

During World War I, many black people were divided on how to think about their relationship to the war. Black people had survived centuries of formal chattel slavery and saw it end through civil war, but now new adapted forms of white supremacy had taken its place. And when the North removed armies from the South after Reconstruction ended, the white backlash against black people was severe. W. E. B. Du Bois, the most preeminent black scholar of his time, saw participation in the Great War as an opportunity to increase democracy at home, but many black leaders disagreed. Ultimately, when black people returned from fighting, they found themselves in an increasingly violent white supremacist Jim Crow social order. In response, Du Bois wrote "Returning Soldiers" as a prophetic condemnation of America's hypocrisy, which claimed to promote democracy abroad while oppressing black people on its own shores. He said, "We return from the slavery of uniform which the world's madness demanded us to don to the freedom of civil garb. We stand again to look America squarely in the face and call a spade a spade. We sing: This country of ours, despite all its better souls have done and dreamed, is yet a shameful land." And despite this, "It lynches." Du Bois could see through the lies of the United States' branding itself as a democracy for justice and equality for all. Instead, "the land that disfranchises its citizens and calls itself a democracy lies and knows it lies." Also, he wrote, "it steals from us." This is how:

> It organizes industry to cheat us. It cheats us out of our land; it cheats us out of our labor. It confiscates our savings. It reduces our wages. It raises our rent. It steals our profits. It taxes us without representation. It keeps us consistently and universally poor, and then feeds us on charity and derides our poverty.

And finally, Du Bois was fed up with the anti-black assaults against his community. America claimed greatness and supremacy while attacking the dignity of black people and treating them as less than human. "It insults us," he wrote. Again, he explains,

> It has organized a nation-wide and latterly a world-wide propaganda of deliberate and continuous insult and defamation of black blood wherever found. It decrees that it shall not be possible in travel nor residence, work nor play, education nor instruction for a black man to exist without tacit or open acknowledgment of his inferiority to the

dirtiest white dog. And it looks upon any attempt to question or even discuss this dogma as arrogance, unwarranted assumption and treason.

Du Bois ended his speech with a divine call to fight the "forces of Hell" and to "make way for Democracy":

> But by the God of Heaven, we are cowards and jackasses if now that that war is over, we do not marshal every ounce of our brain and brawn to fight a sterner, longer, more unbending battle against forces of hell in our own land.[19]

The black prophetic tradition not only fueled the freedom struggle during slavery and under Jim Crow, but was also vital in the civil rights movement. Too often, the freedom struggle of the mid- to late twentieth century gets told in a strange way that molds key figures into the myth of American exceptionalism, rather than revealing them to be its greatest challengers. More than anyone, this is true of how Rev. Dr. Martin Luther King Jr. has been interpreted. There is a reason for this misreading. It is rooted in the extremely selective adoption of his words. For most, King remains frozen in time and place, stuck delivering his "I Have a Dream" speech in 1963 on the National Mall in Washington. Of course, very few have studied the entire speech. Mainstream Americans prefer to isolate one phrase out of context so they can extract it and universalize it as King's once-and-for-all message. Yes, many have heard it so much it runs off the tongue like an evangelical quoting John 3:16, "I have a dream that my four little children will one day live in a nation where they will not be judged by the color of their skin, but by the content of their character." For now, I will bypass explaining how this one sentence has been co-opted to shut down the very things Dr. King struggled for. Rather, I invite you to read the whole speech, and to note how Dr. King's sermon doesn't assume that America actually lives up to its creeds, but instead, with imagination, invites it to do so now.

Dr. King, like every other human being, was not static or one-dimensional. This is most evident when one reads the body of King's writings and speeches over the course of his life. One observation a careful reader will note is that King's content and tone shift dramatically from his early years as one of the leaders in the movement to his final days. There are a few ways to comprehend these changes. For one, we could look at his position in relation to power and describe the adaption he made as he moved from the position of a prophet who had access to the inner court of power to becoming a prophet speaking from the outside. Dr. King, after all, frequently had access to the presidents' ears early on in his career, but that was no longer the case after he strongly spoke out against the Vietnam War. Another way I have looked at it is to see King as more optimistic and rooted in a dream early on, but becoming more frustrated, tired, and angry over time, admitting that he had seen his "dream turn into a nightmare." Most often, I talk about early King and late King. The year 1966 was a significant point in Dr. King's journey. Several things happened around that time, including his attempt to expand the struggle in the South and to turn that attention toward northern cities. Many of the systemic injustices he identified at that time continue to persist today in our ghettos. He also was known in his later years to speak of the giant triplets of racism, militarism, and consumerism. He believed they fed into one another and were not separate issues that people should address independently. Along those lines, he also, as I already mentioned, spoke out against the Vietnam War. This expanded the meaning of the movement beyond parochial limits and connected the dots between poor nonwhite people all around the globe facing poverty and war and the experience of black Americans in the United States. These, along with many other dimensions of his shifts, help illuminate the complexity and maturation of King over his life.

One aspect that was fairly consistent about Dr. King was his ongoing assault against poverty in this country. He believed "there are literally two Americas" that make up our country. While King had no desire to turn our country into a communist nation, and made that plain on several occasions, he also had deep and prophetic criticisms of capitalism. It was inevitably going to create an inequitable schism between the few wealthy and the masses of poor and working-class people struggling to survive. Dr. King said, "One America is flowing with the milk of prosperity and the honey of equality" while the "other America has a daily ugliness about it that transforms the buoyancy of hope into the fatigue of despair. In that other America, millions of people find themselves forced to live in inadequate, substandard, and often dilapidated housing conditions." King's prophetic critique of America's economic order was a common aspect of his framework, an aspect that is often ignored for more superficial quotes that make him appear real cozy with Uncle Sam.[20] Dr. King, especially in his later years, frequently talked back to America, exposing its hypocrisies. He stated it clearly: "Now the problem is America has had a high blood pressure of creeds and an anemia of deeds on the question of justice."[21]

However, America's favorite prophet told the truth to the United States about its militaristic violence all around the world. Despite counsel that there would be social consequences and mainstream backlash for taking a moral and ethical stand on the war, King strived forward anyhow. He understood that other civil rights leaders were not willing to sacrifice donations and public sentiment on behalf of people on the other side of the globe, but he felt that he could do nothing less. What was striking about his 1967 "Beyond Vietnam" speech is that he turned the moral and ethical challenge he had been calling poor and oppressed black people to practice and directed it toward the nation. It seemed hypocritical for a white-controlled nation to want black people crushed under white oppression to respond nonviolently while all the nation's problems were addressed through violence. When he received pushback from black youth on this very point, he heard them, and it transformed his prophetic witness in the public square. As he explained, "Their questions hit home, and I knew that I could never again raise my voice against the violence of the oppressed in the ghettos without having first spoken clearly to the greatest purveyor of violence in the world today—my own government."[22] For someone of his profile to speak so boldly about the nation shook many white people to their core. They were furious. Dr. King, however, knew that this country was steeped in sin, and was abusing its dominance on a global stage for its own profits and to the harm of black and brown people everywhere. So, like a true prophet, he called the country to repentance and rebirth through a "radical revolution of values":

> I am convinced that if we are to get on the right side of the world revolution, we as a nation must undergo a radical revolution of values. We must rapidly begin the shift from a "thing-oriented" society to a "person-oriented" society. When machines and computers, profit motives and property rights are considered more important than people, the giant triplets of racism, materialism, and militarism are incapable of being conquered.[23]

King continued with his diagnosis, highlighting our bloated military budget while we throw a minuscule percentage of the nation's wealth toward empowering poor and vulnerable people: "A nation that continues year after year to spend more money on military defense than on programs of social uplift is approaching spiritual death."[24] Given that our country has dived deeper into this disparity of spending in recent years, one wonders how much more piercing King's words would have been if delivered today. It is interesting that "hate" is usually reserved for groups like the KKK and neo-Nazis, but it is not categorized to name national policies that devastate and destroy people's lives far more effectively than any individual KKK member ever could. This was not the case for Dr. King. In closing his speech he told the truth and held a mirror up to the nation so it could see itself and its role in human history before God: "We can no longer afford to worship the God of hate or bow before the altar of retaliation. The oceans of history are made turbulent by the ever-rising tides of hate. History is cluttered with the wreckage of nations and individuals that pursued this self-defeating path of hate."[25]

While Martin Luther King Jr. has become the most prominent figure remembered during the freedom movement, Ella Baker was a force to be reckoned with in her own way. She mobilized the people themselves for prophetic witness in the midst of national hypocrisy and injustice. She spoke up when necessary, but she focused on cultivating the leadership capabilities of the community rather than just herself. In remembering Ella Baker's prophetic leadership, which was frequently more dialogical and community based than upfront before the cameras, we are reminded that we do not need to wait around for a new Moses. Instead, whole communities (with an inclination toward young people serving a special role) must pursue true freedom together, especially when it means confronting the establishment with faith and courage.

Ella Baker was a force throughout the twentieth century. She was born in Norfolk, Virginia, in 1903, and raised in North Carolina. A part of what shaped her prophetic leadership was her relationship with her grandparents. They were formerly enslaved and yet were generous community-minded leaders who always redistributed their farm-grown excess food generously with others who lacked in the neighborhood. At the age of nine she was baptized. "In Baker's view, baptism called the baptized not only into personal change but also into the work of eradicating sin from society."[26] She excelled in school and after college moved to Harlem where she was exposed to black radical thinking while also deepening her roots in her faith at Friendship Baptist Church. In her twenties and thirties, Baker responded to the mass poverty and hunger she witnessed all around in her northern city by challenging the exploitation of black domestic workers through journalism.[27]

While Ella Baker's whole life was committed to pursuing justice and freedom for oppressed people, she was best known for her participation in the civil rights movement. Baker had a legacy of prophetic leadership that cultivated the leadership, voice, and agency of other oppressed people. For example, she saw firsthand the limitations of an always upfront male dominated leadership style that didn't have authentic space for partnership, collaboration, and dialogue across gender and generations. Baker worked directly with King and the mostly male clergy leadership while also creating new spaces for a more democratic approach for justice organizing. In 1960, thousands of students across the South began disrupting businesses that practiced Jim Crow through sit-ins and mass arrests. They put their bodies on the line in a way that caught the attention of King and the Southern Christian Leadership Conference. They saw the potential in tapping into this youthful energy by absorbing them into the organization as a youth wing under their leadership. Ella Baker, famously, opposed this merge under the SCLC's leadership. Her conviction was that these young adults needed to be free to develop their own agency, goals, and leadership rather than fall within the hierarchical structure at work in the SCLC. During a convening about this very possibility, she urged the young people toward a more democratic path. Despite the urging of the SCLC leaders, the young people took her advice and created an independent organization, the Student Nonviolent Coordinating Committee.[28]

While Ella Baker preferred to practice her prophetic leadership in dialogical community, she did also use her rhetorical gifts to speak back to those in power. For example, in 1964 at the Mississippi Freedom Democratic Party state convention, Baker was troubled that black peoples' lives and concerns were devalued. There was a profound uproar expressed when white civil rights leaders were killed, but when they searched for their bodies in the river and discovered black men's bodies instead by accident, there was no empathetic response for them. No one cared about the death of these black men because they were not killed alongside white people. This angered Baker. In front of everyone at the convention, Baker challenged the hypocrisy of the nation with courage: "Until the killing of black mothers' sons becomes as important to the rest of the country as the killing of white mother's sons, we who believe in freedom cannot rest."[29]

Baker's life, her prophetic leadership oriented toward mobilizing the people (especially the young) rather than creating a singular platform for herself, and her courage to speak back to those in power when needed, provide a great model not just for the emergence of a prophetic leader, but the potential for a prophetic church. That is mobilizing the church into a prophethood of believers. And her legacy widens our imagination for mobilizing communities and indigenous local leadership in our neighborhoods, and the need for dialogue and democratic conversation with a diversity of ideas at the table. She reminds us of the need for a prophetic partnership with black women and black men, young and old, struggling for freedom together, where all voices are heard.

THE WEIGHTIER MATTERS OF THE LAW

In this nation, mainstream Christians have usually tripped up under the demands of speaking truthfully about America. This country has always had lofty ideals that masked ugly realities. For most of this nation's history, blood has been spilling over from the people crushed on its underside. Over these many centuries there has always been a prophetic voice speaking back, and when it is heard it counters America's lies, renounces America's idolatry, and names America's sins while calling for a revolution of values, repentance, and rebirth.

The lie is that, at its heart, America is an innocent nation primarily serving the interests of goodness, justice, and equality. The truth is that the very people who were written out of full belonging and participation in the American experiment are now central to the rebirth of this land and continue to invite everyone to imagine a world beyond what currently exists. Rebirth requires the end of the world as we know it.

Even now, about two million of America's own citizens are locked away in prison thanks to the largest incarceration system in human history. No nation incarcerates its racial minorities at higher rates than the United States. Right now, one of the wealthiest countries to ever exist on this planet refuses to provide access to adequate healthcare for all of its citizens. Healthcare continues to be a marker of social status, when we could easily lift up the quality of life for millions of people through preventative and affordable care. Right now the wealth gap between the richest and the poorest Americans is exposing problems with our economic system, as we watch billionaires hoard wealth while others struggle just to get by. Right now, our poorest neighbors are locked out of owning their own home, stuck in the cycle of high rent and no inter-generational wealth to pass on. Right now, millions of citizens lack affordable, safe, and adequate housing, and unless we ensure access to quality housing for all people regardless of their neighborhood, we will continue to see two Americas persist. If America is exceptional, we could say its greatness is seen in its massive disparities in education, which are designed to ensure that many black and brown people remain a poor working community excluded from the mainstream economy, ultimately finding their way into prison or on probation. Even right now, the top 1 percent are scheming new ways to sup-press wages or exploit their workers out of compensation by hiring people just below full-time so they can maximize profits while not honoring their hard labor with livable pay. Some people only want to talk about the good things happening in our country while turning away from the hardships and suf-fering, but until we look in the mirror and see the American lies we've been telling, we will be a walking hypocrisy.

When Americans proclaim the country to be great and innocent and to demand complete allegiance, no matter what, they participate in American idolatry. One of the most basic commandments from the Decalogue is that we are to have no other god and are not to worship any other object but the one

Creator. Millions of American Christians have had no problem bowing down before Nebuchadnezzar's statue. With religious zeal, many American Christians pledge their allegiance to the nation, without any qualifiers. I remember one semester in college when a friend asked me if I would die for my country. It was a broad question, so I naturally asked for some clarification. Under what circumstances, and for what reason would I die for my country? What came next was a surprise. He said, "No, no that is not the question. The question is, Would you die for your country?" I think we went back and forth one more time basically repeating what we each already had said before it sunk into my thick skull that his point was whether I would die for my country without any qualifications and for any purpose. My answer was easy at that point—"Hell no!" is probably what I said (or was at least thinking). My friend had joined the reserves of one of the branches of the military, and he was all in. But for me, I was confused. There should never be anything that demands your ultimate allegiance as a Christian, regardless of the context and circumstances, except discipleship to the way of Jesus, yielding to the Spirit's activity in the world, and worship of our Creator, and living life committed to loving your neighbor as yourself.

The church must recapture its prophetic witness, and this will only be done if we have a robust, holistic, and multidimensional understanding of sin. Unfortunately, in our society today many employ the language of sin from a thin and narrow understanding. Most people who have not abandoned the language of sin (many progressives and liberals avoid using it) do so in limited ways, and it is an empty shell of its comprehensive significance. Usually it is deployed by conservatives as they discuss sexuality or members of the LGBTQ community, as well as abortion; otherwise, the rest of its usage falls into what I would call the interiorizing of sin. That is, sin is treated mostly as a matter of the inner heart. Sin is viewed as individual and as an internal battle, but has no public or social significance for how we organize our society and the impact it has on others. By manipulating and controlling the category of sin to be primarily deployed in this way, it can be weaponized against others, while rarely having anything to say about one's own participation and complicity in society. For this domesticated version of sin, Christians' duty is to fight against lust or feelings of guilt or shame. Whether they pay fair wages to workers is not a question of sin. Whether they have a "give my kids the best" mentality while other kids live with dilapidated housing and under-resourced and struggling schools apparently is not sin. One must resist anger and a spirit of bitterness, always smile and be nice, but spreading racist scripts and ideologies that harm undocumented people and encourage "tough on crime" policies for "those folks" is not a problem. Denigrating the poor and giving sainthood to people who exploit others, no problem. But if a poor person is deemed to be lazy in their estimation, fire and brimstone. You get my point: something is terribly wrong with our moral and ethical compass, and it has everything to do with how we understand sin.

In the prophetic tradition of the Judeo-Christian Bible, sin has much more to say about what God despises. Consider Amos 5:21-24, a passage frequently quoted by Dr. King. Like many other scriptural passages, here in Amos, God is said to not delight in the worship of a people that engage in injustice, and they need to do justice and set things right for that to change:

> I hate, I despise your festivals,
> and I take no delight in your solemn assemblies.
> Even though you offer me your burnt offerings and
> grain offerings,

I will not accept them;
and the offerings of well-being of your fatted animals
I will not look upon.
Take away from me the noise of your songs;
I will not listen to the melody of your harps.
But let justice roll down like waters,
and righteousness like an ever-flowing stream.

Similar passages exist throughout the Bible. God rejects those who claim to be God's people and desire to worship or give sacrifices when they persist in oppressing others. For a quick sample, consider reading Isaiah 58; Micah 6:6-8; Jeremiah 7:1-11; Zechariah 7; or Ezekiel 34:1-10. They all, in different ways, demonstrate the prophets being a mouthpiece for God expressing divine judgment against people believing themselves to be favored by God and yet engaging in oppression, exploitation, and injustice against poor and vulnerable people. Sin is identified pointedly. It is often a devastating damnation against the people that oppress and exploit vulnerable people. Sin and evil, in Scripture, provide language to identify and challenge personal and social injustice. It is not sufficient to say, "We are all sinners"; we must also note that some people have been significantly sinned against, and God is watching. The language of sin invites us to think about generational responsibility to ongoing injustice, how we show dignity to people made in the image of God, and that no one stands innocent, since sinfulness runs through each and every person. It calls for more than an interior examination of sin, as if the only thing that mattered were our heart: it also calls us to repent and change our practices individually and collectively.

The Judeo-Christian concept of sin, when diagnosed faithfully, is a gift for public discourse. It is an opportunity for a revolution of values, repentance, and rebirth. The prophets focused much of their powerful rhetoric toward addressing two things: idolatry and the rampant injustice in society, which contrasts dramatically with the ways sin language is most frequently weaponized in the public square. This is also the case with Jesus' life and teachings. Jesus, as with much of the Bible, spends very little time on sex and sexuality, and instead focuses more on the harm done against the poor, oppressed, and vulnerable. This might explain the expression of Jesus' compassion toward eunuchs' diverse experiences, since they were a sexual minority in their context (Matthew 19:12).

Jesus frequently embodied and fulfilled the tradition of the Hebrew prophets for his society. One of his most scathing divine judgments was against the establishment religious and political leaders that oppressed and exploited the masses of poor Jewish people. He says, "Woe to you, scribes and Pharisees, hypocrites! For you tithe mint, dill, and cummin, and have neglected the weightier matters of the law: justice and mercy and faith. It is these you ought to have practiced without neglecting the others. You blind guides! You strain out a gnat but swallow a camel!" (Matthew 23:23-24). This follows the exact pattern seen with the prophetic witness in the Old Testament.

I remember when I first moved back to Philly after living in Harrisburg for a few years after college. Moving is always hard. Thankfully, since I had friends and family in the area, I made the necessary calls ahead of time to make it as easy as possible. While I invited a lot of people to help, I invited a few people in particular. I had some heavy items, and I knew I couldn't ask just anyone to help me get them from the rental truck into our home. So I thought about who my strongest friends were who could help carry the heaviest items. On the actual moving day, everyone showed up as planned. It was an encouraging show of support. Immediately people got in the truck and began grabbing items and taking them into the house. Great! Except there was one problem. Some of my strongest friends began grabbing little lamps and small boxes to carry. That was not going to work. I had not called them over to help so they could waste their energy running little boxes back and forth. They were intentionally invited to carry the weightier items on the truck. I had to stop them and have them put down the small stuff, because I needed to get those big items in the house, or all my intentionality around calling them for that purpose would have been a bust.

There is a natural tendency to major in the minors and minor in the majors. This happens when we weaponize the language of sin while avoiding the injustice and idolatry that shape our society. For Jesus in Matthew, he had seen the establishment leaders abuse power and then construct a religious system in which they abdicated what mattered most. Their lives were full of sin, but they had constructed their own framework of sin that fit their lives, so they appeared fine to themselves. There was a gap between how they branded themselves and the actual sin in their lives. Jesus knew they needed a prophetic call to a revolution of their values, to true repentance, and to rebirth, otherwise they would persist in their injustice. Jesus teased them by saying they are out there tithing window plants (mint, dill, and cumin) so meticulously, yet at the heart of the Torah is the call to do justice, and they had completely neglected to do that. Most of the other woes in chapter 23 follow a similar line of them majoring in the minors and minoring in the majors. They devalued what mattered deeply to God. Jesus' powerful prophetic condemnation of their sin held a mirror up to their lives.

Like Jeremiah Wright and many prophetic voices in this land, the church is called to talk back to the nation when it misses its vocation. It is not our responsibility to absolve the nation of its deeds. It is not our responsibility to ensure that American creeds live on. However, it is our responsibility to be a prophethood in the way of Jesus, participating in this living tradition. In the United States, black lived experience has provided one of the most fertile grounds for prophetic witness in our country. From that standpoint, the myths and lies that America has told which erase black and Native voices, along with those of many other vulnerable and marginalized people, are more visible. Talking black has been instrumental for talking back to the powers. And sometimes it is unsettling.

In Kelly Brown Douglas's *Stand Your Ground: Black Bodies and the Justice of God*, she exposed the myth of American exceptionalism that developed from Anglo-Saxon chauvinism, the anti-black racism that frames black bodies as guilty, and the white religious and cultural mission to expand and control this land.[30] In response, she reminds readers of God's freedom and justice, but Douglas also notes that we are in a kairos moment that has emerged out of crisis, which is ripe for prophetic witness. As a black mother, she grappled with the meaning of the death of young unarmed black men and women and the "stand your ground" culture that perpetuates it. Despite the pain of it all, she understood that the prophetic witness of black people gestured toward a better future. For Douglas, "Within the context of the stand-your-ground-culture wars that have violated the freedom and imperiled the lives of black people, prophetic black voices have emerged to hold the nation accountable for its own self-proclaimed history. These black voices have turned the narrative of 'exceptionalism' back upon the nation and called it to live into its very claims to be that 'city on a hill' shining forth divine virtues of morality and freedom."[31] She begins to close her final chapter by saying "This *is* a *kairos* time. It is the time for each of us to be embodied realities of a black prophetic tradition and with moral memory, moral identity, moral participation, and moral imagination begin to create the world we 'crave for our daughters and sons.'"[32]

For mainstream Christians there is a need to first hear black prophetic voices that are willing to truthfully say, "Not God bless America" and instead offer the more truthful word, which is that "God damns" those who build their lives on the backs, necks, and heads of vulnerable people. Jesus' blessings and curses are aligned with this prophetic tradition that reverses social status in God's reign (Luke 6:20-26). And second, mainstream Christians must follow the way of Jesus, which includes a prophetic witness in society capable of naming the "weightier matters" of society, rather than become political puppets for the establishment and their political and partisan agendas. If we are to experience God's deliverance, we need to be set free from the lies, idolatry, and original sin of this nation. May we have the courage to talk back and invite those in society to undergo a radical revolution of values, repentance, and rebirth so that we may begin to experience a taste of beloved community in this land.

5

THE POLITICS OF THE CHURCH

BELONGING, POWER, AND JESUS OUR CENTER

STANDING ON THE TABLE

The church is called to be a counter-witness in society. When hierarchy, domination, institutional and communal bias, violence, greed, and inequity run rampant in society, the church ought to be a community that has adopted Jesus-shaped practices that renounce and resist those social evils in its members' own lives. Jesus should reign so that the lure to lord over others as humans can be rejected. Unfortunately, congregations are known more often for organizing their life around supremacist social norms than for being a visible hope that another world is possible. We must repent of the incongruities of our practice and proclamation if we dare speak to the broader society on its injustices. We have to be able to name the elephant in the room and the principles that organize and shackle the life of the church.

Imagine we were gathered in a room together for conversation. We gather weekly in the same room. And we are seated around a large round table. Everyone is seated around the table except for me. When we meet, I always stand on the table in its very center. Imagine that we have been meeting like this for years. When we come into the room and people take their seats, I habitually take my place at the center of the table. This is the way it always has been. Week after week, this way of organizing our social life feels normal and ordinary for me, and it is the routine everyone else has contorted their own gathering practices around.

Now imagine that one week, seemingly out of nowhere to me, someone speaks up and suggests that this arrangement is not right and not working for them. They believe that I should not place myself at the center of the table for our gatherings. In fact, they do not believe I should be standing on the table at all. Instead of standing, they tell me I should get off and take a seat around the table like everyone else. They suggest that my place at the center is not healthy for everyone else, and is harmful to me. They believe the permanent advantage of my physical location perpetuates troubling social dynamics. A change is needed.

When you think about a person's feelings and expectations, it is no surprise that I might take offense to this request that desires to change the gathering dynamics, and more specifically my placement. I've always stood at the center of the table. I'm not the one trying to change our tradition and practices for meeting. Why am I being picked on? Why am I being targeted and singled out? The normal way of doing things seemed to work just fine as far as I saw. Now I feel judged for just being me. Furthermore, I don't appreciate that I am being marginalized from my place at the table. Marginalizing me is wrong! And I've always tried my best to be a nice person, so shouldn't I use the position I've been blessed with for good? Isn't stewarding my positional advantage the best thing for everyone? Is it not a gift from God to extend God's goodness to others? There is no good reason to marginalize me.

At this point, we can only hope that someone would speak up once again and tell a more truthful story of what was happening. An honest account is needed that is truthful about how and why these shifts need to happen. In response to my complaints it would be appropriate for someone around the table to tell me that while I am claiming to be marginalized by these concerns, that is not what is really happening. I was asked to move from the center and to join everyone else around the side of the table. This, my friends, is not *marginalization*, it is *decentralization*. It is true that my social position was shifting radically from what it traditionally had been. However, I was also invited to join everyone else as equals, to become positioned to recognize the dignity and value inherent in each person.

This decentralization process moves us toward affirming the inherent value and shared humanity of all people. However, it does mean that I am experiencing something. I might have genuine feelings of discomfort. Radical reorganizing of our lives toward a gathering that flattens hierarchy will likely feel disorienting and unsettling for those who had the most advantages by virtue of the original arrangement. I am human, and such changes do not happen separate from human emotion and reaction to changing circumstances. If I am fortunate enough to have a community of people around me who are both truthful and loving, they will help me see that I am not being marginalized but rather decentralized, but they will also recognize that I am a human rather than a machine, and that with change I will undergo a range of emotions and feelings. And I will need to admit that my emotions are real, but they are not a higher priority than the organization of our gathering in a way that allows everyone to be treated with dignity. Communities should not allow the feelings of an individual with social power and advantage to override the reorganizing of our lives toward mutuality and solidarity. People can recognize that socially advantaged people have feelings, even while the community moves forward toward embodying the beloved community. This rhetoric of referring to oneself as marginalized or sometimes even oppressed, when we are really talking about people who have been decentralized, seems to be particularly common right now among many white Christian men (though not exclusive to that demographic, because every person is vulnerable to this skewed interpretation of moments when one's unique social advantages are publicly identified).

Obviously my concern isn't really with how we gather around a table (although these ideas do relate to our mundane everyday life routines). Instead, my desire is to shed light on the need for the church to find deliverance from its mangled politics of belonging and practice of power as we gather together, and then to embody and extend the distinct social practices of local churches when engaging institutions and organizations in society. Basically, I am calling for the church to be righteous in our ecclesial gathering so we can have a prophetic witness of integrity in our social scattering.

Often it seems that the church is hypocritically calling on the broader society to administer justice in ways that it is unwilling to do within the body of Christ. Justice loving Christians want our society to care about vulnerable people, to ensure livable wages, to provide healthcare and housing, to make space for people who have been historically unrepresented in the government, to uplift the gifts of women, to treat every person with dignity and respect, but too often, churches internally are unwilling to radically restructure their own lives to become the beloved community.

Just to be clear, I'm not calling for a moratorium on pursuing justice in the public square, as if the local church should solely do that work (which some conservatives argue for). I believe that one of the main purposes of a society's governing body is to administer justice for the vulnerable and to set things right within oppressive power dynamics that lead to harm. And the church ought to understand this better than most. Instead, I think the church should have enough faith to align its worship and community life in congruity with God's reign on the earth. Out of such faithfulness to God we become a visible manifestation of God's deliverance breaking into our world in a tangible manner. When the church speaks prophetically to society, challenging it to do justice, it ought to be a fraction of what we are already doing in our own life where the Messiah is enfleshed in community. When we hold society to a higher standard than we hold ourselves, we not only become hypocrites, but enact a faithless response that denies the delivering power of God in our lives. The example of someone moving from standing at the center of the table and moving to a position of equality and shared humanity seems to be the very least we should expect from Jesus-shaped community. Our sacred Scripture, and especially the gospel accounts of Jesus, often seem to invite us into an even costlier and revolutionary response to our society's practice of hierarchy and injustice, a response in which the first are last and the last are first.

ACTS 6:1-7: OVERLOOKERS AND THE OVERLOOKED

In Acts, God takes the church on a journey full of growing pains, unanticipated communal challenges, and headfirst into a new belonging in Christ that has room for more and more people. The book helps reveal God's love for all people while remaining attentive to those most vulnerable, which has already been seen in the life and teachings of Jesus. This is the Spirit's continuity with Jesus. Pentecost is a great example. The Spirit descends on the disciples of Jesus while dispersed Jews from around the world are present. There is a miracle of speaking and hearing. The disciples speak, and God accomplishes an intercultural miracle in which everyone hears the words in their own native language. God broke boundaries of culture and region in an intimate way by meeting people through the intimacy of their own home language. This is the opposite of colonizing behavior. God made no demands for cultural assimilation but instead affirmed each of their languages as worthy vehicles for meeting God. This moment brought together into community an interesting mix of Jews who had faith that Jesus was truly God's crucified and resurrected Messiah. Hebraic Jews had retained much of their ancestral language and customs in their homeland, while Hellenized Jews adopted Greek culture and language to varying degrees while living as dispersed people around the world. And now as they came together, the two groups were forming ongoing messianic communities that required different gathering practices and roles where everyone fully belonged.

Early in the book of Acts we read that community and shared life were very important. The Acts community shared all things in common with one another, including their resources. Those with wealth sold their possessions and goods and distributed them according to the needs of everyone. These communities were grounded in faithful teaching of the good news of Jesus by the apostles, eating together in homes, fellowship, prayer, and praise of God. The book of Acts describes a community where God's reign was the new organizing principle for their lives despite Jesus' return not having happened yet. And it was a contagious community that was growing and expanding quickly.

These early Christians are also described as constantly clashing with their social order. From the start they are in trouble with law and order. Despite the amount of times Dr. King was arrested during his day, I think most Christians today would blush if we internalized the portrayal of these early Christians as repeat offenders constantly getting arrested in this Lukan narrative. These Christians were repeat offenders because they had to be faithful to "the stone that the builders rejected," and they knew their ultimate allegiance required them to obey God over human authority. Much of the book of Acts depicts early Christian leaders speaking courageously despite the dangers, disrupting economic currents and money of wealthy people by delivering persons from bondage, experiencing brutality and abuse by soldiers as punishment, being unjustly imprisoned, escaping by God's delivering presence, and then doing something just as subversive once released. If the book of Acts provides a glimpse into actual lived experiences, then there is a correlation between the early church and jail that should make comfortable Christians hesitant about siding with "law and order" in our debates about policing practices, unjust policies, and the prison system.

It is no wonder that the early chapters of Acts describe the formation of a common life among these early Christians, followed by the abuse, arrest, but ultimate freedom of these Christian leaders. Acts then describes an even more intensified form of social and economic shared life in community. These disciples were not participating in status quo conformity with society—it was a subversive counter-witness that brought together Hebraic and Hellenistic Jews into a shared life under the reign of Jesus Christ. These traditional and diaspora Jews were trusting God with this emerging community, seeking to create space where everyone belonged in and through Jesus. We are told that among those who came to this community and bought into the vision of the new community was Barnabas. He sold his field and gave the proceeds to the community, trusting in the Messiah's reign, even while the old order still seemed to be running as usual. The Acts community was a public counter-witness by their existence. It seems like the people were willing to go with God through all the surprises that came their way. What could go wrong?

The faith described by this community was robust, but the community was also fragile. It was fragile because they were joined together only by the space of belonging made for them through Jesus. The push and pull of those who were at home in Jerusalem versus in the broader Roman Empire's Hellenistic culture inevitably would cause conflict. The test was whether their shared common life could be sustained amid the differences that existed.

When we get to chapter 6 of Acts, one of the first things one might notice is that the community had processes of justice already implemented. Specifically, Acts describes an organized system in place designed to take care of the widows in their midst. Anyone who has read their Bible carefully knows that widows are among a sacred list of commonly referred to people (including the poor, foreigners, orphans, and other oppressed people) that the people of God are called to care for, making provisions for their well-being. This Acts community understood their holy vocation and upheld their commitment to vulnerable people. The needs of widows were treated as sacred. They had a system intentionally designed to meet these needs. The people of God are called to embody God's deliverance as a community in the world.

Despite this, a complaint arose that exposed that the daily distribution of food was overlooking its most overlooked and vulnerable members: Hellenistic widows. That's right, a meals on wheels program was in place but it was distributing the resources in an inequitable manner. The systems and structures in the church dedicated for justice were themselves not just. An invisible line had been drawn between those in the community who were treated as though they had full belonging and those whose presence and sense of place in the community was qualified with an asterisk. The asterisk was created by the subtle wink from the insiders who believed that when the rubber hit the road, it was their community and not the outsiders', even while they cared about them. It was inevitable that this fragile community would have to confront the realities of identity, belonging, and power, and to ultimately examine who had become the overlooked, forgotten, or marginalized of the community.

The complaint of overlooking the Hellenistic widows goes all the way to the apostles, and they receive the voiced concern as sacred. Of course, that outcome was not inevitable. The apostles are insiders, they already have full belonging, and their needs are met. The system is working just fine for them. Nonetheless, they've been seized by faith in the new thing God is doing, and because of that they respond as if "whatever affects one directly, affects all indirectly."[1] It is as though their lives have been bound up in common life, as though true justice is not authentic until it is first realized among "the least," "the last," and "the lost." There is no trying to manipulate, control, or drown out this complaint. The voiced concern of the overlooked is prioritized by the apostles, and they bring it to the attention of the whole community. Transparency rather than defensiveness often leads to the decisive implementation of restorative justice and service to those who need it.

After sharing the voiced concern with the entire community, the apostles give the responsibility to the community to choose seven men from among them to oversee that this wrong is righted through ongoing oversight and service. Some people might be troubled that these leaders hand over responsibility for choosing leaders to the community rather than doing it themselves, because whoever does it will oversee the restructuring of the care for these vulnerable widows. Some might interpret their prioritizing their preaching and teaching as a value statement that those gifts are more important to the life of the church than doing justice and serving others. It could even perpetuate American Christian polarization between those who prioritize a "spiritual gospel" over against those who prioritize a "social gospel." We of course do not have to split the gospel into two and choose one or the other. It is more helpful to see the apostles as taking on a shepherding role that empowers the church to be the church. Leaders don't have to do everything. The church is not its leaders; the church is the whole community of disciples committed to following in the way of Jesus and seeking to manifest God's reign on earth. In delegating, they are able to fulfill their distinct vocation, which requires discernment and teaching while wrestling with the Scriptures and remaining attentive to God's active presence. They need to stay attentive to what God is up to and remain formed by the life and teachings of Jesus and the greater scriptural narrative so they can provide pastoral guidance for the community's faithful witness. I think it is precisely because they were prayerfully immersed in God's story and seeking to participate in God's delivering presence that they were prepared to decisively guide and delegate a process for substantive justice for those widows being overlooked. They comprehended that the community must collectively find new social practices and leadership to ensure they embodied the justice of God. Pastors should be empowering their whole community to take responsibility for justice.

In this moment, they are precariously moving toward God's shalom. On one hand, vulnerable women are now honored and their full belonging is being affirmed, yet the irony is that patriarchy is still defining the chosen deacon leadership. All the leaders chosen are men. We know that later in the book of Acts, Priscilla, a significant leader in the church, will directly disciple and instruct Apollos. We also know by Paul's own testimony in Romans 16 that the Spirit of God will move and fall on men and women alike in such a dramatic fashion that we are given a glimpse of women participating in church leadership at every level, from deacons to house church leaders to Junia being named among the apostles. For now, their vision of God's dream for them is only partially realized.

With that restricted imagination named, we should not miss that something powerful is happening nonetheless, something that is breaking this community open toward God's desire for the overlooked and the outsider. A careful reader will notice that all seven of the men chosen have Hellenistic names. None of them have traditional Hebraic names. This suggests that this community discerned collectively what God was doing, and it led them to radically restructure their leadership to such a degree that members representing the once overlooked (Hellenistic Jews) are now the ones doing the overlooking as deacons. They are now overlooking the community's service and processes for internal justice. Moving from overlooked to overlooking the community through service and justice demonstrates God's reign made visible in Jesus, who repeatedly took those on the margins and placed them on the mainstage of God's divine drama.

Notice that the community's leadership structure did not opt for tokenism. That is often the response to such a predicament by those who are decision makers. Some choose to merely tinker with the system, because they do not want to rock the boat that has been working for them. Their decision also was not a matter of simply doing the math, ensuring that the leadership in place is statistically proportional to the community's demographics. A sociological or representative approach might not necessarily be wrong in certain situations, but certainly lacks the radical imagination of God's reign. After careful and prayerful discernment by the people, justice for this Christian community meant taking seriously Jesus' teaching that the first will be last and the last will be first in God's new order. Again, the overlooked were empowered by the community to be the overlookers. This is the church beginning to further realize that yielding to God's Spirit can at times mean reformation, but at times it is a radical revolution of our communal life.

"MAKE YOURSELF AT HOME"

If you came to my home you'd probably hear me greet you with the words "Make yourself at home." This is a common way to welcome others into your home. If I said this to you, there are a few things I'm hoping to accomplish. When guests come over, I want them to feel comfortable. Sometimes when you are at someone else's house, it can be hard to relax. It might not matter how kind people are, it might simply be about wanting to respect their space. So sometimes you feel tight and just can't relax. An invitation to make yourself at home hopefully invites people to more readily adjust and be themselves. To relax their shoulders and take a few deep breaths, putting them at ease. I also greet people this way and sometimes give specific permissions. I invite them to take their shoes off and even to put their feet up. They are welcome to go into the fridge to grab a drink on their own. They are welcome to walk around and explore the house. Again, I want to be hospitable.

However, if I am being honest, when I say make yourself at home, I do not really mean make yourself at home! Certain behaviors would cause some problems if you did them. For example, if you came into my house and started to rearrange the furniture, that would not be okay. It would also be inappropriate for you to come into my house and start taking down my family pictures while putting up your own. Finally, if you dared to go into my bedroom and peruse my closet, and then got the nerve to put on my robe and slippers and walk around the house in them, we would have some words. All that suggests that my invitation to "make yourself at home" is misleading. The truth is, I just want you to be comfortable, but too often I still think of myself as the host and think of you as the guest. That's not really home for you.

I'm married, and Renee (my wife) sometimes changes, rearranges, or renovates our house furniture without telling me in advance. While this would be highly inappropriate behavior for a guest, it is completely acceptable for her because she has full belonging in our home. I expect that she will make changes to our home because she fully belongs. And though I don't like it, she still wears some of my favorite hoodies in the winter to stay warm, and some of my favorite T-shirts in the summer. I have adapted to her doing so because she fully belongs. Sometimes she updates our family pictures while I am out of the house, and enjoys thinking about different paint colors for our walls. Again, these are expected behaviors for someone who fully belongs in our home.

However, her belonging in our home opens up the possibility for more significant changes in our house as well. Our family is made up of Renee, myself, and three growing boys. Since our family has expanded significantly over the past few years, my wife has questioned whether we are maximizing the space in our home the best for all five of us. For example, she has wondered if we should have a second bathroom installed in our house. One bathroom is fine for two of us, but with an expanding family some of our extra space could be converted to better facilitate our whole family, as well as the frequent guests under our roof. On occasion, she has also wondered about knocking down a wall on the first floor to open up the space. Finally, we have even dreamed about one day finishing our basement since it seems like underutilized space right now. These things are not decorative changes. What she is considering are significant structural changes to the building itself so that it can best facilitate everyone who belongs in our home as our numbers increase.

I had the pleasure of leading a small training of local pastors with my Messiah College colleague Robert Reyes. Our sessions complemented one another very well. And I especially appreciated his language of first- and second-order changes, which I believe is more common within behavioral change theory. He explained that first-order changes are symptomatic, that is, surface changes that affect the aesthetics but will not necessarily adapt people toward a different way of living. One example might be taking down all the white Jesuses in the stained glass windows. It is important to do, but there remains something deeper at the root of the white Jesus' existence in the first place.

Second-order changes, however, are deeper institutional changes that affect how everyone behaves and how we define our reality. If you change the rules to a system, everyone who operates within it will have to learn to adapt to a new way of operating within it. An example of this could be a church hiring a worship pastor and for the first time incorporating scriptural and theological themes of God's justice into the music and embedding different interactive and embodied liturgy for the congregation. It could also mean changing books, curriculum, and resources used to equip the congregation on an ongoing basis, which may expand their understanding of who God is and how to participate faithfully in society. This framework does not suggest that first-order changes are unimportant or that churches should only focus on second-order level changes. An image of white Jesus, for example, has centuries of history that reinforced white supremacy, presenting God in the flesh as a mascot of the Western European colonial project. I personally would invite everyone to evaluate the images of Jesus in their decorations and curriculum. However, that change is surface level. One could take down every white Jesus and still have the congregation being discipled after the whitened and westernized Jesus found in so many *theological* portraits and books and living by the ethics of a domesticated and distorted Jesus that doesn't care about oppression and injustice in our world.

Every church believes that it is welcoming. Every congregation believes that they are friendly. Everyone in their own little way tells visitors to their community to "make themselves at home." The question we should ask is how much congregations are willing to transform their current habits and practices as they yield to what God is doing, so that former outsiders are adopted fully as insiders. How do we move from being welcoming to creating true belonging in the body of Jesus? Belonging can't just be a spiritual and abstract truth, it must be lived out, or we deny its reality for our lives. White supremacy, patriarchy, classism, homophobia, and corrosive political partisanship powerfully organize many churches in the United States. A congregation's rules, expectations, habits, decor, and unspoken biases reveal that these forces of oppression still keep Christian gatherings captive.

Christian communities wanting deliverance from the forces that resist belonging and the practice of internal institutional justice must vulnerably yield to the Spirit's invitation to transformation. As in the example I gave of people at my house ultimately being treated like guests by me (God is still working on me), unlike my family members who have full belonging, we are reminded that we must be open to different kinds of change. History teaches us that sometimes the church needs reformation, but sometimes it needs radical reformation. Our congregations need to remain open, rather than defensive, to the possibility that God is taking us on a grand journey that will create us into something new as a people. The Hellenistic Jews and Hebraic Jews were on a journey. God was not inviting Hellenistic Jews to assimilate into Hebraic Jewish culture, erasing their own particularities and culture within the dominant group. This new belonging required that the leaders refuse fragility, renounce supremacy, empower new leadership, and radically restructure the institutional organization by making substantive and comprehensive second-order (as well as first-order) changes.

The historic black church tradition in the United States originally emerged for this very purpose, and ought to be studied accordingly. Too often, Americans conflate the existence and ecclesial practice of the white church with the legacy of the black church. I understand why when one evaluates the two on a superficial level. But once you go beyond the surface, the differences become starkly apparent: the legacy of the black church invites us toward a more radical hope within a white supremacist society. If we stop at the often quoted phrase that "Sunday mornings are the most segregated hour of the week," one might think that the primary goal should be the end of the black church. From an actual historical vantage point this fails to grapple honestly with the meaning of the black church within a white Christian society that organized itself and its church by the rules of racial hierarchy.

The white church was a community that adapted its faith and worship gatherings to align with white supremacy. During slavery the white church in the United States enforced an apartheid system where racial hierarchy defined one's value and belonging. Eventually this would switch to full segregation, in which white churches were spaces for white belonging. In contrast, the black church tradition was created in resistance to the racial hierarchy and segregationist ways of organizing their worship and community. Richard Allen, founder of the AME Church, for example, understood from the start that segregation and racial hierarchy were counter to the way of God while simultaneously recognizing that the church needed to make space for vulnerable black people to be affirmed as made in the image of God. Over the years, they had developed valuable traditions and songs that were especially appropriate for the United States' racist context.

The black church was birthed into the world because it chose to withdraw from white supremacist Christianity. The norm for the black church was that all people came from one single human family and all were welcomed in the worshiping community. This is why Dietrich Bonhoeffer, in 1930, found belonging in the Abyssinian Baptist Church in Harlem and was able to participate at all levels of the church. This historic black congregation, without hesitation, intimately shared life with Bonhoeffer during the heart of Jim Crow in the early twentieth century when northerners were concocting strategies and narratives to bolster anti-black segregation.[2] The invitation into deeper Christian belonging was available to other white Christians throughout the country, but they never opted in, nor even considered, a black church as an option for them. The white church exists because of its segregationist impulses and practices, and for the most part this basic historical fact has never been acknowledged by most white Christians. The black church was born out of withdrawal from that kind of overt white supremacist Christianity. Segregation and withdrawal are not the same thing.

One might wonder what might happen if white churches around the United States confessed their white supremacist and segregationist foundations, and studied the complex and also imperfect social witness of the black church as one pathway toward radically reorganizing their life so that Jesus was at the center and those marginalized and excluded could now experience true belonging. And of course, black congregations have their own issues and challenges to work through as well, and they would do well to wrestle with how God's delivering presence ought to guide our ministry and collective life together in the twenty-first century.

Here are some questions all congregations can grapple with while evaluating their willingness to opening up a space of belonging for others within their institutional and communal life: Where is God's deliverance and justice being stifled in the church? Are there people within the community who have raised concerns about the way the community organizes itself? What would a first-order change look like? What voices would need to be present and listened to to discern what changes are needed? What impact would it have on the people in the community? What behaviors or perspectives would change? What are some possible second-order changes? What anti-oppression or intercultural changes could result from implementing it? Are some people present more as guests than as people who have full belonging? Who is considered for leadership and decision-making? Is the congregation open to surface change as well as radical restructuring of its policies, expectations, and practices? What discipleship must happen to join with the Spirit's radical movement among us in our world?

ADJUSTING THE HEAT IN THE ROOM

In 2018, I was invited to speak at an innovative conference on justice at a Mennonite college. The conference brought together a scriptural theology for doing justice with leadership principles geared to equip people to better do justice work within their communities and organizations. I gave three talks that weekend. First, I delivered the opening plenary, entitled "Eyes Stayed on Freedom," which provided a scriptural theology for justice and shalom. Next, I had a very minor role on Saturday delivering a ten-minute reflection on a scriptural passage that tied into one of the leadership principles being taught. My assigned topic was on adaptive leadership, and I reflected on Jesus' adaptive leadership, which he modeled with his disciples, who were slow in comprehending the significance of the nature of his messianic reign. Finally, I provided the closing sermon for the conference on Sunday morning, entitled "Where Do We Go from Here?," where both conference participants and regular church members attended the service.

Along with my opportunities to share, I appreciated learning from the leadership skills that were taught on Saturday. They were not trivial, but instead were helpful skills and tips for people who wanted to work for systemic change. One of the things I took away from those sessions was something I knew intuitively, but now had a better framework to think about it. It was about the needed skill of intervention, speaking up, and knowing the right thing to say for the right moment, so that when harmful ideas are shared people are prepared to faithfully engage in the moment. People struggle with this all the time. Sometimes someone says something troubling, and no one responds, allowing that to linger as the dominant idea in the room. Having the will to intervene and speak up is important. Likewise, having some sensitivity to what kind of intervention would lead to a more transformative and productive exchange is really important. I have tweaked the analogy slightly, but my ongoing thoughts on intervention originated from those Saturday sessions.

Let's think about adjusting the temperature in a room. If you have a group of people in a room and you decide to adjust the temperature, you have a few different options. You could adjust the thermostat so the room gets colder. Maybe people are too comfortable, and a little discomfort would be better for the conversation you are having. You could make the room really comfortable, so much so that people feel really cozy.

If everyone is stiff and tight, this certainly can let people put their guard down. And you can also turn the heat up in the room. This could intensify the atmosphere, or maybe it could be an attempt to put people to sleep. Of course, when you adjust the thermostat you should have a goal in mind for what you want. What is a conducive atmosphere for transformation in that space?

Speaking up and engaging in prophetic intervention is kind of like adjusting the temperature in the room. Some rooms are status quo and too comfortable. The dialogue is unfruitful, and nothing productive is likely to happen if it continues in the direction it is heading. There need to be people in the room who will courageously, discerningly, and prophetically speak truth in a context-appropriate way. The key is to wisely discern what kind of intervention is right. The goal is always transformation. So if a church is having a dialogue about an unjust way that it organizes its communal life, our goal is to participate in prophetic intervention in such a way as to guide people along the journey of becoming a beloved community. Turning the heat down too much might make the atmosphere frigid and it could tighten everyone up in the room; turning it all the way up may burn everyone by deepening rather than transforming the conflict. Wisdom and discernment seek to offer an appropriately provocative word for what is needed for that group. Sometimes a strong statement is needed, but sometimes a thoughtful and insightful question can be more beneficial. Different situations require different "temperatures" for transformative and productive space. There may be times when turning the heat all the way up is necessary because of the seriousness of the topic. However, if you go with max heat every time, people will not trust your judgment and the atmosphere won't be conducive for growth. Sometimes, people are already hostile and antagonistic toward one another, and we need to find a way to cool people down so they can actually dialogue. Our goal is prophetic intervention that leads to repentance and new life.

Prophetic intervention, however, requires that we speak up. Too often, people remain completely silent when justice requires a prophetic word revealing God's dream for us and our departure from it. There is a false assumption that you have to have some great speech to offer, otherwise you can't say anything at all. Oftentimes, what matters most is not the specific words that flow from your mouth but rather the faithfulness of your witness to stand up for justice and truth through intervening in that space. This is what I frequently tell my white students at my university who worry about what to say when they interact with family or friends who are outspokenly racist. The key, I say, is to speak up. You just need to say something and be fully present. It can be simply saying, "I disagree, and I am disappointed that you believe that about other people." That alone, if you have nothing else to offer, is one thousand percent more valuable than remaining silent because you don't have all the right words at the moment. Your calling isn't necessarily to be a great debater, it is to be a faithful witness, which requires prophetic intervention in the face of untruths about people made in the image of God. Just yield to the Spirit as you step forward in faith, knowing that Jesus the liberator is with you, in you, and guiding you in the moment. God's power is made perfect in weakness, which frees us from the responsibility of needing to be perfect in our response. But it does invite us to be discerning in our moment and where our group is at.

The Sunday morning of the conference on justice and leadership principles, I had my sermon prepared and I was ready to preach. My sermon was on the Acts 6 passage I discussed in this chapter, and I placed it in context within the larger story of Luke and Acts. Since it was Sunday morning worship, there were many other parts of the service before I would speak. There were announcements, gratitude and recognitions for conference planners, worship, and prayer.

The prayer was led by local pastors who did not have the opportunity to participate in the conference. They led a responsive prayer in which they read a line and the congregation replied with the words that were projected on a screen. Even though they did not attend the conference, they clearly were attempting to make the theme of justice and peace central to the prayer. The prayer considered the violence and injustice in the world and sought God to help us to be faithful in our response. However, there was clearly some disconnect between the focus of the prayer and the kinds of conversations we'd been having in the conference. Our conference was attentive to systemic injustice and how it expressed itself through racism, sexism, classism, and so on, and it looked at how those things shape the life of churches and Christian organizations. The prayer, in contrast, turned our attention to violence and injustice "out there" rather than in here, and was more individualistic in focus as well. I particularly noticed it because my sermon was going to revive the themes from the conference to think about how we must be the justice of God as the church. I was immediately conscious of the fact that my sermon would clash with the prayer's language and scope in obvious ways. It happens, but it is not the ideal scenario for the one preaching.

Immediately after the prayer finished I heard a woman's voice yell out from behind me as I sat in the front pew waiting for my turn to go up. This woman's voice yelled out, "Stop, stop, this isn't right!" Since I do a lot of speaking, I have been to many kinds of churches from all different denominations. I usually have a good sense of what is normal for a community. And I immediately knew that this middle- and upper-class white Mennonite congregation didn't typically have people yell and interrupt their well-planned and respectable services. So I turned around, and to my surprise, I knew the woman speaking. She and her husband were also friends with many Anabaptists in Philly, and I'd had the opportunity of meeting her before this conference. She was a Bible professor who did some national speaking, and she enjoyed acting and drama. Knowing this about her, I immediately tried to make sense of what was happening. A lightbulb immediately went off. "Oh," I thought, "she must be doing a church skit that was planned for the conference." Basically, the whole thing was a teachable lesson, and the responsive prayer and the skit together were designed to teach us about speaking up as we'd we learned on Saturday. With that new perspective, I listened as she kept talking. "This isn't right," she continued. "We are praying as though the violence and injustice is out there when we need to confess as a white congregation our complicity to racism and oppression." Two things went through my mind. First was, "Right on." I agreed with everything she said. The second thing, however, was that my analysis of what was happening was off. Something seemed strange. I thought this was a church skit, but as I watched her speak I noticed that her hand was shaking and her voice was quivering. Since I knew she did theater, I couldn't understand why she was so visibly nervous in the moment. It did not add up. No, I immediately realized that this was not a skit, this was an authentic prophetic intervention happening in real time. She had courageously discerned the ways that her own congregation was avoiding the reality of their participation in white supremacy and racism.

She prophetically intervened without a fancy speech, instead choosing to bear witness to a more truthful story that made transformation and repentance possible.

The pastors responded to her prophetic word without any defensiveness or dismissiveness (at least not that I saw). They led the group in prayer again, this time confessing and repenting of the congregation's own role in injustice, historically and in the present. A prophetic intervention, along with the humble response of pastors willing to receive it and respond appropriately, created an opportunity for transformation for everyone in the room. It was in that transformative moment and space, which was now significantly more conducive for repentance and renewal, that I stepped up on the stage to preach my sermon.

NAMING POWER IN THE CHURCH

In the church we often have naive views about our relationship to power. Certainly, there are Christians who recognize the ways the church has pursued social power by any means, and the harm it has caused to our vocation and public witness. Given these ugly realities, more churches need to reflect on their own inclinations toward social dominance. Even fewer churches, however, spend time examining how power dynamics work internally in their communal and institutional life. But whether we name it or not doesn't change the hard fact that it is at work. Our awareness of it does not change its presence and activity in the life of the church. So we should not act like toddlers who close their eyes and think something does not exist because they can't see it. Christians moving from milk to meat need the maturity to reflect on the inevitability of power dynamics happening in our community. When we do, we can consider how to engage it in a Jesus-shaped way and as we are being constantly delivered from the practice of social dominance and concentrated power.

When I was a youth pastor fresh out of college, I was a bit naive myself when it came to power in the church. As I got more involved in the behind-the-scenes decision-making, I quickly realized that church life is often filled with so many contested opinions, visions, and hopes for the community. I mean, everyone knows there are church gossips and egos, but so much more is happening beyond those obvious things. Our church probably had some intensified struggles because it was a historically white church going through growing pains as it sought to become multicultural. When I started there, the worship leaders were all white and led mostly contemporary Christian music, folk worship songs, and Eurocentric hymns. A gospel choir occasionally led special music for the congregation, but the heart of the worship was still white and Eurocentric. As I did my duties there, I began seeing the different ways that the congregation defaulted to white dominant culture, despite having a really beautiful vision statement that described the kind of community they were striving to be. The music wasn't the only manifestation of this, but it certainly was the most obvious and in-your-face contradiction that the congregation had in relation to its own vision statement.

With the opportunity to preach occasionally, I dedicated one sermon to naming some of the challenges that existed that prevented us from becoming the community they themselves had detailed they desired to be. Looking back, my sermon probably was a bit more tame than most of mine are now, but I think it was substantial for where we were as a community at that time. My message drew from Ephesians 2:11-22. This is a popular passage in the "racial reconciliation" movement. However, I focused on the language of breaking down the walls of hostility as an opportunity to talk about community transformation as central for reconciliation. With that in mind, I considered with the congregation where the walls of hostility were still up and what was preventing us from becoming beloved community. I talked about a variety of things that would help us be a multiracial and multicultural community, but I focused on the low-hanging fruit of our worship music as a concrete example. In contrast, I read the congregation's own vision statement, which conflicted with our current practices.

In my sermon, I used an analogy of a remote control to talk about the need to shift the power dynamics in the church. I got the analogy from a Bible professor who had used it a few weeks earlier to talk about his experience on campus. A close friend of mine and I were at his house talking and watching a soccer game. He picked up the remote control in front of him as he spoke. He said that if the school ever wanted real change, they would need to hand over the remote control to nonwhite underrepresented people on campus, and that such people would need to hold that remote until things were more balanced in institutional policy, and then we could share the remote. He stressed, though, that the remote has been in one hand so long that it would take time to create an inclusive place. His concern was that he believed that the institution was not willing to give up the remote.

For my sermon, I just retold that exact story, and what my professor had said to me. Then I applied it to the life of the church and the power dynamics at work that kept reduplicating white power and decision-making in the congregation. I invited the congregation to hand over the remote so we could take the next steps toward becoming beloved community.

Having invited the church to take some next steps toward living into the vision it had claimed, I felt really good after

I finished. Immediately, many of the members of color came up to me thanking me for the sermon. I even received a few phone calls later that afternoon and on the following Monday. The overall gist was that this was a message that needed to be preached. I felt good.

Unfortunately, that feeling didn't last too long. On Monday, I received a phone call from our senior pastor. Apparently, not everyone had appreciated my sermon, and he received some upset phone calls. It was so serious that he was calling a Tuesday morning pastoral meeting (our typical meetings were Wednesday afternoons) because it needed to be dealt with urgently. I was a really young man at that time, and I just remember the sinking feeling in my gut, like I had swallowed a bowling ball. I went from thinking I had given a really meaningful sermon that would help usher us toward greater faithfulness as a church to now thinking I may have stepped over a line and might receive "church discipline" in response. Not sure what to expect, I went to our meeting with a bit of fear and trepidation.

For most of the meeting I sat quietly as the other four pastors spoke. They all went around and shared their thoughts on the sermon. I remember at least a part of what each of them said. The children's pastor, who was a white woman and the next youngest after me, simply said she thought it was a good sermon and didn't understand what the fuss was about. Another pastor whom I deeply respected, and who was the only other African American pastor on staff, said she thought the sermon was good, but she qualified that by saying she thought it was something the senior pastor should preach, that maybe it shouldn't be coming from me. I don't remember everything one of the other white pastors said; I don't think she said much, but I do remember her saying she thought I sounded "angry." That seemed the most ridiculous to me, but I knew that it was something white people sometimes say to dismiss black perspectives. I just let that one roll by. Finally, our senior pastor, an older white man, said that he thought that overall it was a good sermon, but he specifically said that he didn't agree with my remote control analogy. I should have asked some questions in response to that comment, but I still had a bowling ball in my gut, and hadn't yet developed the confidence in situations like that to speak up when needed. He also explained the concerns that some of the worship leaders of the church had about me naming the whiteness in the worship. He agreed with my analysis but also thought that I should sit and talk with them and work through it.

I was happy that I didn't get fired from my first pastoral position, and I certainly never expected such a big backlash to the sermon. While it was difficult for me then, I can look back at that time and laugh about it. For one, compared to most of my sermons now, it really was not that prophetic or unveiling of what was going on. It was light despite the dust it kicked up. But I also recognize that I was a bit naive about power dynamics in the church, even as I was attempting to name them. An older me knows that once you begin naming the concrete worship practices of a church, you are entering into very contested space where people have strong feelings and opinions. It is one thing to speak truthfully, but it is another thing to understand that certain comments will inevitably spark a backlash. I don't think this means we should not do it, but we should be perceptive about the reality of power and its ties to the practices and habits of the church. In our ecclesial context, after naming the imbalanced Eurocentric music, worship at the church would soon begin integrating gospel and other cultural expressions into its life, and new worship teams would begin to emerge that ministered to the community in fresh ways.

That said, I am still disappointed that I never had a conversation with the senior pastor about his disagreement with my "one remote control" analogy. Did he disagree that power dynamics and decision-making power was disproportionately in the hands of white people in the church? Or did he think that the solution of handing over the remote control didn't reflect a Jesus-shaped response to the problem? Did he hear it as a call for him to step down from his role of senior pastor since he was a white male? While I wasn't thinking that when I said it, I wondered later if he heard that and felt targeted. My concern, however, was that he was dismissing the need to take account of how decision-making power was concentrated in white people's grip in the congregation and how race defined leadership and influence institutionally.

It seems that churches notoriously avoid identifying how power dynamics work in their congregations. Power, of course, is complicated and is not necessarily equal to formal leadership roles. Having a formal role in a congregation certainly is a kind of power, but it is not the only power. We need to consider all the different kinds of power that exist in churches, which go beyond clergy and include deacons, trustees, board members, and various paid and unpaid leaders in the congregation that have been given the authority to make decisions. Some of these people with power are visible and up front, but sometimes people can hold decision-making roles that are hidden to most. Does everyone know the various roles and contexts in which decision-making happens?

And then you have informal power in the church as well. If you have been in church long enough you know that it is not just formal leaders making decisions. Sometimes the ones with the most power are people with the right last names who are part of a legacy family in the congregation. Other times, power is expressed through financial giving power. Yes, those who give large sums of money sometimes expect, or are expected, to have disproportionate decision-making power. Sometimes money speaks. And then there is rhetorical power. It can come in two forms. The squeaky wheel often gets the grease. Some people are louder and consistent in making their expectations known, and they have a sense of entitlement that what they say should happen. And their persistence in speaking up can have significant influence over the life of the church. On the other end, some people perform rhetorical power with an ability to persuade. Some people, whether it be through education or gained through experience, are particularly good at making arguments and out-explaining everyone. Sometimes truth doesn't win out, and instead explanatory abilities dominate the life of a congregation. And of course, those deemed respectable and middle-class often have more say than those who don't fit traditional paradigms of what a responsible and trustworthy person looks like. Those perceptions of trustworthiness are often filled with biases that further shape who has decision-making power in the church. Again, this informal power can be visible or invisible. Sometimes everyone knows who wields informal power, but sometimes it is power that remains hidden to most, and only people with formal roles of authority are seeing and responding to it.

My point is that power dynamics are happening in the church. If we refuse to acknowledge this, it will continue unabated, and it cannot be surrendered to the preeminence of Christ. Power dynamics are a part of human relationship. There are also different kinds of power in terms of their relationship to justice and liberation. One can lord power over others, but someone can also share power with others. Power can be concentrated in the hands of a few people, but it can also be dispersed and redistributed to the community. There are churches where pastors act like gods among men, where hierarchy is built into their understanding of leadership. There are churches where the congregation's own decisions perpetuate unjust ecclesial practices, prioritizing their comfort and the status quo. Whether by the pastor or by a congregation, power can be abused.

Our different traditions have different church polity frameworks, and they have their strengths and weaknesses. Given that I am most shaped by black church and Anabaptist church influences, I prefer negotiating power in the church through a dialectical tension rooted in the strengths and weaknesses I see in the two (broad and diverse) traditions. In many black churches, the pastor has a disproportionate amount of power. The strength of it is that prophetic leadership is possible, and a church can be led and challenged beyond its status quo desires and ecclesial preferences with the right leadership. Prophetic leadership is a gift to the church and the broader society. However, abuse of power is likely if the pastor doesn't have accountability and if the pastor doesn't also surrender and submit to the church in meaningful ways.

In many Anabaptist congregations the power is rooted more in the life of the congregation. Communal discernment is prioritized, and the goal of acting from consensus is valued. Consensus doesn't mean every single person agrees exactly, but it also is more than just voting and going by majority rule. It is about trying to arrive at an overall agreement in the community, and about a willingness of outliers to go along with the direction the community is discerning. The strength is the empowerment of the church and a belief that the Spirit can move and be discerned by everyone and not just the pastor. More voices are heard, and a richer, more nuanced perspective can emerge when that is encouraged. A weakness, though, is that sometimes congregations need to be prophetically challenged and shepherded. I've witnessed many Anabaptist congregations that are allergic to strong leadership. But just as the pastor needs accountability, so the church, I believe, needs appointed people who are entrusted to provide faithful leadership and keep the congregation accountable to the gospel of Jesus Christ and God's reign. That is the role of pastors, and if a dialectical tension can be held between pastoral and prophetic leadership that is accountable to the congregation and congregational discernment and consensus-oriented dialogue under the leadership of a faithful shepherd, it seems that some common forms of abuse of power can be overcome.

Every church, though, must reflect on the power dynamics in their congregation, the polity of their tradition, and biblical wisdom culminating in the gospel of Jesus as they seek faithfulness in this area. It is still the case that our Christ was living in coequality with the Father and did not take advantage of that status, but instead emptied himself from divine power into human fragility. Jesus' flesh was not just a generic human life; it was a vulnerable life that Paul calls the form of a "slave." And Jesus, in life, submitted in obedience to God, even to the point of crucifixion. We, then, must have that same mind of Christ, living in mutual submission to one another. This is not a powerless community, because no such thing exists. Such Jesus-shaped communities bear witness to the reign of God by intentionally giving, sharing, and dispersing power in the congregation in ways that make the Jesus story visible in their public witness.

CONCLUSION

The church should not demand that our broader society administer justice and become inclusive when we hypocritically do otherwise. We must radically reorganize our lives so that we not only welcome others but also create communities of belonging through restructuring our lives according to the rule of Christ. The overlooked should become overlookers because in God's reign the first are last and the last are first. We must participate in decentralizing anyone who takes the place of Christ in the community, because that is idolatry. And if they call it marginalization, we need to tell a more truthful story.

We must practice prophetic intervention, allowing ourselves to become a mouthpiece for God in status quo situations. And we need to move from naiveté to maturity in Christ in the face of power dynamics in our community. Becoming Jesus-shaped as a community requires that we participate in Jesus' delivering presence among us. There is no simple answer or formula that will work for every community; the task we have is to creatively discern how to disperse and redistribute power in the church while ultimately yielding to the power of God, who is able to deliver us from captivity and our distorted vision which is leading to domination and abuse. Our gatherings in Christ should make visible that Christ is preeminent in our lives as we struggle for God's dream for us.

6

JUSTICE AND THE WORSHIPING COMMUNITY

The church ought to be a people of justice because we have encountered the God of justice. God is a Mother to the motherless, a Father to the fatherless, and a Friend to the lonely. God is the Waymaker for those who have their backs against the wall and to the poor and oppressed God is also known as a Deliverer. Throughout Scripture, we find the God of Israel to be committed to justice, righteousness, and peace, and habitually expressing solidarity and concern for the most vulnerable in society. If our worship declares the magnificence and faithfulness of the Most High God, then it must be bound to God's own revealed character and activity. Therefore, there ought to be a direct relationship between worshiping God and being formed as people of justice. If we worship, in spirit and in truth, the God described in Scripture instead of our own generic projections of what we want from a god, we will be formed to join God's work of doing justice and setting the oppressed free.

"THAT SOCIAL JUSTICE STUFF"

Although I am not originally from central Pennsylvania, I have lived in the city of Harrisburg twice now. The first time was immediately after graduating college. As mentioned in a previous chapter, I was a youth pastor at a decently sized multiracial Anabaptist church in the city while also working for a neighborhood afterschool program for poor black and brown middle school boys. I returned to Harrisburg in the fall of 2016 after living in Philly for eight years while getting my MDiv and PhD and serving on the pastoral team of my home church for six of those years. Deciding to return to Harrisburg was not simple. I've often called it my second home, since next to Philly I have the most familiarity, community, and networks in Harrisburg. It was where Renee and I first met, and where we got engaged. I formed many important relationships in Harrisburg that continue to be important to me. But being gone for almost a decade means things will not be the same when you return. People's lives go on. Some people leave the area. Everyone changes, including you. People and communities are not static, and Renee and I discussed this before deciding to return.

One of the easiest ways to root oneself in a new place is by joining and participating in a faith community. Renee and I already had relationships with many great people in one worshiping community, but we decided that we hoped to join a local church with a stronger emphasis on the work of justice. So after we returned to Harrisburg we spent several months visiting a lot of congregations in our city. Obviously, we did not visit every church, and most were within a narrow set of ecclesial traditions and denominations, but we visited enough to begin feeling drained and discouraged. We were having trouble finding a congregation committed to doing justice as the body of Christ, although several were multiracial and emphasized internal "racial reconciliation" or did charity or community service. There were even some churches where the pastors seemed personally committed to justice, but it did not seem to include the life of the congregation. Again, our exploration was limited to congregations that I believed were more congruent with our own theological convictions and ecclesial polity preferences, so there were many great churches that we did not visit. Still, much of our first year was a reminder how many churches exist where doing justice is not a part of a congregation's sense of vocation at all.

Eventually, we visited a small multiracial congregation right outside the city that was fairly traditional overall. To my surprise, someone I knew from Philly was guest preaching the day I visited. They told me that the very next Sunday a new couple would be joining the church as a pastoral team, and that I would really vibe with them well. So we returned the next week, and met this fairly young black couple from Philly that worked together as pastors for this small, traditional, and aging congregation. In getting to know them, we discovered we had common friends and networks back in Philly. They were both students and by-products of the black church, while also having a foot in the Anabaptist tradition. In every sermon they preached, they effortlessly interweaved God's justice, the way of Jesus, and contemporary social concerns. While the congregation was not as justice-oriented as I would have liked, the fact that they had invited this couple to co-pastor suggested that they were willing (or desperate enough) to be stretched. So our family decided we would stay and be part of this new phase of the congregation's life, knowing that we probably could be a help in cultivating new life and an awareness of the church's vocation to proclaim and embody good news concretely to our neighbors.

A year went by, and while no great revival dramatically shifted the witness of the church, we remained hopeful that perseverance would eventually bear fruit. I would occasionally be out of town giving sermons, talks, and lectures, or facilitating my "Changing the Way the Church Views Racism" workshops at colleges, conferences, and churches. On one occasion while I was traveling out of state, the congregation held a one-year review of the pastoral couple. From what I heard afterward, the couple was berated and humiliated during the review. The female pastor, in particular, was denigrated for her clothes, the color of her lipstick and nails, and other truly trivial matters that did not conform with the very traditional paradigm of many congregants. In all truthfulness, I do not believe the congregation was ever truly affirming of women in ministry, and I believe that the comments were a passive-aggressive way of responding instead of having to vocalize their actual thoughts. The unstated patriarchy was never acknowledged, and the prophetic voice that the pastoral couple brought to the pulpit was never genuinely embraced by many in the congregation. For example, there were specific comments criticizing the fact that their sermons regularly integrated God's justice and contemporary social concerns. Church, according to many of the stakeholders, should not be consumed with what is happening in the lives of our neighbors outside the four walls of the church.

In response, the couple decided to resign. They realized that the church clearly hired them in hopes of molding them into something they were not, and that the church had never truly caught their vision to be a people sent into their community, sharing God's love and justice. And I suspect the hurtful comments about the one pastor's clothes, lipstick, and such made the decision a bit more immediate and decisive. It is hard to believe that people found those humiliating comments appropriate. And so as quickly as they came from Philly they were making plans to return.

That same day the criticisms were laid out, Renee went to go pick up our boys from the children's program at the end of the service. She spoke with a member of the church about what had unfolded. The member went on to denigrate the pastors' sermons for too frequently addressing justice. In response, Renee said, "That is actually why we started attending in the first place." The member responded with surprise, "Oh, you like that social justice stuff?" And just as quickly Renee retorted back, saying, "Drew would say that is just preaching the gospel and taking Jesus seriously!" Clearly, many of them thought very differently about what faithful preaching sounds like. This conversation was passed on to me secondhand from Renee, but I affirm what she said. Discipleship to Jesus invites us to discover God's commitment to "that social justice stuff." Jesus preached "that social justice stuff" throughout his ministry, always prioritizing the least and last of society in his parables, sermons, and conversations. Jesus lived "that social justice stuff" when he healed the sick, restored the socially ostracized, prophetically challenged the wealthy, and confronted the Jerusalem establishment for "devouring widows' homes." And his promise of a coming reign is overflowing with "that social justice stuff" rooted in Israel's story and the prophetic vision of shalom grounded in divine justice and righteousness. Ultimately, the God in the Old Testament that is described as doing "that social justice stuff" is the one and same God revealed in Jesus Christ.

It is a tragedy that "social justice" in some Christian communities is so stigmatized. How did the church, which is called to do justice (and had, for most of church history, internalized a sense of vocation for justice, even if it wasn't always done well), get to the point where it is problematic to discuss it during its worship? My family's journey of looking for a worshiping community that understood its vocation reminded me how, too often, that very basic Christian teaching and practice is rare in congregational life and is often demeaned in the name of Jesus. The content of our worship misrepresents the worthy God we lift up. I believe that if we were to ground ourselves in the way of Jesus as his disciples, and in the character of the God revealed to Israel in our worship, we would rediscover that the church, if it is to be faithful, must seek justice concretely.

WORSHIP AND THE FORMATION OF THE CHURCH

One of the strangest trends among Christians committed to the work of justice is that many do it alone as individual agents rather than as an organic way of participating in the life of the church. Their faith might ignite them to do justice, but not in concert with their faith community. I know countless people who volunteer with justice organizations, but very few who discover their Christian vocation for doing justice and seeking shalom in their neighborhoods because they worship together with other disciples of Jesus. This may not seem that odd to some, since most people's faith and spirituality is highly individualistic and privatized. Nonetheless, this is not congruent with the image of God's people throughout the biblical narrative whose vocation it is to do justice and bless the nations.

Yet we shouldn't be too quick to blame those who have decided to go it alone as lone rangers for justice. Most churches are not embodying the delivering presence of God in real and concrete ways that lead to actual justice for vulnerable people. In fact, many churches barely or rarely articulate the ecclesial calling to do justice. Mainstream American churches are notorious for creating worship vacuums. That is, sterile spaces where self-professed Christians gather, but only after they have first sucked all the pain and suffering out of their spaces so that comfortable people can remain positive and unbothered by other people's troubles. To take seriously both suffering people and the unjust conditions that produce their hardship is a distraction from their primary work, many assume. This posture inevitably furthers the schism between escapist worshiping communities that have abandoned responsibility to serve their neighborhood and justice-oriented disciples who have taken seriously God's invitation to join in with the work of setting this world right.

Many beliefs undergird the escapist worshiping community. For example, some Christians believe that when they gather, the only faithful way to respond to God is to isolate from the world and focus on God alone. We are called to worship our Creator above all, and doesn't that require blocking out the world? Secondly, for some, Christianity is about attuning to, and privileging, spiritual concerns above earthly and material concerns. Secular society focuses on what can be "seen and felt," but the church, it is claimed, should rise above those carnal desires for the better things (that is, the non-physical world). Of course some recognize how much the Bible is consumed with a focus on justice for the poor and oppressed, but they are convinced that this kind of work is not a vocation for the whole church. Instead, it is the work of super-Christians like Dr. King and Mother Teresa, and all those admirable people deemed saints. Regular Christians must (in this line of thinking) get on with the everyday task of living as normal citizens with typical priorities like everyone else. Providing the best possible home, education, experience, and opportunity for one's own family is central to their sense of calling. Some believe that the church is called to join God's liberative work in the world, pursuing shalom amid so much violence and oppression around the globe, but they assume that as long as their clergy is active or there is a church program dedicated to service and charity, they have fulfilled such calling through their tithes. I guess we could think of it as vicarious representation in exchange for financial giving. Their tithing and attendance at a church where other people actively respond to injustice becomes an umbrella which they fit under, and such righteousness is credited to them. This is not a comprehensive list. Nonetheless, it is helpful to be aware of the ways we justify why the broader church community does not need to get mobilized and organized to do justice in some fashion.

These justifications, however, make sense within mainstream Christianity because our beliefs and practices as worshiping communities are watered down, interiorized, and in some cases, have flipped Jesus' good news to the poor into good news for the wealthy. This is done to accommodate the lives we are already living rather than to invite us into a community embodying the way of Jesus as a witness to the reign of God. My hope in this chapter is to remind us that if we are committed to worshiping God seriously, we should simultaneously be awakening to how love and justice stand at the center of God's character and activity in the world.

In Scripture, God is not only described as *doing* justice. The Bible sometimes describes the central divine attributes of God *as* justice and love itself. In Psalm 89, praise is lifted up to the heavens. And it is said of God, "Righteousness and justice are the foundation of your throne; steadfast love and faithfulness go before you" (v. 14). In Psalm 82, God is described as the One who will judge the wicked on the basis of their injustice toward and mistreatment of the vulnerable. In view of this judgment, the command in verses 3-4 is to do justice: "Give justice to the weak and the orphan; maintain the right of the lowly and the destitute. Rescue the weak and the needy; deliver them from the hand of the wicked." The Prophets make plain who God is in relation to justice. For example, Isaiah 30:18 states, "The Lord is a God of justice."

The entire Bible is full of these descriptions of God; however, the more significant signifier of God's justice flows from the pivotal story in the Old Testament known as the exodus. It is amid Hebrew enslavement that God reveals Godself to Moses as Yahweh, as the One who will deliver the Israelites from bondage. God declares, "I have observed the misery of my people who are in Egypt; I have heard their cry on account of their taskmasters. Indeed, I know their sufferings, and I have come down to deliver them from the Egyptians, and to bring them up out of that land to a good and broad land, a land flowing with milk and honey" (Exodus 3:7-8). In chapter 6, Moses is told to share this message about who Yahweh is (translated in English as Lord): "Say therefore to the Israelites, 'I am the Lord, and I will free you from the burdens of the Egyptians and deliver you from slavery to them. I will redeem you with an outstretched arm and with mighty acts of judgment. I will take you as my people, and I will be your God. You shall know that I am the Lord your God, who has freed you from the burdens of the Egyptians'" (Exodus 6:6-7). It is striking and not accidental that God reveals Godself as Yahweh to the Israelites in the act of delivering them from slavery. From that moment forward God's name and character is remembered and identified with the act of delivering God's people from oppression. Some Christians have missed the significant place the exodus story has in Hebrew Scripture, which shaped the ongoing theological reflection and ethics for generations, including the New Testament Jewish writers.

Previously in this book, we described how justice and deliverance were intertwined in the life and ministry of Jesus, who began to inaugurate God's new society on earth as it is in heaven, right in the midst of this decaying and unjust world. And if God's character is bound to justice and love throughout Scripture—and I would love to see someone argue that it is not—then one must wonder how faithful worship to God does not automatically usher us into a grand awareness of God's justice and deliverance. Said plainly, faithful worship of God ought to enliven us to God's delivering character and presence, and to our participation in divine justice in creation. When our worship strips away that vital characteristic of God, we have fallen into the work of divine construction and projection; one based on the god we want rather than on genuine worship to the Creator of all things. Justice and deliverance are definitive markers for who God has been, who God currently is, and who God will be forevermore.

Worship is a formative experience. When we gather as disciples of Jesus in community to praise our Creator and Deliverer, to remember the faithfulness of God, to recall the incarnation of Jesus, and seek to join the Spirit's ongoing activity, it shapes who we are as people. God is not only justice, God is love, peace, and truth, as well as many other things. However, if something is central to God's character, we as Christians ought to pursue getting to know God as such. We should be seeking to have an authentic encounter and experience with our Creator. We must desire to taste and see that the Lord is good. It is through worshiping God in spirit and truth, rather than merely engaging in mental gymnastics and wishful thinking, that we draw closer and closer to the Sustainer of life. Therefore, encountering the sacred commitment to justice ought to be a seamless part of what it means to worship the God of Israel.

Formative worship will shape the contours of our everyday understanding of the church's vocation. The concept of divine imitation and participation intertwine in the reasoning of Scripture, which initiates the journey into a faithful witness in society. From the very first chapter in the Bible we are told that we are made in the likeness and image of God, although sin wreaks havoc on us, causing us to not bear witness to the image of God as we ought. We often do not reflect God as humanity should, and instead our relationships with God, with our neighbors, with all of creation, and even with ourselves are fractured and too frequently captive to destructive patterns. God's deliverance, beginning with Israel, has the goal of reconciling us so that we emulate God and participate in the divine life of our Creator (2 Corinthians 5:18-19).

True worship of the God who sets the oppressed free creates our own vocational awareness. The character and commitments of our Deliverer become the prize we chase after in our ecclesial life. God's activity is discerned so that we can join it through our social witness and action in the world. How God has definitively acted in the world defines the priorities and agenda for how we are to relate to the most vulnerable. It is not strange, then, to see the command for God's people to care for foreigners, orphans, and widows (those most vulnerable within the political structures of that time), because God first rescued Israel from Egyptian slavery (Deuteronomy 24:17-18; Exodus 20; Leviticus 19:36; 25:38; 26:13; and Numbers 15:41 as a few examples). God's deliverance grounds our moral and ethical life. Leviticus 11:45 invites us to imitate God as such: "For I am the Lord who brought you up from the land of Egypt, to be your God; you shall be holy, for I am holy." God's character defines our own formational goals and priorities.

Micah 6:8 is one of the most quoted texts with regard to understanding justice as integral to living in a manner that pleases God. God "has told you, O mortal, what is good; and what does the Lord require of you but to do justice, and to love kindness, and to walk humbly with your God?" Ironically, the verse is often stripped of its context, as with many other popular verses in the Bible. But instead of lifting the verse up by itself, reading more carefully provides a deeper challenge to our vocation of justice. Most people are familiar with verses 6 and 7 as well, which demonstrate that the kind of worship that God desires is not more sacrifice, but justice. It is reading from the start of the chapter, however, that makes clear that God's character grounds what God requires of humanity. In particular, verses 3 and 4 read, "O my people, what have I done to you? In what have I wearied you? Answer me! For I brought you up from the land of Egypt, and redeemed you from the house of slavery." Therefore, the context in which God desires justice and kindness from God's people is an organic outflow of our imitating God, who delivers the enslaved, oppressed, and exploited.

Our worship as the church should discipline us to stay attentive to God's activity and character. While God can never be mastered and systematized (as if the Most High God could be figured out through intellect and expertise!), this does not mean that no vital dimensions of God have been revealed to us. As God's people, we are expected to encounter God's self-revelation to us. Without sounding too much like the theologian Karl Barth, God reveals Godself to us, and we should hold our fragile interpretations of those divine self-disclosures with care. God's love for humanity and God's justice for the vulnerable and commitment to right what is wrong are characteristics that should be clear for any community that worships God. Jeremiah 9:23-24 frames our knowledge of God's character and activity as such:

> Thus says the Lord: Do not let the wise boast in their wisdom, do not let the mighty boast in their might, do not let the wealthy boast in their wealth; but let those who boast boast in this, that they understand and know me, that I am the Lord; I act with steadfast love, justice, and righteousness in the earth, for in these things I delight, says the Lord.

American Christians gather frequently, but it is not always clear who exactly is being worshiped when we do. Is the focus of our worship awakening our awareness of the One who delivers people from slavery and who intimately hears the pain and suffering of the poor, oppressed, foreigner, orphan, and widow? Or have many of us merely been worshiping the American god of our own projections, who cares only about our interior struggles and first-world problems, and who wants us to focus on seeking the best for our families and waiting for the afterlife while remaining apathetic to the suffering of others? If our church's songs, liturgy, Scripture reading, preaching, communal life, discipleship, and dialogue do not reveal to us the God of justice and deliverance, and if it does not form a people called to be an extension of our

Creator's love and justice for the vulnerable, then something is off with our worship. Worshiping communities are called to assemble where the liberation of God disrupts our lives and the neighborhoods and lands we inhabit. Not only are worshiping communities conducive for doing justice work locally; it is the faithful response that God desires of us. And it is the kind of community the world needs.

THE WORSHIPING COMMUNITY

If God is a God of justice, then worshiping communities that radically reorganize their lives to the reality of the Most High God will increasingly, and inevitably, begin participating in the revolutionary vocation of the church. When that isn't happening, it would be appropriate to question whether the one we worship is actually the God revealed to Abraham and Sarah and made flesh in Jesus, and to grapple with the degree to which our perceptions of the divine are distorted. A faithful worshiping community already includes habits of justice, and it disciples people who do justice as they go.

Comfortable mainstream religion is primed to support the status quo. The gods of insatiable consumerism, coercive domination, and hierarchical denigration invite people to adore the beauty of their "exceptional" nation. When a congregation also aligns with the status quo and religious nationalism, its formative practices confuse faithful discipleship with the nation's definition of a good citizen. Disciples, they teach, are able to demonstrate faithfulness through their allegiance to their nation and its flag. Bible lessons turn a household's attention away from the most vulnerable and toward developing an inward-looking nuclear family. Given that the Bible says so much about the poor and our call to love others, comfortable mainstream Christians opt to ignore the passages calling for justice (which suggest we would have to arrange our lives differently) for the less inconvenient act of charity. Nothing is more praised in status quo religious communities than abhorrently wealthy people donating proportionately small amounts out of their abundance while remaining committed to never changing the broader conditions and systems that make such charity necessary in the first place.

The character of our community's discipleship needs to be prayerfully diagnosed. What kind of lives, in the most holistic sense, do people who regularly gather for worship live? Are we a community that makes manifest the delivering presence of God in our neighborhood? What formative practices do we lead our people through that would help them know and join the justice of God in their everyday mundane routines? Do our sermons, Bible studies, prayer time, distribution of resources, budgets, programming, song selection, public witness, church polity, and leadership gesture people toward the liberation of God in our world or toward the status quo? How does our church relate to the social order? In the words of pastor Michael-Ray Mathews, "Are you a chaplain to the Empire or a prophet of the Resistance?"[1] Our worshiping together ought to help us see and experience God's justice and goodness toward those in need.

> I will praise the name of God with a song;
> I will magnify him with thanksgiving.
> This will please the Lord more than an ox
> or a bull with horns and hoofs.
> Let the oppressed see it and be glad;
> you who seek God, let your hearts revive.
> For the Lord hears the needy,
> and does not despise his own that are in bonds.
> (Psalm 69:30-33)

One glaring failure forming communities to be in allegiance to this old order more than to the God who promises new creation is because we no longer remember what genuine Christian conversion demands of us. It is often cliché to talk about being "born again" or "reborn," or to claim that the old person has died and a new person has risen up in its place. While the language of conversion has remained, it is an empty shell of itself when we interrogate what we often mean with this language. In my own experience, people typically either mean they have accepted Jesus as their *personal* Savior, or have said "the sinner's prayer," or have asked Jesus into their hearts, or are referring to a prayerful acceptance of God's forgiveness of one's *personal* sins. If not that, then people usually mean they were baptized into the church. Unfortunately, none of these things necessarily grasp the formational and radical multidimensional change a catechumen underwent in the early church during conversion.

After the original apostles began dying off, and then their followers as well, the early church began formalizing processes for discipleship. They did so to provide continuity with apostolic teaching and habits in their community, with the root of their faith built on the teachings of Jesus and the apostles. Jesus, and the apostles, may have died decades before, but they understood that "the way" of Jesus' followers still demanded a costly conversion. Alan Kreider, an early church historian, helped illuminate these ancient processes of the church by exploring how historical sources detail the way that catechumenates, or "candidates," seeking to join the church went through a rigorous catechism journey before baptism was provided. The goal was genuine conversion. These stages were not designed to just fill a person with head knowledge; rather, they were designed to facilitate the change of the whole person. Even before getting to the stage focused on learning the Scriptures and Christian teaching, these candidates often learned to embody the ethical way of the life of the church. Conversion assumed a way of life as much as it did a way of understanding our world. Conversion, Kreider hammers home throughout his book, always included a dynamic change in belief, behavior, and belonging for these early Christians. He explains, "As I read the records of the early Christians, I am struck by the way in which conversion involved change not just of belief but also of belonging and behavior."[2]

The process of conversion was not a cookie-cutter program that was exactly identical for each community. Some were particularly rigorous, taking as many as three years for candidates to complete the catechism process before baptism, but we do not see evidence of that everywhere. Likewise, while definitive patterns about the content and nature of catechism from that time are visible, there were also different emphases and approaches that existed within different regions and times before catechism was completely overhauled. I introduce you to this history not to compel you to play "Simon says" with the early church by imitating every practice you discover. Rather, we ought to wrestle with the spirit of what the church only a few generations removed from Jesus and the apostles was trying to implement, and how it understood Christian conversion. We have much to learn from the traditions of the early church that significantly facilitated discipling a people that understood their responsibility to serve the poor among them, especially as their own communities frequently comprised many people low in the social hierarchy of the Roman Empire.

Of course, Kreider also narrates the way that the church after Constantine continued to domesticate and water down the meaning of conversion. For Kreider, one cause was the social shift that Christian leaders made during that time: "So much changed, not least (in view of the contributions of fourth-century Christians to the theological formulations of the church) the locus of theologizing: from the margins of society the theologians moved to its centre, including the imperial court."[3] Under Constantine's reign, people began coming to the church in droves. This is not necessarily a problem, even if one is curious about the motivation. To meet the demands of the masses, along with the shifting theological framing of the church in relation to the social order, the catechism process was changed. After the fourth century many could be functionally Christians without being baptized, leaving that until their deathbed. Likewise, those who were baptized no longer underwent a comprehensive multistage catechism that converted one's belief, behavior, and belonging. Baptism now occurred before rather than after any rigorous conversion process that included embodying the ethical way of Jesus. People could opt out of continuing through the whole catechism process because they were already baptized. Another shift includes an emphasis on the teachings of Jesus slowly being replaced with a greater emphasis on the creed, the Lord's Prayer, the patriarchs, and behavioral guidelines from the Proverbs. Catechism never disappeared, but as Western Christendom emerged, it now came after baptism, and its content was less rooted in the way of Jesus.[4]

To take this one step further, many who refer to themselves as "born-again Christians" have not gone through any substantive Christian formation with the goal of comprehensive conversion. "Born again" conversion, in this scenario, usually means saying a variation of prayers that confess sin and ask for salvation through Jesus' death, but is mostly severed from the kind of costly life changes that sever one's allegiance to the social order and its priorities. In its place are membership classes lasting anywhere from six weeks to an hour, which are created to orient new members to the mission and values of that particular church. This is still better than those that do nothing, but the concept of conversion here means something entirely different from what it once did. Very rarely, though not never, does such a membership class guide its participants through holistic conversion so that they are living disciples of Jesus who, among other things, serve and do justice for the poor and have a new sense of belonging in the church. For many people, most dimensions of their life stay the same.

Discipleship leading to conversion is necessary, but how a community cultivates Christian formation in a worshiping community must also be as responsive as Jesus himself was to the various social contexts and challenges of different people. On one hand, Jesus' invitation was to follow after him, and the task of being a people that are changed by walking in the living presence of the risen Christ, and norming our belief and practices with biblical wisdom, culminating in the life and teachings of Jesus, is pivotal. The call to follow Jesus is a universal call for humanity to discover the things that make for peace and justice as God desires. Yet on the other hand, when we hear the words "Come, follow me" from our Messiah, there is a distinctive meaning for discipleship in view of the spiritual, social, political, economic, physical, and psychological conditions one finds oneself in. The call to follow Jesus is a specific invitation that includes God's good news to and for the poor. As quickly as we acknowledge the universal call we simultaneously must explain the particular significance for different individuals and different social groups.

The universality and particularity of the gospel gets ignored, leading to a dangerous misappropriation of Jesus' teachings.

Even a surface reading of Matthew, Mark, Luke, and John quickly reveals that Jesus does not have a one-size-fits-all gospel message. Jesus does not invite every person to enter the reign of God in the same way. While all the gospel writers help the church to see this phenomenon, Luke's account of Jesus' birth, teachings, death, and resurrection throws it in your face from start to finish. There Jesus makes it evidently clear that the first will be last and the last first. Nonetheless, all four gospels bear witness to this truth. Constantly, Jesus preaches, ministers, speaks, and interacts with different people in vividly distinct ways. The poor, the hungry, the vulnerable women, the sick, the socially excluded, those deemed sinners, and anyone who has fallen into the cracks of humanity's oppressive roads are prioritized and privileged in Jesus' ministry. For "the least," "the last," and "the lost" at the margins and periphery of society, and for those whom mainstream society exploits and excludes, our Messiah's invitation defiantly proclaims that the coming new order has been inaugurated for them. Likewise, it should not be lost on readers that sometimes the invitation to follow after Jesus is deemed "costly," while at other times it is described as "easy" and "light" (Luke 14:25-33; Matthew 11:28-30).

In *Becoming a Just Church* by Adam Gustine, this same point is explained for those who are socially advantaged.[5] As an upwardly mobile straight white man relationally networked with many white evangelicals, Gustine understood that discipleship needs to account for their socioeconomic realities. In agreement with my assessment (that this is basic New Testament scholarship and not innovative), discipleship to Jesus has very particular implications for socially advantaged, or what he calls "high ground," people. In his estimation, "even a cursory reading of the life of Jesus leaves us with substantial evidence that we have seriously missed the boat as it relates to how a person's social reality influences the path of discipleship. The scriptures give us example after example where Jesus makes the characteristics of a person's social location central to the vision he casts for their faithful discipleship."[6] The kinds of past and present systemic injustice a people group experiences are all factors that should shape every dimension of a worshiping community's life. Jesus did not say blessed are the poor *and the rich*. Comfortable Christians despise or just ignore Jesus' actual teachings, but he said blessed are the poor and woe to you who are rich (read Luke 6). In fact, for the wealthy, according to Jesus, nothing short of a divine miracle could get them into the reign of God—it would be easier for a camel to make it through the eye of a needle (Luke 18:18-26). This is not a one-time comment, as if Jesus detoured from his normal message when he said that. The "good news for the poor" (Jesus' own words) is a distinct feature of his message and ministry (Luke 4:18-19). As Gustine explains, self-emptying and movement toward solidarity with the oppressed are the way of Jesus:

> We must be willing to engage the social location of the upwardly mobile and invite them to empty themselves in order to faithfully follow the way of Jesus. Not doing this is selling a false bill of goods, a gospel devoid of some of the essential postures required for living it out. . . . The rich young ruler had fallen into the false gospel of religious performance that excluded his social location. We are selling that false gospel when we pretend the gospel is one-size-fits-all. Instead, there is a bigger, better, and more beautiful gospel and way of life that comes through emptying ourselves, because it is from the low ground that we taste the resurrection power of God.[7]

Therefore, not only do our worshiping communities need to disciple toward authentic conversion, but to do so requires a truthful accounting of our place on the social ladder. Jesus proclaimed release to the captives, recovery of sight to the blind, and liberation for the oppressed. Jesus also prophetically challenged the leaders, the establishment, and the wealthy because he understood (unlike many Americans) that there is an interconnected relationship between those on opposite sides of inequity. Our faith communities must develop Jesus-shaped, contextually aware, forms of discipleship. For the church that is yielding in worship to the liberating activity of God, this is not a choice. For Gustine, "A church committed to justice will ensure that a person's social location is woven into their discipleship framework because social location shapes the way people hear, receive, and respond to the gospel."[8] If the church does not do so already, it must sermonize in jazz, recognizing not only the right song to play, but the audience and mood in the room, so the melody of Jesus can groove appropriately in the lives of all of us, and each of us.

A COMMUNITY OF FAITHFULNESS AND EFFECTIVENESS

For the worshiping community to discover the ecclesial vocation of justice in alignment with what God is doing, even its traditions and customs need to be delivered from the captivity of the status quo. We underestimate how the inertia of Christendom and colonialism continues to shape how we gather as the church, and in particular, the way it teaches us to value inequitable wealth, the military industrial complex, and white supremacy. What we need is a careful scrutiny of our various communal practices. When worshiping communities yield to the Spirit's presence and activity, we pursue faithfulness, but that does not mean we cannot also be effective conduits of justice for our neighbors.

Talking about effectiveness is a contested concept theologically for some Christians. Many readers may not even know that effectiveness can be a potentially warped value for the church and that some theologians actually warn against thinking in such pragmatic ways. Very often, effectiveness is *the* deciding factor for many churches' short- and long-term decisions. Today, churches are trying to do what works. The church growth movement certainly encouraged that priority by providing tips and tricks to increase church membership. Unfortunately, churches too often forget to transparently discern whether our practices and choices are also faithful to the God we serve. For this reason, the politics, ethics, and means of many local churches are often no different from those of corporations, the military, or politicians. It seems so common sense that the principles that "work" in the broader society should be adopted in the church. How the meaning of Christ crucified disrupts our understanding of "what works" from a cosmic and eschatological vantage point is not considered. The biblical account and its collective wisdom force careful readers to grapple with the way God is at work in the world. Jesus' birth, life, teachings, ministry, death, and resurrection become the definitive interpretive lens through which we read Scripture and work through this theological and ethical conundrum.

For Jesus it is sheep, serpents, and doves that help clarify the way the church pursues justice. In Matthew 10, the twelve disciples are sent by Jesus to bring the good news of God's reign to people in several towns. They are given authority to extend God's holistic deliverance to people who need it. Jesus said, "As you go, proclaim the good news, 'The kingdom of heaven has come near.' Cure the sick, raise the dead, cleanse the lepers, cast out demons" (Matthew 10:7-8). However, Jesus' instructions are more comprehensive than the type of deliverance to provide; they also describe how the disciples are to face antagonism and hostility, and particularly before those controlling the political system who will arrest and brutalize them. It is in that context that Jesus says, "See, I am sending you out like sheep into the midst of wolves; so be wise as serpents and innocent as doves" (v. 16).

As in many other passages scattered throughout the Bible, sheep are vulnerable. Sometimes Scripture describes them as peacefully being led to the slaughter. In the Prophets, often the shepherds themselves are the ones harming the sheep. And in this case, it is wolves who prey on the sheep. They all emphasize different points, but in each passage the sheep are vulnerable. In a broader reading of the Old Testament, we are frequently reminded that powerful nations have horses and chariots at their disposal, but instead of an impressive military arsenal to trust in, it is the almighty God whom this set-apart people has at their disposal. For the enslaved Hebrews being chased by Pharaoh, for Gideon and the three hundred soldiers, and for David before Goliath, we are reminded that the people are vulnerable before the nations but that God is able to overcome their dangerous and daunting enemies. So Moses puts a staff in the waters and splits the sea, Gideon's soldiers act a fool and scare away their opponents, and young David is victorious over the imposing giant.

Each of these stories is meant to brag on our God who is able to overcome the seemingly impossible. They teach us that the way things seem are not ultimate, and they are not the final word on the matter. This is grounded solely in the logics of faith. Sometimes Christian communities forget to cultivate faith and instead lean only on what seems to work for those in power. The church at its most faithful was so not because it merely trusted in the logics of how the world works, but because the people believed that God is able, then walked courageously forward in light of that. Dr. King frequently did the same in his own talks. For that reason he is known for often quoting the line "The arc of the moral universe is long, but it bends towards justice." His faith in the cosmic and eschatological justice of God led him to align with that and to move forward believing that the way of truth and love is faithful and effective because it is God's way.

Our vulnerability doesn't mean we are to sit around twiddling our thumbs; instead, we are to engage in discovering the way of Jesus which leads to shalom. In view of our vulnerability as sheep in a world of wolves, we are not called to be like wolves but are encouraged to be like serpents and doves. People have concocted strange interpretations of what it means to be like a serpent or a dove. Usually that is because people want to construct their own ethics for its meaning. We need not waste our time, though, because Jesus says exactly what he meant. First he said, "Be wise as serpents." Here we are reminded of the crafty ways of a serpent. Jesus, as well as many individuals in the Bible (indeed, this is frequently seen in many non-Western traditions), values the "trickster" figure. African people and many descendants from Africa tell trickster stories in which smaller vulnerable animals are cunning and outwit larger dangerous predators. In the United States, Brer Rabbit stories told by enslaved communities carried on that tradition. To be wise as serpents is to intentionally scheme and undermine daunting and powerful figures and situations. Disciples of Jesus, then, ought to be tricksters, putting together our best minds to be crafty on behalf of God's reign. We scheme and plot on behalf of goodness, justice, and peace so that our world experiences the flourishing of God. But we do this from below, as the vulnerable ones who place our faith in God.

Likewise, as we steal away outside the visibility of those who dominate and control society, we can plot and plan our next moves to subvert this old order, but we do so as "innocent as doves." The means matter. Innocence, in contrast to the wolves that abuse power and cause physical harm through the formal systems of government, turns us away from perpetuating cycles of violence to get the job done. I'm not calling for an intricate ethical system of pacifism but instead to simply turn to the way of Jesus, which teaches us to love our enemies. We are not a death-dealing force, and we must remain innocent of the temptation to use coercive, top-down, violent means that cause destruction in the name of peace. This is not about legalistic rules but instead about faith in who God is and how God acts; ultimately, it is about how we participate in God's delivering presence in the world. We must disciple our communities in a way that opens local churches to the reality of our vulnerability while also yielding to the God who is able to do more than we can ever conceive.

For this reason, doing justice in the way of Jesus is not only faithful but inevitably effective. Anything that God's hand is upon will be effective within the "moral arc of the universe." Some pacifists have scorned the goal of being effective and all forms of pragmatism, and they shake their heads in shame at anyone who deploys these words. Often, though, they are comfortable white middle-class Christians not directly harmed by the ugly effects of white supremacy, cycles of intergenerational poverty, or patriarchal violence. Those who have tasted the vicious dimensions of these oppressions hunger and thirst for those realities to come to an end. If you actually love people who are violated by the cyclones of exploitation and marginalization, you care about actually ending them. The difference for followers of Jesus comes down to faith in God. True faith(fulness) leads us to believe that God's means lead to shalom. Seeking justice through our faith is effectively pursuing and embodying God's shalom in creation. Authentic faith does not turn away from the vulnerable and remain neutral to oppressive society. Authentic faith is the kind that enables people to seek the end of slavery in America despite it seeming like an impossible pipe dream. It emboldened folks like Ida B. Wells to challenge the lynching that wreaked havoc after slavery, despite white-controlled newspapers and white mainstream "common sense" justifying the violence by scapegoating black men. Today, when our country has the largest incarceration system in the world, some resist anyhow, imagining a world in which such dehumanizing institutions no longer exist. Authentic faith is often radical and effective in view of the larger story of human history that God shepherds along. The question is whether local churches today will disciple people toward such faithfulness.

In *Faith-Rooted Organizing*, Alexia Salvatierra and Peter Heltzel bring together faithfulness and effectiveness, organizing people toward service and justice. I want to turn our attention to some of the opportunities they identify for mobilizing the church toward doing justice. They note that many of our liturgies are oriented to do this work, we just need to tap into that. For example, "Activities such as seder meals ritually celebrating the liberation of Hebrew slaves from Egypt (in the Jewish community) or *posadas* (a Hispanic ritual in which processions reenact Mary and Joseph's search for a place to give birth) awaken hearts and minds to a re-energizing and sustaining message." Within Jewish and Christian traditions are plenty of liturgical practices that could help disciple, convert, and mobilize our people to join God's justice. Another one is music. The authors write, "Paul Gilroy argues in *The Black Atlantic* that music was integral to identity formation among the African diaspora because it could express the horror of the Middle Passage and slavery through primarily nonrepresentational forms. From the Underground Railroad for escaping slaves to the civil rights movement, music has fueled struggle for justice."[9] It is worth critically reflecting on the nature of our music sung in worship. If our music lacks the capacity to form people into an awareness of our full vocation, then we must become students of those who have created songs from within the sites of suffering and oppression. Music has the capacity to awaken us to God and our hurting world while igniting and sustaining our action through deep spirituality.

The authors of *Faith-Rooted Organizing* share about various other gifts that Christ-centered community provides for local organizing work, but I want to highlight one more. They also discuss prayer. Returning to my earlier point, we must have faith that God is able. Salvatierra and Heltzel remind us that prayer is "the lifeblood of spiritual communities" and ought not be treated merely as "a strategy," because it is in fact "a way of life." But more important than that, they remind us "that prayer has power, and it is no shame to use our power for God's purposes." The authors describe their own experience: "In faith-rooted organizing, we have learned on the ground that prayer is as effective in the public arena as it is in the private arena."[10] Not only have I witnessed this as well, but I have had multiple opportunities to pray in public while participating with faith-based organizations struggling for justice in my city. And for those watching politicians who are also believers, they are reminded of their own faith commitments and that God is active everywhere, including in our public square.

Some may be surprised I did not begin by discussing preaching, but I do want to discuss it now. Preaching must faithfully proclaim the whole gospel. And for churches that do not have a vibrant discipling culture in their community, the preaching might be the only opportunity you have to reorient those who gather into participating in God's justice. Preaching is one of the easiest opportunities we have to align and overlap the troubles of our world with God's activities that lead to shalom. Too often, sermons are preached as though people were not suffering outside our walls. And we preach as though biblical wisdom and the story of Jesus have nothing to say about the social concerns we are confronting. That should not be so. Our preaching ought to lean into, and embrace, the pain and suffering in our world. And while it ought never become a platform for partisan politics, it ought to have a moral and ethical grounding that has a fresh word for our times. In *How To Preach A Dangerous Sermon*, Frank Thomas explains his own approach to talking about issues like healthcare in our country: "This for me is fundamentally a moral issue, an issue of being humane one to another. I do not allow people to make it a political issue between Democrats, Independents, and Republicans. I argue this: preach the moral base of issues, and though you will be accused of preaching politics, you will in fact be preaching dangerous sermons."[11] In a different text on the practice of African American preaching, Frank Thomas also invites us to critically question what we are preaching about while movements for justice are happening all around us in society: "What will we preach? Will we push deeper and deeper into these bigger subjects with real honesty and search for truth?"[12]

However, as long as congregations remain monological spaces where people's voices are passive and silenced, there will always be limits to how much formation toward God's justice will happen. I sincerely believe congregations need to create dialogical space for worshiping communities. That is, communities that practice open, authentic conversation for the whole church, believing that the Holy Spirit is not limited to speaking only through the pastor or preacher for the day, but through everyone. This transitions congregations from being a passive audience into active and genuine community. Many churches that in theory profess the priesthood of all believers in actuality do not create any space or culture for communal discernment and dialogue. The two most prominent examples of dialogical community I've witnessed come from the black church tradition and the Anabaptist tradition. The black church tradition has many streams within it that have practiced call-and-response during the preaching moment:

> The call and response nature of the sermon—call and response refers to the interaction between preachers and congregations all over black America that allows the audience to partner in shaping and directing the sermon. Based on oral traditions in west and central Africa, the preacher says something and the congregation says something back. The preacher often makes a sermonic plan in the study, but feedback from the audience often leads to improvisations initially unforeseen by the preacher.[13]

Through call-and-response, congregants are not merely passive consumers, but participate in the preaching event by speaking back to the preacher, in affirmation, through worship, and also providing clues to the preacher if something is not resonating or making sense. It is not strange for the congregation to direct the preacher on what to do. They might say, "Make it plain," or "Tell the story," providing directions on what is needed. These responses are provided through an understanding of their oral tradition, culturally speaking back within the rhythms and grammar of the community. Thus some unwritten rules guide the preaching event so that it is dialogical without slipping into chaos.

Many Anabaptist congregations, though certainly not all of them, have a tradition of fostering open and authentic dialogue as well. Traditionally, these communities engage in dialogue, but instead of while the preaching is happening it usually commences immediately afterward. I have been invited to preach at Anabaptist communities that practiced open dialogue. After I finished speaking it was followed by a meaningful time of dialogue, providing space for questions and dialogue from the congregation, as well as providing the preacher (in this case me) an opportunity to respond. I have noticed that some leaders find the idea threatening but I have always seen the value in creating these spaces based on my own experience.

In *The Power of All*, Stuart Murray makes a scriptural, theological, historical, and practical argument for dialogically empowered communities, which he calls "multivoiced" congregations:

> In relation to discernment it means believing that the community can seek the mind of Christ together, confident in the direction of the Spirit and hopeful of reaching a united decision. It means drawing out the reticent, including the marginalized, listening for the prophetic minority, and developing processes to ensure all are heard and that decisions are made without undue delay. This does not abolish vision casting and decisive action, but it dramatically increases the community's ownership of what is decided.[14]

Open conversation filled with honest reflections and questions after I preach has become something I look forward to whenever it happens. Sometimes, there are different angles by which to see a topic, and it usually is enriching to add layers of wisdom on top of what was already preached. There also have been times when someone in the congregation struggled with something I said, especially since I am often invited to preach on racism and how it affects the church. While many are receptive, there will always be some who struggle. Their questions are actually a great time to listen well to where people are at as well as an opportunity to further clarify what exactly I mean. My experience is that allowing conflicting perspectives to be shared in the open (rather than existing in private and remaining dormant) provides teachable moments and opportunities that are ripe for transformation and growth. Honestly, it is difficult to imagine trying to disciple people while not providing dialogical space where they can be open and honest about where they are. For many mainline and evangelical churches, I've witnessed all across the country a dramatic difference in views between the clergy who personally believe in the church's vocation of justice and the congregation members who differ quietly but rarely talk about it openly. Creating space for patient and authentic conversation is needed for these congregatoins. Dialogical community is vital for the formation of a worshiping community.

Therefore preaching is important, but just as vital is our capacity to dialogue together as an actual community that finds our belonging in Christ. Our preaching must speak prophetically to the reality of suffering that exists. Frank Thomas argues, "If preaching does not engage the biggest subjects with real depth and honesty, then preaching itself will go the way of disco and the blues."[15] More than that, though, we must also cultivate communities that resist the urge to silence the wisdom of the whole church and thus the potential to hear the Spirit's voice speaking through anyone she chooses. Murray reminds us that "multivoiced church is an alternative to the dominant tradition in which large numbers of the Christian community are passive consumers instead of active participants."[16] From an even broader perspective, everything we do as a worshiping community ought to bear witness to the character and activity of God, including divine justice. Our liturgy, music, small groups and Bible studies, programming, fellowship, and leadership should facilitate true transformation in the way of Jesus and participation in God's reign. Pastor Sandra Maria Van Opstal writes:

> Expressions of worship help capture the imagination of congregants. And through worship we experience the now-but-not-yet of God's kingdom: unity, freedom and justice now—but not yet. Therefore we must create worship services that enable prophetic imagination in which people can see the future reality of God's kingdom breaking into the present. Justo González says, "Christian worship is, among other things, the place where we catch a glimpse of 'the future Reign from which and toward which God calls us'—a glimpse that both supports us in our pilgrimage and judges us in our attempts to be too settled."[17]

7

ECONOMIC INJUSTICE AND THE CHURCH

My mom occasionally reminds my siblings and me of the hard financial struggles we went through as a young family. Things changed dramatically after my dad became a pastor and the church grew stable enough to provide a decent salary. She brings it up to remind herself of, and to teach us, an ethic for how to live today and how we are to treat others. Usually whenever she mentions our past financial hardships, she is directly challenging us to remember that we were once in a similar situation as those struggling now, so that we remain compassionate and aware of the different socioeconomic realities people find themselves in. She often tells one story in particular to make her point. Before our family joined the middle class after my dad became a pastor, life was precarious.

Back in the day, the women's group at our church would ask for five dollars in dues from everyone to support the ministry. On the surface that sounds fair. If everyone chips in just five dollars, then they would have what they needed to accomplish their goals. It allows the whole community to participate, and no one person or small group has to bear the burden of the costs.

My mom, however, reminds us that in those days our family was barely squeaking by. Not everyone was aware of the financial struggle we were going through. So she recalls on one particular occasion when the women's group was collecting dues, that she had only five dollars left. Not just five dollars left in her purse, but five dollars *total*. She had to make those five dollars last until our family got more money. Back then my family comprised my parents, my two older siblings, and myself. My youngest brother and my oldest niece would also join the clan down the road. The decision around whether to pay the dues was really about whether my mom was going to choose the ministry or the well-being and provision of her family. Of course, any religious system that puts the survival of people up against the ministry of the church has gaps in its awareness and flaws in its practice.

From the very start, the Torah in the Old Testament taught that it was the responsibility of the people of God to protect and care for the poor, the orphans, and the widows in their midst. At the heart of our faith is the ethical vocation to bring life rather than death to the poorest among us. This simple, clear, and straightforward teaching culminates in Jesus. Yet it is frequently ignored, dismissed, or explained away. Ignoring such ethics does not change God's commitment to those crushed by the inequities and unjust economic systems designed to advantage the greed of the wealthy and powerful.

In my mom's case, our family experienced miracles every day. My mom was the queen of making "sumpthin out of nothin" and finding a way to see just a little bit stretch, and last, beyond what seemed possible. If you have been through similar circumstances then you know the tricks. Like when you run out of ketchup. By this point, you have already turned it upside down, shaken it, wound it up, and got a few more blotches of ketchup to slide out. After you have done all that, then comes the miracle. With just a little water, and a few love shakes, you've suddenly got more ketchup to go around. I know somebody knows what I am talking about. We were not fancy, but Mom knew how to make things stretch to feed her family and we never went to bed hungry.

In Mark 12:38-44, we are reminded that poor widows were exploited by the Jerusalem establishment. Jesus, by this point in Mark's gospel, has already come to Jerusalem, where spiritual, economic, political, and social power was concentrated in the hands of a few leaders. Jesus has already come to the temple, he has already called the temple authorities a den of thieves, and he has already flipped the tables of those exploiting the poor. And Jesus, after enacting these and other revolutionary demonstrations, begins his temple takeover of the temple teaching ministry. This Occupy-style movement by Jesus was radical because he engaged in disruptive and escalating actions that demonstrated the tensions between him and the ruling class. This direct confrontation added injury to insult since he engaged in prophetic judgment of the temple and how it was organized and designed to exploit poor worshipers.

Jesus was known for providing for the poor as he went town by town preaching the coming of God's new society. However, there was no single miracle that ended all poverty, or that with a snap of the finger made all the economic injustices disappear. Jesus never worked like that. Instead, Jesus intervenes, not with a Thanos snap, but with prophetic presence while discipling people into his new society. Jesus was not apolitical in his teaching, so he turns his attention toward the Jerusalem leaders, and he highlights their hypocrisy. In particular, he calls them out publicly because they love their privileged status in society, and they ridicule faith in God through public prayers that further elevate themselves socially. He claims that they are consumed by the social honor they received. There is something else Jesus mentions that does not always get a lot of attention. They also, according to Jesus, "devour widows' houses" (Luke 20:47; Mark 12:40). Yes, Jesus explicitly mentions how the religious system exploits these poor, vulnerable women, when its vocation is to do the opposite. Jesus says that these powerful and religious people will be judged the most harshly.

If you keep reading, Jesus moves from his prophetic judgment about robbing widows of their homes to observing the activities happening in real time in the temple. He doesn't just observe everything, though; we are told that he has a particular interest in watching the temple treasury box. He is observing the crowd's giving with a class consciousness that would make most Americans very uncomfortable. Jesus carefully watches as the rich give a lot of money but only out of their abundance, and then he observes a poor widow give her two last coins, worth a penny, literally giving all the money she has.

After watching this, Jesus calls his disciples to him so he can carefully unveil for them what is really happening. The mainstream American Christian narrative would say that the wealthy are blessed, and the poor widow is not. Jesus wants them to see and understand, from his perspective, that the wealthy gave out of their abundance, but it was just spare change proportionally. In contrast, this poor woman has just given all that she had. Everything. We should read this with Jesus' comments about devouring widows' homes still in mind. These two accounts are back-to-back. We often miss that Jesus' comments about this widow who has given everything are both an affirmation and a critical lament. Jesus affirms the character and faith of the woman because in the gospel of Mark the quality needed to be a disciple of Jesus is the willingness to risk everything to follow the Messiah. This widow is ready to follow Jesus, unlike the wealthy whose lives are comfortable with this old order instead of filled with longing for God's new society. But the other side of the coin is Jesus' prophetic lament. Jesus laments that a (religious, political, and social) system exists that would devour and take everything from a widow, when the purpose of God's people was to protect, provide, and care for the poor. Jesus laments the kind of religion that has lost its way and justifies the exploitation and cheating of the poor and most vulnerable.

The church ought to participate in God's deliverance for the poor, helping them not only survive but thrive by creating new economic currents not bound by our current economic reasoning, and concretely seeking the flourishing of all people in our society.

FUNCTIONALLY PROSPERITY GOSPEL

While local churches are frequently known for being charitable, they usually operate out of the mainstream economic reasoning of our society. Many mainstream Christians assume that our current economic system is divinely chosen. Christians have adopted market logics and have tightly woven them into their belief and practice. Clearly this is the case with the prosperity gospel that promises that if you believe you can achieve, just blab and grab, name it and claim it. This theological distortion of the gospel ties the myth of meritocracy (which correlates hard work with success) with one's faith in God. Faith, they claim, will open up the windows and doors to health and wealth. God's blessing (defined by American consumeristic tastes) is yours for the taking if you would just have enough faith. Churches that push the prosperity gospel are an obvious example of taking Christian teaching and blending it with our society's economic reasoning.

But let's turn the mirror on our own Christian communities. I don't believe that most local churches blatantly teach the prosperity gospel. However, what is taught and what is caught are two different things. My observation has been that most mainstream Christians are *functionally prosperity gospel adherents*. By this, I mean they espouse more traditionally orthodox beliefs but live the logics of the prosperity gospel more than Jesus' radical ethics about money and wealth. In fact, I imagine that it would be nearly impossible to distinguish the economic and consumer practices of most American Christians from those who explicitly adhere to the prosperity gospel. If you observed what homes, cars, and products people bought, how they budgeted, or how their money was used, I imagine that it would be difficult to discern who was a prosperity gospeler and who was not. But you only have to listen carefully to how a person uses the word *blessing* to find out if they are functionally following the prosperity gospel. The gospel of Jesus has not redefined "blessings" for most Christians. Where Jesus pronounces blessings on the poor and woes toward the rich, most comfortable Christians do the opposite. Anytime they increase their wealth they claim that God did it. When they talk about their big homes, those homes are *assumed* to be a blessing. Our economic reasoning is frequently the opposite of Jesus' teachings.

Since large numbers of comfortable Christians have internalized and given sacred approval to the economic forces and currents of their society, it becomes hard to pronounce and embody good news for the poor. Even among so-called liberal and progressive Christians, poverty is frequently an inconsequential reality. It is one thing to support a presidential candidate who advocates for the working class, but when one's own life remains fully congruent with the economic machinery, that reveals what lies beneath the thin veneer. Our habits are fairly predictable and too often are based on our socioeconomic status, revealing a failure in our economic discipleship.

OUR STRANGE ECONOMIC REASONING

Few comfortable Christian leaders are willing to even consider how economic ethics in Scripture ought to shape our everyday discipleship. Our commitments to consumerism, maximizing profits, increasing capacity to generate wealth, private ownership, and a general belief in the good of unregulated markets are markers of our derailed economic reasoning in the church. Contrast the silence on scriptural reasoning on wealth with the current obsession over contemporary sexual ethics, which is barely touched on in Scripture but is nonetheless dividing the church in the United States, and you begin to see how much Christian ethics are determined by culture wars rather than formed from ethical wisdom and inspiration from biblical texts.

For example, there are just a small handful of passages that traditionalists draw from to condemn homosexuality. Ironically, the word *homosexuality* was introduced as a translation into English Bibles for the very first time in the 1940s.

Furthermore, scholars currently debate the meaning of those handful of passages, because it seems like many interpreters have been imposing twentieth- and twenty-first-century understandings of sexuality onto these ancient texts that were written in communities that were not having the same cultural debates we are today. Nonetheless, denominations are splitting over differences in interpretation and practice in the local church. At the same time, there are over two thousand Bible verses about wealth. And the gospel narratives of Jesus spend a lot of time redefining our relationship to wealth. However, there are almost no expectations for economic discipleship for comfortable Christians in most churches in the United States. Local churches either teach the exact opposite of what Jesus taught so that Christian economics fits into the American dream or suggest that it is not the church's business to interfere in the economic lives of parishioners. It's these kinds of hypocrisies that turn people away from the church and malign our witness in the public square.

The worst thing a person can do, according to those who follow an Americanized Christianity, is advocate for something that appears closer to socialism than capitalism. Bishop Hélder Câmara's popular quote comes to mind: "When I give food to the poor, they call me a saint. When I ask why the poor have no food, they call me a communist."[1] To be clear, I'm not suggesting that socialism ought to be conflated with the reign of God either. But even a cursory reading of Scripture would readily find some deeper resonances with socialist principles than with capitalism's individualistic values. Only by carefully cherry-picking random verses and recompiling them together could one claim that the Bible from Genesis to Revelation suggests that what God wants is unregulated capitalism. Now, there certainly are plenty of ways to regulate capitalism in a more economically just way than we currently do. I'm not convinced any system is perfect, since humans will always be the ones running it. Nonetheless, I am confident that certain approaches for organizing the flow of wealth in society will inevitably result in massive economic inequality. But frank conversations about this in the church, despite Jesus' own solidarity with poor people, are considered to be off limits.

Our comfortable Christian sensibilities would be horrified if we grasped how early Christian leaders talked about wealth. In contrast to assuming it was a blessing from God, amassed wealth was often framed as resources *stolen* from the poor. Rather than approaching it through a hyper-individualistic lens, or as an issue of rights and private property, early Christian leaders often began from a different point. Nothing was solely yours to do with however you desired. Everything was from God and was to be shared with all humanity. With this reasoning, they frequently suggested that people that hoard wealth and then give to the poor are not actually engaging in charity. They are merely returning what was stolen and what was rightfully always theirs. Ambrose, an influential church leader in the late fourth century, provides a great example of this logic: "You are not making a gift of your possessions to the poor person. You are handing over to him what is his. For what has been given in common for the use of all, you have arrogated to yourself. The world is given to all, and not only to the rich."[2] Basil of Caesarea, also in the fourth century, said it with more punch: "The bread in your cupboard belongs to the hungry man; the coat hanging in your closet belongs to the man who needs it; the shoes rotting in your closet belong to the man who has no shoes; the money which you put into the bank belongs to the poor. You do wrong to everyone you could help but fail to help."[3]

For early Christians, the practice of giving alms to the poor was taught with an eye toward redistribution and not merely comfortable charity. Irenaeus, who came a few centuries before Ambrose and Basil, and who embodied a sense of deep solidarity with the poor after his conversion, called for Christian redistribution. He said, "Instead of the tithes which the law commanded, the Lord said to divide everything we have with the poor."[4] One of the earliest extra-biblical sources that give us a glimpse into early Christian community belief and practice is the Didache, which tradition taught was teachings passed down from the apostles. It says, "Share everything with your brother. Do not say, 'It is private property.' If you share what is everlasting, you should be that much more willing to share things which do not last."[5] And John Chrysostom, who was known for his fiery speech on wealth, wrote: "Not to enable the poor to share in our goods is to steal from them and deprive them of life. The goods we possess are not ours but theirs." These teachings, which are just a tiny fraction of what was said and taught on wealth by early Christians, ought to at least cause some self-examination around our own economic reasoning.[6]

Our goal is not to merely mimic everything the early church did and said, but to have our lives seized by the economic revolution of God. We ought to participate in the new thing God is doing, and it cannot exclude our economic discipleship and our relationship to wealth and poverty. There is significant dissonance between the American church and the thrust of biblical teaching on wealth and poverty, especially when we see that scriptural wisdom climaxes in the life and teachings of Jesus. We will not find a faithful way of participating in God's economy until we are converted from our internalized thinking, which is apathetic to poverty and triggered by any form of redistribution of resources.

While there are lots of provisions within the Torah on behalf of the poor, Jubilee in the book of Leviticus has a uniquely vital role in shaping later Christian ethics. This is especially true for Luke's account of the Jesus story. You won't fully understand what Jesus teaches unless Jubilee is living in the forefront of your consciousness as you move through the story. Jubilee is a gripping and decisive concept for Christian practice and prophetic judgment, and it provides an anticipatory glimpse of God's future for us.

At its heart, Jubilee is a divine call to hit the restart button that liberates those shackled by compounding inequality and bondage. Basically, every fifty years the Israelites were to practice Jubilee, in which deliverance would be experienced throughout the land for (almost) all its inhabitants. Many focus on whether this was practiced by the original hearers. Honestly, it does not matter. Even if it were never practiced, disobedience should not be a reason for us to not wrestle with Scripture's wisdom for us today. The meaning of Jubilee is summed up in Leviticus 25:10, "And you shall hallow the fiftieth year and you shall proclaim liberty throughout the land to all its inhabitants. It shall be a jubilee for you: you shall return, every one of you, to your property and every one of you to your family." Not only are we told when it would happen, but we see that houses and property are to be returned to their original family owners. Verse 13 says, "In this year of jubilee you shall return, every one of you, to your property." In this case, the land itself, not just the property, will be returned. The ancestral lands will be back in the family, so no matter how bad things got, your family would never be permanently landless.

The rationale for Jubilee is rooted in God's character as a liberator of the Israelites. In Leviticus 25:38, God explains,

"I am the Lord your God, who brought you out of the land of Egypt, to give you the land of Canaan, to be your God." Once again in the final verse of the chapter (v. 55) we hear again, "For to me the people of Israel are servants; they are my servants whom I brought out from the land of Egypt: I am the Lord your God." This reminder that God is their liberator also extends to liberating Israelites who are indebted servants to another Israelite. Verses 39-41 detail the expectation of freedom for the enslaved: "If any who are dependent on you become so impoverished that they sell themselves to you, you shall not make them serve as slaves. They shall remain with you as hired or bound laborers. They shall serve with you until the year of the jubilee. Then they and their children with them shall be free from your authority; they shall go back to their own family and return to their ancestral property."

Again, this will become a powerful and captivating scriptural vision for Christian practice and hope, but it isn't without moral gaps. Most notably, a careful reading of Jubilee in Leviticus reveals, freedom from bondage was a provision only for the Israelites. Non-Israelites are explicitly named as people who are eligible for slavery. Early on, the call for Jubilee is only partly liberative because it does not provide an expansive vision of deliverance for all people. This text by itself opens up our imagination for what is possible, but it is only in conversation with the rest of the Bible that we arrive at a trajectory of universal deliverance. Some of the prophets, for example, were already anticipating salvation extending to all humanity. This continues in the gospel of Luke and the narrative of Acts. These texts begin with a vision focused on salvation for the Jews, but as the narrative unfolds, so do the boundaries of God's promise: it is for all flesh. Our Jubilee ethics must follow that same biblical trajectory.

Some of my family likes to play Monopoly when we are on vacation. This game encourages vicious economic sensibilities not much different from what we frequently see in real life. It only takes a few laps around the board before everyone has converted fully into cutthroat capitalists in pursuit of economic domination. Winning by all means, increasing our wealth and properties, seeing most players as competitors rather than collaborators, until we have dominated the board by hoarding everything, is the pattern I've witnessed (and participated in) every time. My family gets particularly cutthroat, making some of the in-laws a little intimidated about joining in on the "fun." There always is one winner, who gloats in all their glory at the end of the game. Of course, the game is temporary and we always must pack up the box after we are done. We then move on to a more holistic way of interacting with one another.

Using the Monopoly analogy, I've heard some preachers remind their congregation that when "our box" (meaning our coffin) closes, those things we have accumulated won't matter anymore. This is a good reminder. However, I wonder if we ought to not only consider how those things won't matter after we are dead, but also reflect on how we can play the game differently. Technically, no one is stopping us from operating differently, even within the confines of the game. What would it look like to have a Jubilee mindset, or to adopt the reasoning of early Christian leaders when we play? What if we refused to enter our role and play by the designed goals? What if we redefined winning or we shared the properties cooperatively? What if we rebooted the game if things became too lopsided and inequitable? Honestly, that probably would not be tons of fun in Monopoly, but it certainly would bring joy in real life while facilitating God's flourishing desires for humanity.

As I mentioned already, the whole biblical narrative is overwhelmed with wisdom and reasoning that run counter to the logic of mainstream economics. This is especially obvious in the gospel of Luke, though it is a feature in all the gospel narratives. Read Luke's account and you find that the poor are distinctly being lifted up, while the wealthy are constantly being chastised. They are invited to voluntarily walk away from hoarding the resources God intended for everyone and to redistribute their wealth to the poor. The book of Acts follows this theme while describing radical communities of mutual economic sharing so that no one was in need. Unlike the rich young ruler who walks away from Jesus, we are told that Barnabas freely sells his field and brings the proceeds to the church to be used for the well-being of all. Some join this radical community yet deceptively withhold resources rather than share all things, and the book of Acts claims they experience God's judgment.

But the New Testament illuminates different ways that Jubilee can happen. It's not always from one shared purse; sometimes on a larger scale Scripture is fostering a Jubilee consciousness of interconnectedness. Paul, for example, invites the Corinthian church to redistribute their abundant resources to another community in extreme poverty. The example, for Paul, with this generous redistribution is Jesus. Although rich, he became poor, so that we might be rich in Christ. The goal for Paul is that they pursue equilibrium and balance: "I do not mean that there should be relief for others and pressure on you, but it is a question of a fair balance between your present abundance and their need, so that their abundance may be for your need, in order that there may be a fair balance" (2 Corinthians 8:13-14). We give, receive, and share all things, which includes economic resources, but it should not be limited to that. Everyone has gifts to share and everyone has needs. Jubilee ethics are part of the wisdom of Jesus-shaped economic reasoning.

MAXIMIZING PROFITS

Jubilee ethics fulfilled in Christ directly clash with the values and principles of mainstream society. Unregulated capitalism does drive innovation, but it also encourages corporations to maximize their profits by any means available to them, to pursue limitless expansion and growth, and to approach their business in the spirit of competitiveness rather than collaboration. These goals usually harm workers, do damage to the earth, and foster apathy and selfishness in relation to the well-being of others. Global and multinational corporations function like empires seeking to exploit the labor of others. They rarely recognize the inherent dignity of all labor, and intentionally pay as little tax as they can get away with so those at the top can stuff their pockets.

Grassroots movements have been decrying the suppression of wages that large corporations have engaged in for a long time. Corporations like Amazon, Walmart, Apple, Nike, and so on are not small businesses trying to squeeze by. They are accumulating billions of dollars of profits while paying as little as possible to their workers, whether here or abroad. We constantly hear about increasing productivity of laborers (or scrapping workers for robots) and growing stocks, profits, and economies, yet wages, when inflation is accounted for, have not kept up. In most cases, they have been stagnant and with inflation, they technically have been in decline. It is near impossible for poor and working-class families to survive on minimum- and low-wage jobs. Ironically, these companies expect the American people to foot the bill for their low wages and jobs that don't provide healthcare. People's tax dollars have to be spent to fill the gap for low-wage workers because fair wages and healthcare are denied by these companies. Simultaneously, these same corporations can publicly brag about all their profits and soaring stock valuations.

In *Unified We Are a Force*, Joerg Rieger and Rosemarie Henkel-Rieger describe some of the ways the dignity of labor has been under attack and devalued in the United States. I appreciate that they remind us that the trends we see are not a natural phenomenon. The growing inequitable divide between employers and employees is a problem engineered by humans. The authors highlight that "it has become the generally accepted dogma for corporations that their primary responsibility is to their stockholders rather than to their workers."[7] The well-being of working-class employees is not prioritized, and they become targets for exploitation to meet corporate goals. The denial of the dignity of all labor is visible through the massive wage theft that corporations engage in. This occurs when corporations illegally withhold pay from their employees. In the United States, "day after day millions of dollars are withheld and thus stolen from workers. Agriculture, poultry processing, janitorial services, restaurant work, garment manufacturing, long-term care, home health care, and retail are the industries with the most reported cases of wage theft."[8]

To grasp the scope of the problem, we can consider the amount of property stolen through burglary and robbery in 2012 and compare it to the wage theft that occurred in the same year. In total, robberies in 2012 account for close to $340 million. That is a lot, but it is dwarfed by the amount of stolen wages that were *recovered* that year: about $933 million. And that only represents the money recovered from corporations in cases that were resolved—it does not include the frequent theft that happens without people's knowledge, or wage theft committed against vulnerable people (e.g., people who are undocumented) who are afraid to report what happened.[9]

Every summer break during college, when many of my peers were enjoying their break or working as camp counselors, I was working in warehouses. I needed to pay the bills, and picking a job for the sake of fun was out of the option. I worked in warehouses because they always seemed to be the best option for saving as much money as I could without having any job experience or connections to higher-paying options. It was hot and often arduous labor, and I did overtime many days so I could save up for the next school year. Every summer I ended up working at a different warehouse because I would go wherever there was an opening.

One summer that included working at a Walmart warehouse focused on renovating the local store in our area. This particular job was temporary, so they attracted many college-age workers who were okay with a limited gig for the summer. The pay was a little less than some of my other warehouse jobs, but it still beat working a bare minimum-wage job. So at the end of the summer my pockets were a little thinner than in other years, but the job was a bit more enjoyable because many fellow employees were my age (unlike my other summer jobs) and I always was amused by the young adult drama and gossip that inevitably occurred each week. As quickly as the summer began, it also ended. I went back to school, where I lived on campus, studied biblical studies, and enjoyed the college life. Years went by: I moved back to Philly, got married, started my MDiv, bought a home, and had my first child. And then suddenly, seemingly out of nowhere, I received a check in the mail for a few hundred dollars. Apparently, Walmart had been sued for employment theft and I was unknowingly one of its victims. It was strange because receiving the check felt like being given extra money, as if a church mother had quietly slipped money into my hands. However, the truth was that Walmart had stolen my hard-earned money without me even knowing it was happening. Wage theft is one obvious and illegal way in which the dignity of labor is attacked and undervalued.

The truth, however, is that wage theft is merely a symptom, and the bigger problem causes less outrage and is perfectly legal. *Wage suppression* is the greater concern that we need to be attentive to if we want to affirm the dignity of all labor and the well-being of all workers. Wage suppression is the "widespread efforts to push down compensation for working people."[10] Again, places like Walmart and Amazon are great examples of this. Walmart "is making enormous profits by pushing down wages, cutting or eliminating benefits, and preventing workers from full-time employment, thus forming an on-demand workforce with nontransparent scheduling."[11] *Unified We Are a Force* details the low compensation of Walmart workers compared to the inequitable wealth of the six family members who own the corporation:

> Walmart is ranked at the very top of global Fortune 500 companies according to its own website. The company has 2.2 million employees and made $16.4 billion in profits in 2014. The combined wealth (in assets, capital, stock, and securities) of the six heirs of Sam Walton, the founder of the company, who hold more than 50 percent of the shares of the company, is greater than that of 42 percent of all Americans. This means that six people own more than 49 million American families put together.[12]

When *United We Are a Force* was written, the average Walmart worker made $8.81 an hour, or $15,500 in annual earnings. The choice Walmart makes to redirect their profits away from those who labor for the company so that stockholders can increase their wealth results in the American people paying for Walmart's poor treatment of their workers. As much as $1,750,000 per store is picked up by taxpayers so that Walmart heirs and other stockholders can see stocks rise. There are additional insults. For example, an Ohio Walmart, instead of just providing workers with livable wages, asked its own employees to donate canned goods to aid other employees who were struggling to get by. And these days, Amazon is often outdoing Walmart at its own rigged game.

The intentional suppression of wages by global corporations creates a culture that normalizes exploitation and inequality of workers. As the church situates itself in its context, it must recognize the forces and trends at work in our time that diminish the chances that poor and working-class people can flourish. It is not enough to do charity, and not even distributing our own wealth provides the full answer. We must have prophetic courage to tell Pharaoh to stop exploiting his workers, and to release them into a life of flourishing. We need local organizing and movement work that insists on the dignity of all labor and affirms our social responsibility for the well-being of all workers and employees.

FINANCIAL APARTHEID

Dr. King decried that there were two Americas, one flowing in prosperity, the other existing in poverty and dilapidated housing. The existence of two Americas, in view of our racial history, is not because of the natural flow of market forces. Instead, it exists because elites designed and structured our society so that the majority of poor people, and especially black people, would not have access to the same capital as everyone else. Too often when we speak about economic inequality and the wealth gap, it is framed ahistorically, making black poverty appear to be the result of a failure of black people rather than the result of an intentional financial apartheid system that was rigged by the white majority. Intergenerational black poverty was imposed through laws and policies that excluded the black community from full participation in the mainstream economy. While poverty in general is a problem, until we acknowledge how black poverty was designed through policies, we will continue putting Band-Aids on bullet wounds.

My neighbor Rafik, whom I spoke of earlier in the book, returned to Philly after serving time in prison. I mentioned that we would talk about all sorts of stuff, including touchy issues like religion and politics. But Rafik also knew that I was a graduate student and a pastor at the time. I represented access to communities, organizations, and networks that he would not have connections to otherwise. So frequently, he would ask me to keep my ear open for available jobs. Particularly, though, he wanted to know if I knew of any jobs that were hiring people who had a conviction. He was hoping to find a job that paid a livable wage but was facing the discouraging experience of having door after door close on him because of his record. Scholars like Michelle Alexander have documented well how the mass incarceration of black men has created a caste system in which people are permanently and legally discriminated against even after they have done their time (often for nonviolent offenses).[13] Other studies have shown that black men with and without convictions are especially targeted with racial discrimination in the employment process when compared to their white counterparts. It is no surprise that my friend continued to struggle to find employers that paid a living wage and were willing to give him an opportunity.

But the existing financial apartheid runs deeper than the problems that mass incarceration has created, although that legalized form of discrimination certainly perpetuates the already existing wealth gaps. At every stage of this nation's history, racist policies and customs have been engineered to block the majority of black people from full access and participation in the mainstream economy. Obviously, the enslaved labor of black people laid the foundation for this nation's wealth. Black people toiled under the brutality of the white whip and produced billions of dollars for the U.S. economy. That capital was the engine for all sorts of economic growth.

However, going into the twentieth century, most white workers were also still being left out of that prosperity. So the government intervened. The early and mid-twentieth century saw the creation of the white middle class through a series of policies and programs designed to help them create and build wealth. The Progressive Era and the New Deal ushered countless poor and working families from poverty into middle-class life. Federal Housing Administration and student loans were subsidized by the government, making it easier to buy a home than to rent. G.I. Bills, Homestead Acts (which started in the 1860s), and many other policies created wealth stability for so many white families. What is amazing about this period is that the government saw a problem, intervened in the economic sphere, and successfully guided millions of families out of poverty. Most white families benefited from one or more of these programs. Ironically, many white families today tell stories about how one or more of their past family members from the early and mid-twentieth century picked themselves up by their own bootstraps, when in fact they were beneficiaries of government handouts intentionally designed to provide an uplift out of poverty. It doesn't mean they didn't also work hard, it just means they were given an opportunity, through favorable conditions created by government policies and programs, for their hard work to be productive.

Meanwhile, black families were forced into social and economic segregation and denied access to these government programs designed to create and build wealth, and instead were handed decades of the most horrific forms of terrorism this nation has undergone. While the twentieth century was a time of empowerment for many white Americans, black people were navigating Jim Crow, neo-slavery, and the lynching era. Black people obviously experienced discrimination in employment throughout the twentieth century. That needs to be stated, but need not be argued. What is ignored is how black people were explicitly denied access to the same Progressive Era–government programs that were designed to lead white Americans from poverty to middle-class stability. FHA loans and student loans were not provided to black people at that time. In fact, 98 percent of FHA loans went to white families. The same thing is true of the G.I. Bill. Black soldiers who fought for their homeland discovered that allegiance to their country did not translate into their country having an allegiance to them. The Homestead Acts, which gave away acres of land on the penny, were denied to most black people. Even basic access to the new credit system was not available to black people, while white families in the mid-twentieth century leveraged it to increase their standard of living. The housing, land, and investment of wealth that people received reshaped the United States, but black people were intentionally barred from participation. They were economically segregated and redlined into ghettos, where intentional disinvestment was occurring. Furthermore, black people's money went in every direction, including to many white-owned businesses, but white people's money and investments rarely supported black businesses. It was financial apartheid.

The few white families that did not use these government handouts directly were still able to fully participate in these flourishing economies, while black people found themselves constantly trapped in the cycle of holding the lowest and least desirable jobs, like service work and field work. They were completely locked out of the mainstream economic system. Even Irish and Italian communities that had historically been ostracized by white Anglo-Saxon Protestants were able, in the twentieth century, to become "American" through white social performance strategies. Despite their experience of discrimination, their newfound white status allowed them to benefit from government intervention and to gain access to financial sectors that were for whites only. And when black communities somehow began climbing out of poverty, white backlash was sure to follow, destroying that emerging (yet ultimately small) financial power back to the ground. The most famous example of this was the legacy of "Black Wall Street," a famous community in Tulsa, Oklahoma, that had an emerging neighborhood of successful black businesses. The wealth gap was not going to close by this alone, but its existence provided hope that economic stability with a safety net was possible as black businesses thrived. Leaders like Booker T. Washington had claimed that if the black community developed financially, then white people would respect them. He thought the path of economic power, rather than political power (as advocated by W. E. B. Du Bois), was the pathway to true freedom. In the end, he was wrong, because he underestimated white backlash to the rise of black business in the twentieth century. In

1921, during just one of many race riots during that time, white residents destroyed and burned down black businesses and homes, demolishing the Greenwood community and its economic development.

Even today, the proverb in the black community that we are "the last hired and the first fired" persists. Financial apartheid is still a reality for many in the black community. Of course some will protest this point. What about the existence of black millionaires? What about the black middle class? Isn't this a sign that financial apartheid is finally over? But black millionaires are clearly the exception to the rule. For example, in 2017, the *Washington Post* reported that one in seven white families were millionaires, compared to one in fifty black families.[14] Wealth is not evenly distributed. Proportionately, many black families continue to reside in "the other America" Dr. King spoke of. To comprehend the ongoing financial apartheid that affects large segments of the black community today, one needs only to see the persistent lack of wealth the community holds collectively. Mehrsa Baradaran details this shocking inequality in *The Color of Money*:

> When the Emancipation Proclamation was signed in 1863, the black community owned a total of 0.5 percent of the total wealth in the United States. This number is not surprising; slaves were forbidden to own anything, and the few freed blacks living in the North had few opportunities to accumulate wealth. What is staggering is that more than 150 years later, that number has barely budged—blacks still own only about 1 percent of the wealth in the United States.[15]

It is a sleight of hand to turn our attention to black millionaires and billionaires when such examples are nothing but fantasies for the average black working-class family. From the beginning of the nation's founding until today, anti-black policies, laws, and customs have intentionally blocked the black community from full participation in the economy. A closer and careful study of this subject (and I highly recommend *The Color of Money* and *The Color of Law*) reveals that it will take the same intentionality in law and policy to fix the system as it did to create the problem. We need to create access into the mainstream economy through the redistribution of resources and through investment in poor black neighborhoods in the twenty-first-century as was done for white people through government intervention in the twentieth century. Neither black people nor the church should hold its breath that this will actually happen (our racist history says it is very unlikely), but that doesn't change the prophetic task to tell the truth about setting things right. I believe white churches should begin a Jubilee-shaped redistribution of resources and economic investment in communities that are still suffering in their racially and economically segregated zip codes.

Jeremiah the prophet also called out the sons of Josiah for the exploitation of laborers and oppression of the poor during his own time. For Jeremiah, God was decisively on the side of the poor and oppressed:

> Woe to him who builds his house by unrighteousness,
> and his upper rooms by injustice;
> who makes his neighbors work for nothing,
> and does not give them their wages;
> who says, "I will build myself a spacious house
> with large upper rooms,"
> and who cuts out windows for it,
> paneling it with cedar,
> and painting it with vermilion.
> Are you a king

because you compete in cedar?
Did not your father eat and drink
and do justice and righteousness?
Then it was well with him.
He judged the cause of the poor and needy;
then it was well.
Is not this to know me?
says the Lord.
But your eyes and heart
are only on your dishonest gain,
for shedding innocent blood,
and for practicing oppression and violence.
(Jeremiah 22:13-17)

THE CHURCH'S ROLE

What is the church to do in the face of such devastating economic inequality and oppression? If the church is not called to mirror the empire, or to respond in kind, then how do we live in the face of such top-down coercive economic oppression and financial apartheid, where wages are diminished, the dignity of labor is devalued, and entire people groups are denied access to economic participation? When our economic system encourages individualism, competition, maximizing profits, and ongoing expansion rather than flourishing communities, collaboration and mutuality, and maximizing the common good through a sustainable future, what might the vocation of the church require of us? How might a Jubilee ethic fulfilled in Christ get reimagined for our twenty-first century, and how do we begin to embody that through Christ's presence in our community?

Today the church is in need of a radical imagination capable of perceiving God's new society, where new economic relations are concretely embodied. The church needs to actually live in accordance with the reign of the Messiah, in which economic domination is defeated. It ought to be a community where a Jubilee ethic fulfilled in Christ results in creative and contextualized redistribution of wealth while confronting the death-dealing material arrangements of this old order. God's dream for creation is a flourishing and sustaining world for all inhabitants in which we live interdependently with one another in peace and justice. Manifesting God's reign as followers of Jesus while participating in the delivering presence of God must never be a hypothetical, abstract, or spiritual idea that does not correspond with faithful living that bears witness to Christ's resurrection and victory over this world. For this reason, the church must have courage to follow the living presence of Jesus, to be guided by his way, allowing the Messiah's reign and the Spirit's guidance to interrupt our economic practices. We proclaim that Jubilee is fulfilled in Christ, and that is good news to the poor.

As already stated, Luke's gospel account is the most direct about Jesus' life and teachings on wealth and God's dream for new economic relations. Those who desire to hoard wealth, exploit their workers, or scapegoat the poor using the myth of meritocracy and rugged individualism will be severely disappointed with the gospel of Luke. Jesus relentlessly castigates the wealthy while remaining unconditionally affirming of the poor. While some Christians have tried to spiritualize some of the gospel accounts and thereby avoid their implications, it is not so simple to do so with Luke's account. Comfortable Christians have worked hard, performing quite impressive mental gymnastics to marginalize Jesus' hard teachings on wealth, or to make them say the opposite of what they appear to be saying. Again, that can only work in Luke's account if you never read the whole thing and instead cherry-pick isolated verses. If you immerse yourself in Luke's gospel story, remaining open to the hard teachings of Jesus, you discover a Jesus that reverses the economic hierarchy and flips the table (literally and figuratively) on who is honored and who is shamed in society.

For Jesus, the year of God's favor (a euphemism for Jubilee) is proclaimed in Luke 4:18-19, setting the stage for Jesus' ministry. From there, the poor are blessed and the wealthy are condemned (Luke 6). A gospel for the poor is pronounced, while a radical message of repentance for the wealthy is offered. Even before those words of Jesus we witness the revolutionary praise of Mary anticipating God's new social arrangement. Mary understands who God is and how God continues to work: "He has brought down the powerful from their thrones, and lifted up the lowly; he has filled the hungry with good things, and sent the rich away empty" (Luke 1:52-53). Even John the Baptist understood from the beginning that God's reign means a new society is being birthed that will end the reign of the wealthy ruling class. Through the Messiah, "every valley shall be filled, and every mountain and hill shall be made low, and the crooked shall be made straight, and the rough ways made smooth; and all flesh shall see the salvation of God" (Luke 3:5-6). A careful reader will notice that the application of Luke 3:4-14 is economically focused, which is why John the Baptist calls for the redistribution and sharing of goods and the end of exploitation to prepare for the Messiah's coming : "'Whoever has two coats must share with anyone who has none; and whoever has food must do likewise.' Even tax collectors came to be baptized, and they asked him, 'Teacher, what should we do?' He said to them, 'Collect no more than the amount prescribed for you.' Soldiers also asked him, 'And we, what should we do?' He said to them, 'Do not extort money from anyone by threats or false accusation, and be satisfied with your wages'" (vv. 11-14). John the Baptist was all about redistributing resources and ending exploitation.

After his baptism, Jesus is sent to the wilderness, where he renounces the devil's offers to lord over the kingdoms of the world or to control resources as the miracle bread king, and instead remains dependent on God's promise. John the Baptist's disciples are said to have recognized Jesus as the Messiah because, among other things, the poor had good news preached to them. Jesus provided nourishment to the masses by praying to God and demonstrating that his good news is truly good for the poor. Jesus told the parable of the rich fool who hoarded wealth and then died. Then there is the story of the rich man who lived luxuriously while Lazarus was neglected and suffered through life. They both die, but the punch line is that their fortunes are reversed in the after-life. Abraham refuses to allow the rich man to be comforted: "Abraham said, 'Child, remember that during your lifetime you received your good things, and Lazarus in like manner evil things; but now he is comforted here, and you are in agony'" (Luke 16:25). The passage concludes by arguing that even before Christ came, everything needed to understand our ethical responsibility to one another was present in the Torah and prophetic texts of the Hebrew Bible.

One of the more troubling passages on wealth for many comfortable Christians is found in Luke 18. This passage is one which people read in isolation and then attempt to make it not say what it directly says. We are told that a wealthy ruler came to Jesus asking how he can inherit eternal life. Appar-ently, he faithfully kept the law, but Jesus assures him that there was one thing he had not done. He had not embraced the spirit of the Jubilee ethic that Jesus was fulfilling in his ministry. Jesus told him, "There is still one thing lacking. Sell all that you own and distribute the money to the poor, and you will have treasure in heaven; then come, follow me" (Luke 18:22). At that moment the man became sad and walked away because he had great wealth. Just so people don't domesticate the meaning of the story, Jesus provides it for us directly: "How hard it is for those who have wealth to enter the kingdom of God! Indeed, it is easier for a camel to go through the eye of a needle than for someone who is rich to enter the kingdom of God" (vv. 24-25). Despite Jesus' own explanation of the parable, I've still witnessed comfortable Christians do all sorts of heavy intellectual labor so they can deny and domesticate Jesus' challenging words. For some, "It had nothing to do with wealth specifically, it was just his heart that wasn't all in for God." For comfortable Christians it is always a matter of the heart when it comes to wealth, which means one can claim a heart change rather than actually repent from our economic practices. Even after we have surrendered over our last idol in our heart, we can continue to hoard resources for ourselves without regard for the well-being of poor people.

Another story in Luke functions as a foil to the rich ruler account. It is Zacchaeus's story, which begins in the very next chapter. Just as the economic implications of the rich ruler story are avoided and replaced with an ethic concerned only with matters of the heart, so the meaning of the Zacchaeus story is also watered down and domesticated, making Jesus' revolutionary ministry safe and Santa Claus-ified. Just think about it, most people know this story primarily through the popular Sunday school song, which intentionally leaves out the punch line of the passage:

Zacchaeus was a wee little man,
and a wee little man was he.
He climbed up in a sycamore tree,
for the Lord he wanted to see.

And as the Savior passed that way,
he looked up in the tree
and said, "Zacchaeus, you come down!
For I'm going to your house today!
For I'm going to your house today!"

Whoever created this song was particularly crafty. It is such a catchy song that teaches people from a young age about Zacchaeus, but it actually lays a different meaning over the Lukan story. Most people know that Zacchaeus was a tax collector who exploited his own people by performing a role for the empire of overseeing the collection of taxes. This was a lucrative job. This is unjust wealth at its finest. Given this reality, Zacchaeus was an outcast in the community. He would have clearly been defined as a sinner among the Jews, and he would have known it. So when Jesus called Zacchaeus to come down (I think the language of *coming down* can be understood to have a symbolic meaning in relation to economic domination) and announced that he had decided to go to his home, this would have been scandalous on Jesus' part. Zacchaeus was part of the lost children of Abraham living directly counter to the Torah and the ethic of Jubilee. Jesus' fellowship with him was perceived as making him unclean to many observers.

When Jesus spoke to Zacchaeus, we do not know exactly what Jesus said to him. A great line from the musical *Hamilton* is fitting: "No one else was in the room where it happened." That is how I feel about this moment. It is not hard to imagine some possibilities, given how Jesus is typically portrayed. Zacchaeus was a wealthy man who exploited the masses of

poor Jews in his community, severing him from being in relationship with God, with his community, and with himself. He
was under the power of evil forces and greed that led him to
maximize his wealth rather than pursue the flourishing and
well-being of all people within God's reign. It was clear that
Zacchaeus needed God's deliverance through an invitation to
repent from those harmful exploitative practices and to courageously practice Jubilee ethics in response to Jesus. Jesus
may very well have told Zacchaeus something similar to what
he told the rich ruler. All we know is that Zacchaeus had a
deep and transformative encounter with Jesus which radically
changed his economic practices with his neighbors:

> "Look, half of my possessions, Lord, I will give to the poor;
> and if I have defrauded anyone of anything, I will pay back
> four times as much." Then Jesus said to him, "Today sal-
> vation has come to this house, because he too is a son of
> Abraham. For the Son of Man came to seek out and to save
> the lost." (Luke 19:8-10)

This is a powerful liberative story that contrasts radically
with the rich ruler encounter. Zacchaeus voluntarily practices
a Jubilee ethic through two distinct actions. First, he recognizes that he has a responsibility to all people living in poverty. Half of his possessions will be given to people living in
poverty. Secondly, Zacchaeus understood that his wealth was
accumulated through exploitation and by harming those who
already had a foot on their neck by an unjust system. Therefore, Zacchaeus plans to make amends by paying reparations
to all his victims. He knows that righteousness requires setting
things right and restoring people to wholeness and well-being.
He not only will give back what he took, but will give four
times that so they can flourish. In many ways, Zacchaeus is

much more than a foil to the rich ruler, he embodies faithful economic action in his neighborhood where the Jubilee ethic fulfilled in Christ is visibly manifested. His life becomes good news for the poor. He freely redistributes his wealth, and this is enough for Jesus to declare that he has experienced true salvation. Salvation, for Jesus, is not merely an afterlife issue. Salvation is about experiencing God's deliverance even right now, from below the powers, amid the sinful forces and evil systemic patterns that keep people captive. Zacchaeus was lost and now is saved.

Zacchaeus seems to provide a really powerful starting point for a theology of reparations in the church. His practice of jubilee, not only through a redistribution of half his wealth, but his giving back four times what he exploited for his victims has the potential to reframe reparations conversations in this country. Too often, opponents of reparations will say there is no price that can be put on what was done. This is partly true. We can calculate numeric numbers for stolen wealth from free labor and other forms of exploitation, but that by itself will never do justice to the harm done. However, this argument is usually said to actually justify doing *nothing* at all. In contrast, Zacchaeus's ultimate goal, however, was not limited to putting a price tag on the harm done so he could pay that debt. He went above and beyond the amount of money he exploited and instead sought to repair the harm with the goal of wholeness and flourishing for those he wronged. Making amends and setting things right in broken relationships is at the heart of a Christian theology of reparations. The ultimate goal is shalom.

Jesus' good news applied to our economic practices and reasoning has everything to do with our individual and collective lives as his followers. What Jesus' deliverance means for the poor and the wealthy provides the theological and ethical launching pad for creative, contextual, and historically informed Jubilee ministry. The church is not called to be the empire nor to replicate its exploitative and death-dealing ways of constructing society. God's deliverance begins where God's reign is taking root, from below the powers and authorities. It is in solidarity with the poor that the church practices Jubilee ethics on behalf of its neighbors.

The church is the community of called-out ones seeking the common good and flourishing of our neighborhoods and all creation. The vocation of the church is to join God's vocation of setting the world right. Rather than a top-down approach, the church is with the poor, for the poor, and ultimately is the poor (in that its members include those in poverty and those in solidarity as the poor in spirit). Any community that rejects the Jubilee ethic fulfilled in Jesus has rejected God's deliverance from our oppressive economic arrangements.

CONCLUSION

We've witnessed how prioritizing profits over people leads to denying the dignity of all labor and to the suppression of wages. Furthermore, particular people groups and communities have been intentionally disinvested and blocked from participation in the broader economy. And our globalized economy means that exploitative practices are not bound by national borders; they take as much advantage of workers everywhere as our world will allow. Yet Christ came in the flesh preaching good news to the poor and had an invitation into God's reign for the wealthy as well. They too could be delivered from their captivity, but that deliverance requires repentance from exploitation, greed, and hoarding. The option of redistributing wealth and setting things right with those harmed is always a concrete option.

My friend and colleague Richard Crane sometimes jokes that we treat Jesus like we treat our crazy uncle at our family gatherings. You know, that one relative that says outlandish things and no one bothers to correct him because they don't take him seriously. Well, for too long, Jesus has been treated like our crazy uncle in the church, which has allowed for Christians to think and live in ways so contradictory to the life and teachings of Christ. Therefore we resist being set free and participating in God's deliverance for the poor. White Christians in particular need not think about poverty through the framework of charity. Centuries of policy have advantaged white people and economically plundered black and many other nonwhite communities. The church, like Zacchaeus, must set right the wrongs committed against its siblings, along with the broader vocation of pursuing the flourishing of all people. Until the church renounces its false economic gospel and accepts Jesus' reign, its story will continue to look more like that of the rich ruler than that of Zacchaeus. Most days it seems impossible that the mainstream church will ever seek the flourishing of all economically or make reparations for past and ongoing harm. The good news is that all things are possible with God.

8

THE THINGS THAT MAKE FOR PEACE

CONDUCIVE STRATEGIES FOR ECCLESIAL GRASSROOTS JUSTICE WORK

In the summer of 2018 the Poor People's Campaign publicly launched across the country with a series of weekly escalating actions that climaxed with a large rally in our nation's capital. Fifty years after Martin Luther King Jr.'s own Poor People's Campaign, his ideas were revived with the help of Rev. William Barber's national profile and growing network of organizations across the nation. The campaign's goal was "to challenge the evils of systemic racism, poverty, the war economy, ecological devastation and the nation's distorted morality." The launch was happening in about forty states, with the participation of many local community organizations across each state. Pennsylvania, my own state, had brought together many organizations from across the commonwealth to link arms in solidarity in this movement. And since I was once again living in Harrisburg, the state capital, I was at ground zero for the targeted rallies and actions that summer.

My own journey toward nonviolent action and struggle derived from my scriptural and theological understanding of Jesus as a nonviolent Messiah coupled with my ongoing study, since graduating college, of Dr. King and his philosophy, as well as the broader freedom movement of the 1950s and '60s. As a student of King, I had delved into many of his writings and speeches. I had watched documentaries like *Eyes on the Prize*, documenting the civil rights struggle. And on three occasions between 2005 and 2010 I attended a ten-day trip entitled "Returning to the Roots of the Civil Rights Bus Tour" led by my friend and Messiah College colleague, Todd Allen, bringing groups from Philly and Harrisburg along with me two of those times. I was a student of King's successes and failures, but most importantly, I had caught his vision for a Jesus-shaped way of resisting injustice and seeking social transformation.

When the revived Poor People's Campaign came to my city, I knew I was going to participate. Many Christians celebrate Dr. King in January, pretending that they would have supported him and his agenda, but at the time many Christians were hostile or apathetic to his work. For me the test of what we would have done back in the '60s should only be assessed by what we are doing now, rather than engaging in wishful thinking through hypothetical scenarios. I had the desire to join the reviving of his campaign, and to be honest,

I also had a job that made participation more feasible than it was for many others. Having vocational freedom to be out of the office multiple Mondays in a row requires either radical sacrifice or social advantages. I had just completed my second full year teaching as a professor of theology, which provided an advantage for me to get involved over the summer. Classes are out for the break and I get to schedule my agenda for the summer. Not everyone has that.

With the cover of a stable and flexible job, extra free time, and financial safety, I decided that I shouldn't only participate, but should take the added risk of engaging in civil disobedience and get arrested. Each week different actions were planned, with the intention of disrupting the status quo and elevating the awareness of our campaign in Pennsylvania. I knew I couldn't get arrested every week, since most weeks I actually did have other responsibilities (and I also had been working closely with a community organization that had some of its own plans unfolding that summer as well). But I figured that I should offer my time and body at least once by getting arrested, since the consequences for that action would not sting for me the way it could for other people in different professions. Pastors and professors, among other professions, continue to have an umbrella of protection when getting arrested for civil disobedience which allows for greater radical action. There should be no shaming of people who do not have that social advantage.

After looking at my schedule for the summer, along with the plans of Pennsylvania's Poor People's Campaign, I decided that I could participate in four out of the six weeks, while getting arrested would be most feasible for me the final week of the demonstrations. So I went to most of the rallies and actions, but held off getting arrested in the beginning weeks.

As always, I was moved by my fellow organizers and activists taking action on behalf of their neighbors each week. Some of my Harrisburg friends spoke at the rallies. People from across the state engaged in civil disobedience as they blocked the street in front of the capitol and blocked doorways and walkways. Each week was something new, keeping the capitol complex police on their toes as they tried to anticipate what we had up our sleeves next. When the final week came, I was a bit anxious. You have to go through mental, emotional, and spiritual preparation if you are going to willingly get arrested. On one hand, I thought of intentionally getting arrested as something honorable, since many generations have engaged in civil disobedience as a means of standing up for justice while joining a great cloud of witnesses. On the other hand, it still involved getting arrested, interfacing with police, going through the system, and getting locked up. Sometimes things do not go as planned during strategic civil disobedience. Who hasn't watched videos of police using unnecessary violence while arresting people? So yeah, I was still anxious as the time approached.

I arrived early for our pre-meeting before the rally. It was held in the basement of a local church building in downtown Harrisburg that was within walking distance of the capitol complex. I was at peace that morning as I arrived. There was a good turnout. Harrisburg friends were there, as well as new friends I'd made during the past month and a half. The meeting got started on time, but after a few minutes those gathered were quickly informed that there would be no civil disobedience action after the rally that day! Yes, you read that right, no action was planned for that day. I think my mouth literally dropped. It took a few minutes to sink in. I would not be getting arrested that day. Several people expressed their disappointment about this news. I was disappointed, but I understood the challenging decision that the lead organizers had faced. So I went to the rally as I had every other week, and when it ended we left without engaging in any strategic nonviolent disruptions.

All I could think about afterward was the irony. I had literally been planning to get arrested for weeks, intentionally willing to use my body and time as a means for struggling for justice. I did so as my feeble attempt to follow Jesus in my neighborhood and as an act of love for my neighbors. I did not believe it was any grand salvific act that would instantly flip the tables of injustice, but it was going to be my small ripple in the ancient river that has flowed with courageous resistance and peacemaking for centuries.[1] The irony of not getting arrested was intensified by the reality that both of my brothers have been arrested and been racially profiled by police. I have personally witnessed neighbors and community members being involuntarily arrested countless times. On the national level, almost one out of three African American men will be arrested at some point in their lifetime. And here I was, one of the few black men in America who desired to get arrested, and I somehow failed to do so.

In the end, getting arrested or not doesn't matter very much in contrast to an ongoing commitment to seek justice in the way of Jesus, in whatever kind of action is needed. In fact, while it would have been an honor to affirm with Augustine and Dr. King that "an unjust law is no law at all" by engaging in civil disobedience, the truth is, I was already working for justice in many ways, with deeper participation and commitment than that one act I had put on a pedestal. I already was working closely with a faith-based organizing group, I attended countless actions and spoke and marched at rallies, and I was a co-leader for a relational network in Harrisburg committed to doing justice locally by encouraging action through partnership across ecclesial and organizational boundaries.

After writing *Trouble I've Seen*, and after speaking all over the country (especially to local congregations), I began to realize that many Christians have no clue where to begin pursuing justice in their neighborhoods as followers of Jesus. While some Christians have completely avoided the call to do justice, others recognize the work is needed and sacred but do not know where to begin. Many only think about the electoral process or who their favorite candidate is. Over and over again, I heard Christians thank me for my book and the charge to work for racial justice, but then say they did not know how they should move forward with that goal. Eventually it became clear that I needed to assist congregations in getting their feet wet beyond the simple directives I provided at the end of *Trouble I've Seen*. A focus on a variety of strategies conducive for those committed to faithfully following Jesus seemed necessary. Praxis matters. At the same time, the challenges we have ahead of us not only are about action but also include the work of delivering our sociopolitical imagination from captivity to sinful social forces and patterns that turn us against God's deliverance and justice. This book has been an attempt to do that very thing. Now it is time to explicitly turn our focus toward some introductory strategies and tactics that are faithful to Jesus and are also conducive to doing justice and peacemaking within our troubled republic.

In Luke 19, Jesus mourns Jerusalem's impending destruction by the Roman Empire. He wishes that they had only known "the things that make for peace" (v. 42). What is missed in this is that Jesus seems to imply that there are some things that make for shalom (wholeness, well-being, and the presence of justice), and there are some things that do not. Said another way, there are social change strategies that are effective, pragmatic, and faithful for setting things right, and there are some that are not. There are some social change strategies and tactics that align with God's deliverance and peacemaking, while others require abandoning our faith in God and core ethical convictions. What I propose below are some select strategies and tactics that are not uniquely Christian, and I will refuse to pretend that they are—while also recognizing that they easily align with God's peacemaking and justice. These strategies and tactics are conducive for the church because they do not require abandoning the way of Jesus. Jesus was a revolutionary peacemaker who subversively ushered in God's reign as a grassroots movement under the empire's rule, and he did so while recognizing the dignity of the poor and vulnerable rather than by centralizing coercive power over society. However, Jesus did engage the ruling powers through prophetic witness and faithful confrontation instead of engaging in apolitical apathy. While Jesus had many things in common with some of the Jewish sects and movements of his day (especially the revolutionaries and radicals), he refused to allow any group to control the narrative about God's justice and the means by which it will be accomplished.

The church must be as wise as serpents and as innocent as doves as we learn the things that actually bring peace and justice. Our minds are set on God's shalom and the sacred dream for all creation. The strategies and tactics below are possible methods to take up within a local congregation. We must resist baptizing anything as the sole and single way. We yield everything to the preeminence of Christ. We must continue to "study war no more" and improvise with our peacemaking strategies that aid in our struggle for shalom (see

Isaiah 2:4; Micah 4:3). In particular, I will focus on nonviolent resistance, social movements, community organizing, electoral politics, hybrid approaches, community development, and will conclude by reviving a conversation on reparations. There are other ways to pursue social change, including through the arts and through legal work (think about Bryan Stevenson and the Equal Justice Initiative, the development of cooperative businesses, etc.).

NONVIOLENT RESISTANCE AND STRUGGLE

The first conducive strategy for the church to pursue social change is through nonviolent action and resistance. This, of course, is a broad umbrella category that overlaps significantly with other methods. Hopefully some of the earlier chapters of the book have sufficiently provided the scriptural, theological, and ethical reasoning for why there is a deep convergence with this broad strategy and the peacemaking of God revealed in Jesus Christ. Even in the Old Testament, where God is *sometimes* described as utilizing violence, we see an ongoing effort to bind the evil of violence with tighter and tighter restraints, so by the time you get to the prophetic texts in the Hebrew Scriptures there is already an anticipation, in many of them, of the end of all violence. Shalom is envisioned, and pursuing peace is frequently lifted up. This biblical trajectory takes unequivocal sides in view of Jesus' witness to peacemaking, enemy love, and directly confronting and clashing with the Jerusalem establishment. Jesus accepted the backlash of disrupting the status quo and the economic flow of money in the temple, which inevitably led to his own death instead of taking the lives of those in power. His life (as described by each gospel writer) portrays what we would call a nonviolent Messiah engaging in revolutionary speech and action, but of a different variety than most revolutionaries. As such, nonviolent resistance and struggle as a strategy aligns well with the very witness of Jesus' peacemaking.

For me, following the peacemaking of Jesus requires a particular way of life that cannot be sidestepped in the church's pursuit for justice. For starters, as Christians, we must affirm the dignity, sacredness, and value of each and every life. This is true of the violated and the violator. Jesus does this through his attentiveness to the vulnerable and stigmatized while still refusing to take the life of those who do harm to others. While prioritizing those most harmed, Jesus still shared meals with tax collectors and the Pharisees, dialoguing about God's reign. Vital to Christian faith is the belief that all humanity is made in the image of God, and that conviction must be the beginning point for nonviolent action strategies. We recognize the inherit value and sacredness of the life of each and every person.

Second, Jesus calls us to love our enemies. This has always been a tricky concept that we are often quick to claim while nonetheless perpetuating harm to our political enemies. Sometimes we claim that we are just practicing "tough love," when in fact we are not concerned with their well-being at all. The test for whether we truly love our enemies should be discerned by our ability to treat our enemy as we would treat someone we care about deeply if they were in that same situation. Imagine how you would respond to a beloved family member. Or better yet, how we would desire to be treated if we were in that place. Take the famous hypothetical of an intruder breaking into your home. Our first instincts are to take out anyone who might harm our loved ones. What does it mean to love our enemies as Jesus taught? This is not usually on the table of consideration for many churches. To be upfront, I'm not a doctrinal pacifist; I believe there are scenarios where you may need to physically restrain or possibly physically harm someone you love deeply to limit the violence occurring, but if you truly love them, it would be a pained decision that would push you to creatively do *everything* in your might to avoid using violence. Loving your enemy, when considering the peacemaking of Jesus, challenges us to care about the actual well-being of oppressors just as much as we do our own loved ones. This is a hard teaching of Jesus, but it clearly has the capacity to break cycles of violence that frequently spiral out of control in our society.

Third, Jesus engaged in a prophetic witness that confronted the evil practices and teachings in society that harmed vulnerable people, and he did so knowing that there would be an inevitable backlash from those in power. There is always a backlash, and pretending that there will be no consequences is naive. Christian discipleship has always required accepting risks through courageous and costly action. Anyone trying to "sell" you Jesus without including costly discipleship is hoodwinking you. The love of God is best demonstrated by Jesus, who laid down his life for us. Therefore, we are told that we ought to lay down our lives for one another (1 John 3:16-18). To be clear, so my words are not twisted into a harmful ideology, I am not advocating a martyrdom complex! I believe that Jesus came so that we might have an overflowing, abundant life. Life is good. We should not be looking to die. The problem is that some people are disproportionately bearing the brunt of death-dealing systems and policies. So we risk personal harm at times as a protest against death and in solidarity with others who also should have a chance to flourish in life-giving community. Accepting the consequences for faithfully following Jesus through actual sacrificial action is the meaning of "take up your cross and follow me." There is no resurrection except through death itself, and there is no participation in the life of

Jesus that rejects accepting the risk of the cross. Confronting the powers and establishments in society that oppress others by taking up our cross is probably the most revolutionary and subversive dimension of Jesus' peacemaking.

More nuanced aspects to Jesus' peacemaking exist which are relevant for the church's engaging in nonviolent resistance. But these three things (the dignity and value of human life, enemy love, and taking up the cross) seem important for shaping the character and nature of our nonviolent struggle. The church's goal is to seek justice, but it is also to do so faithfully before God while allowing our lives to make the Jesus story visible for our neighbors. This is about being the good news to the world in our embodied action.

It is also helpful to think about nonviolence through the six principles that Dr. Martin Luther King Jr. himself described:

Principle 1: Nonviolence is a way of life for courageous people. It is active nonviolent resistance to evil. It is aggressive spiritually, mentally and emotionally.

Principle 2: Nonviolence seeks to win friendship and understanding. The end result of nonviolence is redemption and reconciliation. The purpose of nonviolence is the creation of the Beloved Community.

Principle 3: Nonviolence seeks to defeat injustice not people. Nonviolence recognizes that evildoers are also victims and are not evil people. The nonviolent resister seeks to defeat evil not people.

Principle 4: Nonviolence holds that suffering can educate and transform. Nonviolence accepts suffering without retaliation. Unearned suffering is redemptive and has tremendous educational and transforming possibilities.

Principle 5: Nonviolence chooses love instead of hate. Nonviolence resists violence of the spirit as well as the body. Nonviolent love is spontaneous, unmotivated, unselfish and creative.

Principle 6: Nonviolence believes that the universe is on the side of justice. The nonviolent resister has deep faith that justice will eventually win. Nonviolence believes that God is a God of justice.[2]

A brief look at Dr. King's approach to nonviolence reveals that there is nothing passive about his understanding of nonviolent action. Occasionally the words *nonviolence* and *pacifism* are used interchangeably. While pacifism isn't necessarily passivism either, there is an error in conflating the two terms. Pacifism, in my unpopular interpretation, is a doctrinal system advocating for a life of peace and the renunciation of violence in all areas of one's life. Nonviolence, as Dr. King describes, is a philosophy and method for resisting injustice and seeking to transform one's society. For Dr. King it was also a complete way of life because it was shaped by his faith in Jesus; however, many have adopted it solely as a strategy for social change without making it a life commitment.

Another mistake people make is to hear the word *nonviolence* and then merely equate it with certain marches and boycotts. When people think of nonviolent action, often the Montgomery bus boycott or the Selma to Montgomery marches come to mind. Those were famous actions that continue to live on in our present consciousness. However, there is a danger of limiting our imagination for doing justice to those narrow options. Just take a cursory look at the 1950s and '60s alone, and one will find a range of nonviolent resistance tactics. Some people used their own bodies to integrate spaces, such as white schools that hoarded resources while black institutions were deprived of an equitable distribution of money. Groups creatively decided to ride buses to challenge the white supremacist hierarchy that dominated interstate travel. Thousands of students participated in extremely disruptive sit-ins. Some actions were designed to put pressure on economic centers in an effort to ensure jobs and livable wages for black people. Some symbolic actions were organized, like carrying Jimmy Lee Jackson's dead body to the capitol steps in Montgomery, Alabama. Downtown business centers were disrupted and shut down, young people left schools, people filled jails, tent cities were built, demands and negotiations were held, electoral officials were challenged, letters and pamphlets were written and disseminated, voter registration drives were pushed, rallies in churches were held, fundraising was ongoing, sometimes presidential appeals and court injunctions were disregarded, and national campaigns were launched. Songs of resistance and resilience were sung and sermons were preached in church buildings, in the streets, and in prisons. This is not a comprehensive list, but all these things were a part of what we now call the civil rights movement.

Not only should you not conflate nonviolent struggle strictly with large political marches (although marching certainly is a nonviolent action), but you also should not restrict nonviolent tactics to what was done in the 1950s and '60s freedom movement. If we were to step back and pay attention to the history of global nonviolent strategies and tactics, we would find a long list of strategic and creative actions. In fact, Gene Sharp, a renowned academic theorist on nonviolent action, compiled and categorized a list of different types of nonviolent campaigns and tactics that have been used around the world. Eventually his list included 198 different tactics, a far cry from the puny one-hit wonder of marching that restricts our imagination. One can find all of these listed in Sharp's seminal work *The Politics of Nonviolent Action*, a three-volume work, published in 1973.[3]

Sharp believed that nonviolent action was "political jiu-jitsu" because the people could "turn repression into a weakness for those in power" by practicing it.[4] In fact, while Sharp believed in nonviolence as a principled way of life for himself, he did not care as much about whether those who used it were committed to it. He played a large role in debunking the myth that nonviolent action was less effective. For him, oppressed people ought to use it precisely because it worked.

Political scientist Erica Chenoweth, however, strengthened the narrative around the effectiveness of nonviolent campaigns by dedicating her scholarship and energy to doing quantitative research comparing violent and nonviolent movements. She examined over three hundred campaigns and to her surprise "found that nonviolent movements worldwide were twice as likely to succeed as violent ones."[5] This runs counter to common assumptions about how the world works. We have been falsely convinced that violence is the final word on the matter. In fact, nonviolent campaigns have actually increased in effectiveness as time has passed, while violent campaigns have been becoming even less successful as the years go by. More interesting, from a social science standpoint, is the power of mobilizing the masses and its relation to an effective campaign. Nonviolent campaigns do not require as many participants as one might think to successfully reach their strategic goals. Chenoweth found that campaigns that reached sustained and active involvement from 3.5 percent of a population were successful. Many accomplished their goals with even less participation. This is notably less than earlier research, which suggested that 5 percent of a population participating in an ongoing nonviolent grassroots campaign would be unsustainable for any regime.[6] Despite many people's assumptions, nonviolent action has statistically been more effective for societal change than violent uprisings. While stats should not override our faith, because we trust in the unseen God, they do align with a Christian cosmic and eschatological conviction about "the things that make for peace."

One of the reasons many people who are not directly involved in sustained and active nonviolent struggle are surprised by the effectiveness of nonviolence is because they misunderstand the strategy. Too often we make everything about a single scapegoat rather than seeing the power systems in society that give them authority in the first place. For example, under the Trump administration, many called for Donald Trump to step down as the solution to their problems. Nonviolent strategies, however, turn their attention to *the pillars* that hold up a regime, policy, institution, or system rather than just targeting an individual. The power and authority that regimes and authoritarian leaders have are possible only if the broader society grants it to them through obedience and submission. Once society itself becomes disobedient to the ruling powers doing the harm, that social power cannot be sustained. For example, Hitler did not execute the Third Reich single-handedly, it took a German citizenry that was obedient and subservient to him. Consider this: "If people refuse to cooperate with a regime—if civil servants stop carrying out the functions of the state, if merchants suspend economic activity, if soldiers stop obeying orders—even an entrenched dictator will find himself handicapped. And if popular disobedience is sufficiently widespread and prolonged, no regime can survive."[7]

This is where the "pillars of power" come in. It is a metaphor for the different sectors and institutions in society that bolster sociopolitical domination and control. Once you "knock down" or sufficiently shake enough pillars, the social, political, and economic support for an oppressive establishment will fall, much like Pharaoh's power began to crumble under the widespread deterioration of his empire during the ten plagues. It is no wonder that Jesus took his struggle straight to the temple in Jerusalem, since the leaders there held concentrated social, cultural, political, economic, and religious power. Many pillars existed in one place, but faithful worshipers remained obedient to the Jerusalem establishment. Jesus explained that its power was not as permanent as it seemed. That "mountain" could be moved.

For example, Srđa Popović of the Otpor! movement in Serbia said, "Every tyrant rests on economic pillars, and economic pillars are much easier targets than military bases or presidential palaces. Shake them, and the tyrant will eventually fall."[8] In our society, we must identify the pillars that uphold economic, social, and political domination. There are political parties and institutions, business and commerce, financial partners, stockholders, faith communities, neighborhood organizations, educational institutions, media and news, unions and lobbyists, customers and consumers, and many others that represent pillars of support depending on the nature of the problem. Each plays a role in constituting social power. People engaging in nonviolent struggle need to identify what pillars in their contextual situation need to be addressed for the domination to crumble like a game of Jenga. The authors of *This Is an Uprising* write:

> The pillars concept offers a catchy visual metaphor for the social theory of power. Imagine the various institutions of society as columns holding up the roof of a Roman temple. Social movements are pulling at the various columns. If they remove one or two of the pillars of support, the

building would be weakened, but it might still stand. However, if people pull out enough of the pillars, the temple is sure to topple, and the movements will triumph.[9]

It is important to remember, especially as followers of Jesus, that our goal is not to destroy people but to bring an end to systems of injustice that are destroying the lives of our neighbors. When we remember that our battle is not against flesh and blood but against both spiritual and sociopolitical forces and systems, we will be able to uphold the peacemaking of Jesus while also pursuing concrete justice for our communities (Ephesians 6:12). It will also aid us in seeing how power functions in our society in ways that are not always obvious. Typically, when we think of how power works we often focus on who is at the top rather than on what enables and bolsters the systems in the first place. Consider divisive issues in a local congregation. People often think that the power solely resides in a visible authority figure like the pastor. However, as we've discussed, congregations have all sorts of power dynamics at work. Elders, a church board, or deacons and trustees might wield significant power. Knowing who actually holds power is important. And there are informal and invisible forms of power as well. Which member has influence simply because they have been there a long time and therefore wield disproportionate power when they speak up? Sometimes being the squeaky wheel or a big donor or having a particular last name provides people with power. If this is the case in a congregation, how much more is this at work in our society? The church must learn to be as wise as serpents, and to not be so naive and unschooled when it comes to the fact that power dynamics are always at work in our world.

At the same time, the temptation can very easily turn into thinking, "If we can't beat them, join them," which was the mistake the church made as it increasingly practiced Christian supremacy over society beginning with Constantine's reign. The challenge we have, which nonviolent struggle helps to address, is to embrace strategies and tactics conducive for engaging and negotiating power in society while also remaining faithful to the way of Jesus. There are certainly ways in which some nonviolent campaigns might not align well with the revolutionary yet peacemaking way of Jesus. It is the church's work to carefully discern when it engages in any work for social change so that the story of Jesus is made visible and so shalom may flourish in our world.

SOCIAL MOVEMENT PROTEST (TAPPING INTO SOCIAL AND CULTURAL MOMENTUM)

In 2011, shortly after I finished my master of divinity program and was preparing for and applying to PhD programs, the Occupy Wall Street movement shocked the United States through a whirlwind of mass protests, marches, disruptive actions, and encampments. Before that time, I was more a student of social activism than an actual activist. I had been studying the black freedom struggle long before that, and arguing that Jesus was a nonviolent revolutionary, but none of my more radical Christian convictions and ethics had yet translated into much praxis. With the scale of the Occupy movement suddenly unfolding all around the country, including in my own city (Philly), I was compelled to get more active. There was a clear convergence of goals between Jesus' prophetic witness, his good news to the poor, and his Jubilee ethics, which called for a radical redistribution of resources, and that of the Occupy movement's unequivocal challenge to the economic structure of our society, which left poor and working-class people close to, or below, the poverty level.

Given that convergence, I decided I would partially participate. I hadn't fully bought into the movement's approach and its centralizing of white people's voices. So at no point was I involved in any strategic planning or organizing anything with the Occupy movement. Initially, I just went to visit the Center City encampments in Philadelphia with no plans on actually living in a tent myself. My participation was limited to getting my body in proximity, checking out what was happening, and later it included marching on a couple of occasions.

Some of what helped the Occupy movement spark a national conversation on poverty and concentrated wealth was the widespread and varied levels of participation that people could choose. The national news highlighted limited groups of people engaging in civil disobedience, sometimes getting arrested or pepper-sprayed as a consequence for participation. More broadly, across the country, mini tent camps were set up in downtown business sectors; the first one was launched in Manhattan. And then there was space for even broader involvement with lower commitment levels from people like myself who didn't join the mostly young and white occupiers but nonetheless supported the conversation about poverty, wealth, and livable wages that was happening.

There are different ways to assess the significance of the Occupy movement now that we have several years' distance from it. Despite some very valid critiques about its unsustainable model, the movement has had a long-lasting legacy on our class consciousness as a society. Prior to the movement, mainstream politicians rarely spoke about poverty and the well-being of working-class people. Policy and political rhetoric usually centered on CEOs, stockholders, and the middle class. Occupy Wall Street restructured the debate altogether by helping the average citizen realize that the top 1 percent held over 40 percent of the wealth of this country. In contrast, the bottom 80 percent owned about 7 percent of the wealth. These staggering statistics became mainstream rhetoric directly because of the Occupy movement, provoking the media and some politicians to engage with its core concerns. The protest movement did not sustain itself long enough to create the conditions for actual policy change, but the cultural and rhetorical impact it sparked continues to shape ongoing political goals in mainstream politics today that would have been inconceivable or impossible before 2011.

The Occupy movement is only one example of protest movements for social change, which usually fall under the umbrella of nonviolent struggle. In 2014, after the death of Michael Brown in Ferguson, Missouri, I began to increase my participation in protest movements. I attended protests organized by Christian leaders in Philadelphia around the Black Lives Matter movement. I also participated in actions planned by young activists, often college students. With them, I marched, I handed out pamphlets, I chanted, and I participated in a "die in" outside Philadelphia's City Hall in the winter. Along with that I attended large marches, most notably one organized by POWER Philadelphia and other organizations that linked arms to address criminal reform, the education system, and livable wages. Much of this was while I was a PhD student at the historic Lutheran Seminary in Philadelphia while also serving as an associate pastor at my church. I could not commit to deeper involvement than what I was doing, but I had deep convictions and desired for my body and time to bear witness to God's justice. Protest movements make room for broad participation without requiring deep and ongoing commitment from all the participants.

One of the strengths of protest movements is their ability to mobilize masses of people while tapping into the cultural and social momentum that exists. If I were to pick one word to characterize protest movements, it would be *mobilization*. Protest movements usually try to mobilize people into public action. Broad mass participation is desired with protest movements, making it easy for people to join in where they fit in. When a protest movement has broad visible engagement, it makes it less scary for newbies to join in as well. While there are some exceptions, this type of movement work usually does not facilitate ongoing commitments to the work.

Another defining characteristic of some protest movements is their willingness to be disruptive and to seek social change outside the formal channels that have been designated by society. Theorists of protest movements have argued that they are especially helpful for groups that do not hold social power in society or when access to formal channels to voice concerns and to truly be heard are not provided. This would explain why so many within the civil rights movement used disruptive protest movement techniques; black people were officially denied access to voting. A willingness to disrupt, and to do so strategically through escalating actions, provides a different kind of power to oppressed people. Again, statistics show that movements that are able to do this with broad, sustainable participation (remember 3.5 percent) are successful.

A final note: Protest movements sometimes produce enormous change in a very short time, especially when they have mobilized masses of people and are able to put sustained pressure on the pillars of society. Protest movements usually tap into, or create, social and cultural waves, which they can ride to the shores of social change. For example, when the Black Lives Matter hashtag first appeared in 2013, there was no initial large protest movement. But even before that, and after, tensions and anger bubbled below the surface in many black neighborhoods across the country. When the Ferguson uprisings happened, they were documented live through social media. This created a broader social and cultural wave that quickly mobilized more and more people for the movement. With growing cell phone and social media technology, awareness about police brutality, which had always existed, was suddenly being distributed widely across the country. The grassroots protests and waves on social media forced many media corporations to take note. The movement both expanded and rode the preexisting wave of social frustration.

One of the strengths of protest movements is also their weakness. A protest movement can quickly change the social atmosphere like a storm, but it can disappear just as easily as a storm as well. In fact, many protest movements are usually not organized for long-term sustainability. There are multiple reasons for this. For one, the attention span of mainstream society is short. In a 24/7 news cycle, it's hard to remember what the big news was from two days ago, so it is extremely difficult to sustain popular concern for social change. However, another big reason is because protest movements attract people that have made no ongoing commitment. The very thing that allows for mass participation can often result in a short-term movement. Requiring higher degrees of commitment will create long-term sustainable movements, but they will likely result in less involvement. Having no expectations around people's dedication to the struggle could ignite broad engagement, but if those people are not committed for the long haul, you will have them until the wave dissipates.

One might think that this critique means that protest movements are useless. That is simply untrue. Countless protest movements have accomplished significant social change in relatively short periods of time. Protest movements can bring policy change and redirect social norms. This usually occurs when movements are able to strike while the social and cultural iron is hot. In fact, even after the protest movement dissipates, its ongoing impact and influence often linger and take new forms. The mass protests for the Occupy movement, the Black Lives Matter movement, and the Me Too movement are not what they once were. Yet the aftershocks of each are still being felt and fleshed out today. These protest movements created many converts who are looking for ways to make change through policy, institutional initiatives, classroom learning, and political campaigns, and the rhetoric of these movements is an inseparable part of our current discourse. Changing the public narrative is an essential part of social change. Sometimes mobilizing enough people and letting them disperse into society will have an unquantifiable impact that will only be fully understood decades later. Certainly, the much older and longer black freedom struggle that began under slavery and still exists in new forms today bears witness to the ongoing ripples that can continue to expand in all directions.

When it was first reported that the Trump administration was detaining and separating children from their parents or guardians at the southern border, there was a large uproar and outraged response. Since moving back to Harrisburg in 2016, I have worked closely with a variety of organizers and activists in my community. Because of this work I was invited to speak at a very large rally and march hosted by MILPA (Movement of Immigrant Leaders in Pennsylvania) and a few other organizations that had been working on immigrant rights in our city.

When I arrived at the rally I was surprised to see how many people came out. It was probably the largest march I had participated in while in Harrisburg. We started in a garden by the river, where some initial speeches were given and some freedom songs were sung. Then we chanted and marched a few blocks to the governor's mansion. We marched around the entire block, and so many people were present that all sides of the city block were full simultaneously. In fact, when it was time for me to speak in front of the governor's mansion, I am pretty sure that only about a quarter of the people even saw me, and even less probably heard what I said. The event was a powerful and symbolic demonstration of our collective voice. We marched around the governor's mansion in particular because (at the time of this writing) Pennsylvania actually has a detention center that has been operating for years. The governor has the legal power to shut it down through an emergency removal order. Despite being on the side of justice in many other ways, he has refused (again, up to the writing of this chapter) to end Pennsylvania's cooperation. There has been an ongoing movement to shut down the Berks County detention center, and this rally brought more attention to this local work while also proclaiming boldly that we stood against what was happening at the national border as well.

This struggle for our immigrant neighbors has continued, but not with the same mass demonstrations. For example, in the spring of 2019, I attended another event hosted by MILPA and a few other organizations in Harrisburg. This time about thirty to forty people showed up. Without the momentum of popular dissent in mainstream society, the group comprised mostly activists and organizers with higher levels of commitment, and only a few people came out who did not have that level of dedication. In fact, the capitol complex police showed up and tried to intimidate and deter our small group from gathering by making up (as we found out at the end of the night) a false ordinance. But the nonviolent struggle is continuing. Right now there are local leaders working together, planning and plotting justice for their neighbors. And while not everyone is showing up for community demonstrations, I believe that many of the people who were initially mobilized into mass protest do care on some level and will continue to speak up for justice on behalf of their neighbors.

There are plenty of ways that local churches can participate in protest movements. Certainly there are supportive roles they can play, like providing space for planning meetings and rallies. Most churches are capable of providing food and drink for protesters. Churches can also participate directly in protest movements. In fact, if networks of congregations, rather than just individual congregations, decide they will support a particular protest movement, it can provide a significant boost of people presence. Of course, congregations are also free to put their minds together to plan their own actions at times as well. A community of Christians could identify an injustice in their community and plan a creative nonviolent disruption or action and invite neighbors to participate. Since you are already beginning with a set number of people and should be able to draw sister or neighboring churches into solidarity with your activism, you provide a great starting point for mobilizing people in your neighborhood while bearing witness to the way of Jesus as you do so. Of course, local congregations should avoid re-creating the wheel by duplicating the work of organizations that are already doing good work locally. It is always a best practice to follow the leadership of those most affected by an injustice instead of operating out of a savior complex. Protest movements, with their strengths and weaknesses, are viable options for local congregations.

ORGANIZING PEOPLE POWER

When I returned to Harrisburg to start teaching in the fall of 2016, my oldest son was about to start kindergarten. Harrisburg School District has always struggled to adequately educate its children. Inequitable funding, concentrated intergenerational poverty, a long history of being on the painful side of racist discrimination and neglect, failures in administration, and a stifling national philosophy of education that measures success by encouraging educators to teach to a test rather than contextualizing education for students all came together to produce our struggling school system. As I write, our school district has been taken over by Pennsylvania and is in a state of receivership. My wife and I love Harrisburg and were committed to living there when we returned, including raising our kids there and fighting for change as well. So the school district would eventually be a very important place for all of our children. We knew that we had to be present and working for change over the long haul and that there would be no quick and easy fixes, because the problems were complicated, multilayered, and part of much older forms of injustice that preceded us. My wife joined the PTA and has continued to play a significant role in our kids' school. I along with other faith leaders and friends turned attention to some larger systemic issues that affected the school, like the inequitable state funding practices in Pennsylvania that were robbing Harrisburg students of millions of dollars every year. To address this we worked with POWER, a local faith-based organization that was trying to expand from Philadelphia to Harrisburg. I already was familiar with them from Philadelphia, but this time I was ready to commit to working with their campaign more closely.

Community organizing seeks to empower and give voice directly to the people affected so they can change their communities through ongoing campaigns. If you want to understand organizing, then the keyword really is *organization*. Justice work through this model is done through official and formal organizations. These organizations have definitive structures, which include a hierarchy of leadership. They are developed and designed to listen to and empower the concerns of the collective participants. And yes, there usually is actual membership in community organizations. People are asked to formally join and commit to the work. While there are paid organizers, the work is expected to be carried out by everyone because they all must own the objectives and campaigns being addressed.

With the emphasis on membership and commitment, organizations are able to struggle for justice over the long haul. Deeply integrated into the philosophy of organizing is the belief that real change requires long ongoing struggle. Organizations are usually not seeking any quick fix or shortcut. They believe deep structural and institutional barriers exist that create the conditions which harm vulnerable communities. The answer to this problem is building grassroots power and striving after incremental steps toward justice for the long haul. Typically, organizers try to make realistic and measurable goals that they believe are achievable. You may start small, and as you grow in membership, develop a power base, and produce wins, you continue to take on larger and larger campaigns.

Building power, then, is an important aspect of community organizing. What is intriguing about the nature of this power is that it is not top-down, concentrated power from a ruling class. Instead, power is redistributed back to the people, especially those who are oppressed and violated. This is dispersed grassroots power exercised from below. It is important to note that it is power, and not top-down domination. Sometimes people think of power in only one way. They falsely assume that the only kind of power is when you "lord it over others," but there are other kinds of power beyond tyranny, hegemony, or plutocracy. In fact, everyone has power, because everyone has some agency, even when it is constrained. This doesn't mean that bottom-up power cannot be abused as well; poor whites have often used their collective bottom-up power to support elite white domination and to "keep black people in their place."

Community organizing grows its power through relationship and solidarity. Rather than starting with a big rally or march, organizers usually prefer to begin with one-on-ones. They start building power by meeting with one person at a time, hearing their concerns, explaining who they are and the significance of community organizing, and inviting them either to see more or to join. The official "ask" may come later, when residents are gathered together. Either way, getting to know people, hearing their stories, and letting them express their own struggles and obstacles is really important for organizers.

In many other forms of activism, participants are merely told what the agenda is going to be, and you sign on (or not) on the basis of the predefined focus. The philosophy of organizing runs counter to this approach. Instead, the people are gathered, and together they identify all the different concerns they have in their neighborhood, and then discern together which ones they will prioritize. In actuality, this philosophy is not *always* practiced, because some particular issues that the paid organizers are committed to already are going to be lifted up. Usually it is a hybrid of agendas between that of the people in conversation with the structure of leadership. Nonetheless, do not discount how empowering it is to let people speak for themselves, voicing their own suffering, frustrations, and hopes.

Organizations, however, must eventually demonstrate their power. At this point the numbers do matter. Organizations want to show that they have people power, which gets the attention of policy makers. This is usually accomplished by publicly rallying together masses of people who are committed to and passionate about whatever injustice they are addressing. A march or rally often serves well for this, so long as it is public and visible to the decision makers. For organizers, though, the rally is not "the work" of organizing, it is merely a demonstration of the people power and a space where people can make their concerns heard. If done through an organizing model, a rally like this will likely have a variety of voices. Some organizers might speak, as well as experts and even some politicians that support the policy change being proposed. More vital, though, are the voices of the people being directly affected. I have seen young children give voice, at organizing rallies, to the atrocious learning environments they are expected to be educated in, as well as undocumented people sharing the pain of Immigration and Customs Enforcement agents arresting their family members. People are not spoken for, they are speaking for themselves. Too often poor people are discounted, and it is believed that only highly educated people are capable of communicating these matters. For community organizers, there is room for everyone's voice, but those affected most are especially privileged.

Community organizing demonstrates a group's power to power brokers and policy makers directly. They go straight to the formal channels of decision-making power while making clear they have a power base whom they represent. My personal experience has been that a small handful of people who represent leadership, expertise, and those personally affected will meet directly with a particular politician. Simultaneously, outside the office doors singing, praying, and chanting continues. Most of the community organizing experiences I have had were with faith-based organizers. During these actions, faith leaders are invited to offer a prayer, lead a song, or encourage the people. I have prayed to let "justice roll down like waters and righteousness like ever-flowing streams"; the Spirit has been invoked to touch the hearts of the politicians so they would do what was right. And some of my favorite protest chants have been learned during these rallies.

Finally, it needs to be noted that philosophically, faith-based organizers are strategically nonpartisan. They do not endorse political parties. This is extremely important because when you are working locally, you realize that you cannot blindly support any party; instead, you are focused on transforming the injustice and achieving the policy goals set by the people themselves. Community organizers may find themselves receiving affirmation and resistance from politicians from different political parties. Furthermore, you may find that support or apathy will change with a single politician depending on what you are working on at any given moment. The one resisting you now may later support you, and the one who won't grant you a meeting at the moment may later be an early supporter for something else you propose down the road. The official nonpartisan stance of organizing runs counter to the logic of merely adopting the top-down political platforms of a particular party.

There are obviously many strengths to community organizing. First, faith-based organizing is often very conducive for this work. Some of the most effective and influential organizations are faith-based. This makes an easy entry point for churches wanting to link arms with such work. The commitment to long-term change is especially helpful for when mainstream consciousness or conversations are not attentive to particular concerns affecting your local neighborhood. Organizing provides a steady and focused community structure to empower its people to make change over the long haul. Its incremental approach can help community members realize that they actually do have power, power that is usually untapped and sitting dormant. You are encouraged to start small with attainable goals, and then build from there. The nonpartisan commitment of community organizing aligns well with how the church ought to have a liberated ethic that remains free from the captivity of the top-down corrosive partisan platforms that are handed to society. The relational aspect also humanizes everything through personal story, commitment, and solidarity. Even the structure and leadership provides formal processes, making decision-making and action smoother. When done well, organizing can empower communities to bring ongoing change on a variety of specific local issues. It does not rely on the cool, new, and sexy topic in national news, but it is an old faithful friend that is always there when you need it.

However, community organizing is not a perfect model for doing justice, and it has its own limitations. Typically, one of its greatest weaknesses is its rigid approach, which is not usually adaptable or open to different methods or attentive to cultural moments. Organizers usually frown on protest movements. Since such mobilizing efforts are usually looking for a quick fix and are usually short-lived, and since they do not always empower communities to address their own list of specific local concerns, they often have a bad reputation among organizers. Community organizations usually highlight the failures of protest movements to convince people of the value of structure and power-building found in organizing. Some of these critiques are legitimate concerns, but it can result in throwing the baby out with the bathwater.

History and social science point to a plethora of effective protest movement tactics. Sometimes something is in the air and change is emerging and on its way, and it just needs a movement to tip the balance. Consider the enormous reshaping of the U.S. landscape after the massive sit-in movements around 1960. One could argue about whether every civil rights movement protest always targeted the right goal, whatever that means, or whether they sometimes claimed victory too quickly when further institutional change was possible, but one cannot argue that these movements did not make significant change in a relatively short time. Is it possible that many organizations need a greater spirit of adaptability to the varying contexts and conditions we find ourselves in? Further, organizers typically focus their attention directly on the formal channels and power brokers themselves. This is admirable, but some communities are less likely to be recognized by such power brokers, no matter how much people power they have. Organizers usually do not engage in nonviolent disruption as a strategy, because they want to keep lines of communication open with the formal decision makers. However, there are times when the formal channels are broken or not working for more vulnerable and oppressed members of society. It is precisely in that moment that a willingness to seek change outside working with those at the top can be necessary. Here the metaphor of knocking down the pillars through negotiation and strategic nonviolent protest could be helpful. The realism of incremental change is especially helpful when the wind is against you, but when it is pushing with you it can become a barrier. Because of ideological commitments, sometimes organizers, who have people power and experience, refuse to assist in working for dramatic change that is actually possible.

These limitations, however, do not erase the significance of community organizing as a conducive strategy that churches ought to take seriously. Faith-based organizing, in particular, makes perfect sense for the church. You begin with an already existing network of solidarity because the church is the place where people's belonging has been realigned in Christ. The church renounces top-down coercive domination, but certainly can participate in redistributing power back to the people. The church affirms that each person has dignity and ought to be able to speak for themselves about their concerns, prayers, and hopes. The church lets suffering speak. The church's ethical and sociopolitical imagination has been delivered from captivity, which makes it an ideal community to come alongside local neighbors toward a nonpartisan agenda of local concerns. The local church that is bound to the ruling-class platform that is handed to them is not existing as the church by definition (that is, as called-out ones). Ultimately, local churches must choose to follow the way of Jesus, embrace scriptural wisdom, and yield to the Spirit in this work. Just because power isn't top-down coercive domination doesn't mean that it cannot be used unjustly. The vision for faith-based organizing for the church must always be oriented toward shalom and the flourishing of all creatures and creation within the reign of God.

My main experience with organizing has been with POWER Interfaith in Harrisburg. I've primarily worked with them in their effort to bring justice and equity to Pennsylvania's education funding. A statistician researched and charted how racially discriminatory our state's funding practices were. To even my surprise, race rather than class was the greatest determining factor for whether a school district was being underfunded by the state. The more white students in a school district, the more likely that state funds were providing more than their fair share, and the more students of color in a school district, the more likely the district was being underfunded. Pennsylvania eventually adopted a fair funding formula, but they do not actually use it entirely. Only a small portion of state funds goes through the formula while the rest is still distributed by the original racist patterns. If Pennsylvania ran all its education funds through the fair funding formula, a small city like Harrisburg with a majority of students of color would receive about $30 million more each year. And this is just state funding, which is about 35 to 40 percent of funds; the rest comes from local taxes, which are just as problematic. So I have worked with POWER to address this education apartheid distribution of funds. I have attended monthly meetings, I have been one of the main speakers at a large rally in Pennsylvania's capitol building, I have prayed and chanted outside the doors of politicians, I have helped to develop a workshop to be used with faith communities, and I have provided support in other ways. I have witnessed firsthand how faith-based organizing can be a conducive strategy for the church to seek justice locally in partnership with one's neighbors and alongside other faith communities.

ELECTORAL POLITICS (OR WHEN THE TAIL WAGS THE DOG)

Taking action is one thing, but electoral politics is a minefield of its own. It is extremely jarring that a nation could elect Barack Obama for two terms and elect Donald Trump immediately after him. They represent deeply conflicting personalities and political agendas (although most presidents are consistent in their commitment to warmongering militarism and nationalism). Some may see this as the inevitable swings of a democratic society, while others believe it is more symptomatic of rising political struggle caused by a declining white majority that is seeking to hold on to their social dominance.

My first time ever participating in a presidential election was for President Obama. I will not lie, it felt pretty historic. Given that our country had, for so long, denied and suppressed the vote of black people, that we could elect our first black president in my lifetime was powerful and previously inconceivable. My joy in participating in such a historic moment in the nation's history, however, was tempered by a disappointment in many of President Obama's positions and policies. I was disappointed that he scapegoated his former pastor, Jeremiah Wright. There was also his troubling use of drone warfare, the continuation of global military overreach, some neoliberal rhetoric and politics, and his cozy response to the big banks that caused the Great Recession. On the other hand, he made some concrete strides, amid corrosive partisan opposition, to expand healthcare for all. What eventually was implemented lacked the teeth to make a difference because of significant Republican opposition. That he was able to accomplish anything at all, given the racist resistance he experienced, while remaining fairly poised throughout, was admirable and was characteristic of his administration.

A greater disappointment for me was with so many Democrats who voted for him but failed to provide a prophetic voice to the president because they thought their primary responsibility was to defend him against the nasty GOP right-wing smear campaigns. I get it, that is a natural response. And when we compare him to many other presidents, it doesn't take long before you feel grateful for many aspects of his leadership. But the church has a responsibility to hold all politicians accountable to their constituents, pushing them to do better. The awkwardness and lack of desire from Democrats and progressive Christians to challenge the first black president reveals the limits and dangers of our participation in electoral politics. Democracy works best when there is political accountability from the grassroots, regardless of whether "our guy" (or "gal") is in office. I won't even get started on how the Republican Party fell into the pocket of Donald Trump.

So how should the church think about voting and the electoral system in the first place? The church should not engage society merely out of a generic "common sense" derived from mainstream society; instead, we are called to think faithfully as Christians. There are many different ways that Christian traditions have thought about how to engage and participate in a democratic republic. In fact, some Christians have intentionally decided not to vote at all. They claim that electoral politics is coercive and amounts to not much more than a tyranny of the majority. It is not hard to see how one might land there, given that most of the United States' history is overflowing with white supremacist and oppressive laws and policies instituted by elected officials. A white majority abused their electoral power to maintain their concentrated political control over nonwhite people for centuries. If voting is merely about social domination, then you can understand why some Christians believe the only right response is to opt out of the system and find another way to pursue social change and a faithful Christian witness. In fact, some Christian communities have argued that there are no models for voting in the New Testament or among early Christians, which for them suggests that electoral politics is outside the church's responsibility. Again, they seek to live out the political dimension of the church through other means. In this line of thinking, scriptural silence on voting, as well as the model and reasoning of Jesus and the early church alone, ought to define the contours of our political action today.

In contrast, other Christians believe that it is your responsibility and duty to vote. As a citizen in this country you have the honor and obligation to participate in the political process and to shape the future of the society. Some have used the language of stewardship over creation as a framework to describe the human responsibility to share in this holy mandate of shared governance. So important is your vote, they argue, that to abstain is to abdicate one's voice. In fact, I have heard it said multiple times that if someone does not vote, then they have lost their right to speak up about the issues facing our society. In the black community, in particular, it is not strange to hear appeals reminding young people that their ancestors died so they could vote, and therefore they have an obligation to cast their ballot for that reason. Overall, voting as a duty has been the dominant position for most mainstream American Christians, who believe that our citizenship requires social responsibility through the ballot box.

Christians who advocate for voting are not homogenous for why they believe so. For some, voting as Christians is an opportunity to institute Christian laws and policies. Their concern might be that they perceive an increasing secularization of society and a loss of Christian laws and values. This is claimed to be the primary cause of our decaying moral foundations in society. They think that if we can just get "our folks" (usually white conservative Christians) in leadership, or at least people who align with our concerns, we can help make this country "Christian again." In contrast, other Christians see their responsibility to vote as more in line with their call to love their neighbor, to care for vulnerable people by doing justice and by seeking the common good and flourishing of all society regardless of their faith. For these Christians, you should not try to legislate Christianity, but you should allow your Christian faith to guide your awareness of what is needed to cultivate a just pluralistic society where everyone can flourish and live out their religious convictions without persecution. For them, Christian morality and ethics must always be voluntarily practiced and never coerced in any form.

The challenge in all this is that we really have no clue what Jesus or the early church would have thought about living in a democratic republic (if we even are). There is a deep contrast between living in the Roman Empire, where Caesar was blasphemously lifted up as lord and a divine being, claiming ultimate political power over his territories, and living in a society structured like ours. For our situation, sometimes it seems like once you have political access to the vote, then we all share in *Caesaring* whether we like it or not. This sounds bad at first, since Caesar definitely should not be our model for political action. However, it is precisely in redistributing Caesar's power (though in actuality, only partially) that electoral politics is at least partly compelling since the process is not completely top-down and the power is more dispersed than concentrated. It isn't parallel with being an emperor. To complicate things further, once you have that political access, it is yours regardless of whether you use it directly. At the end of the day, even a no vote is a political choice and a kind of voice. Truly, opting out of the political system is not easily accomplished. That point alone does not necessarily mean that one must vote, but our nonparticipation is uncontrollably caught in a complex and tangled web of politics. In one way or another, those who have citizenship and the right to vote are still part of the political system.

If we are going to participate in the things that make for peace and justice, it is necessary that we think deeply and carefully about our Christian relationship to voting. If we desire to join God's delivering presence in the world, we must think about even our voting habits, and what it means for the church to live within the complexity of our flawed political system. Therefore, let's think a bit more about the electoral system and whether there is a viable means for the church to seek justice.

Rather than just share my own thoughts, I want to help us feel some of the tension that probably should exist for us as Christians if we are to live in nonconformity to the logics and reasoning of our society. I want to stretch us in both directions. Let's begin by thinking about why Christians might choose not to vote. I know several Christians who take this posture. Had I not known them I might have thought that this was the most socially irresponsible choice as a Christian. Further, I might have believed that such a choice was socially and politically passive, one that neglected the responsibility to love our neighbors concretely and to do justice in society, as we are called to do as the church. This is not true, though. The Christians I know who have intentionally chosen not to vote out of conviction (which is different from those who are too lazy or too disengaged to vote) are extremely engaged in grassroots justice work. They are involved in movement work in their neighborhoods.

Ironically, intentional Christian nonvoters charge those who do vote with being politically pacified by the system. Some studies suggest that this is not just an empty charge. Nekeisha Alexis-Baker argues for freeing one's voice through nonvoting and cites the work of Benjamin Ginsberg as supporting evidence for the pacification of voters that leads to decreased activity outside the electoral system. She notes his

studies from 1965 and 1972 which suggest that "frequent voters are less attracted to disorderly forms of political engagement." This differs from those outside or on the margins of
the system who, as Ginsberg writes, "are much more likely to
press their demands in a disruptive" way.[10] Ultimately, it suggests that regular voters are more inclined to be aligned with
the status quo than to seek significant social change. The more
dependency people have on the formal channels of electoral
politics leads to severely limiting their social activism.

Along those lines, voting as a primary means for seeking
change leads to the captivity of people's political imagination.
The moment you begin to see the government as the primary
dispenser of justice, you tend to cut off all the other viable
avenues available to you. The resources and potential in one's
faith community and broader neighborhood are overlooked.
This is particularly evident in some of the language in my own
community. I have heard all my life that our elders died for the
vote, and so therefore it is a disgrace for black people not to
vote today. But this historical narrative is only half true. The
reality is that black people resisted and struggled for a lot of
things; some even wanted to opt out of the system altogether.
One thing is for sure, though: people resisted. They resisted for
about 250 years under slavery in this land. They resisted for
another hundred years of legalized Jim Crow and white terrorism. And it was not until the mid- to late twentieth century
that the Voting Rights Act was installed. The irony is that so
much attention is placed on voting and very little attention is
placed on the strategies that actually won the right to vote in
the first place. It is not as if black people were sitting around
waiting for 350 years until the right to vote came. If that were
the case, we would still likely be enslaved today. No, black
people resisted through a variety of grassroots activism, civil

disobedience, boycotting, organizing, protesting, speeches, investigative journalism, marching, and so forth. It is odd that large portions of the black community have turned their back on the very methods and means that got us the vote in the first place, and now insist that voting is our exclusive sacred birthright. It seems that our political imagination has been severely restricted.

Another reason a Christian might be against voting is because they reject the logic that not voting equates to abdicating your political voice. Nonvoters question if their voice has anything to do with the electoral system. Alexis-Baker once again makes a compelling argument on this front:

> Voting advocates often overlook a simple fact: there is no space on ballots for people to share thoughts on issues that concern them. Ballots do not contain room for voters to indicate why they have chosen a particular candidate or to identify agreeable policies. A ballot only has room to affirm prepackaged candidates whose vague plans have been publicized via sound bites, by negative campaign ads, in speeches, and in televised debates.[11]

Electoral politics gives the impression of voice when in fact it is merely cosigning prepackaged candidates and platforms. Even the candidates you vote for do not represent your unique voice and concerns, and the gap grows once they get in office. Very often, political party insiders and those with money decide what the platform is going to be and provide party members talking points so they stay on script. Is this process really about giving voice to the people? For nonvoting Christians, the prophetic voice of the church is too valuable for it to be domesticated or co-opted by prepackaged partisan platforms.

From a theological and ethical view, the issue that the church must wrestle with is whether such an emphasis of top-down politics distorts the church's vocation and witness. The long history of Christians practicing supremacy over society rather than taking the grassroots path of Jesus is an often ignored challenge to our current predicament in a partially democratic republic. If we are constantly consumed with imposing our preferred laws and policies on society, are we choosing societal coercion over the voluntary reign of God? Plus, do we even want "our guy" (or "gal") to be the face of the empire? The United States continues to be a complicated global presence. Despite some good things we could note, our country has caused, and continues to cause, a lot of harm globally, especially in light of the economic and military power that we exert over other nations. We seem to assume that if we can pick our pharaoh, we can somehow control and direct the outcome of history. Biblical wisdom and the revelation of Jesus suggest that history is not determined by the powers that be; instead, the gears of God's deliverance turn toward justice among the most vulnerable of society.

Finally, nonvoting Christians would highlight how broken our electoral system is anyway. Big money is spent buying politicians to ensure that they are in the pockets of billionaires and large corporations. Then there is intentional corruption to our democracy, such as when Russia interfered in our 2016 elections without consequence. And the misinformation campaigns are just as frequent from within our nation as they are from beyond our walls. Unjust and evil forces are at work behind the scenes manipulating our political system. Black voters know better than anyone in this nation that there have always been unjust efforts to suppress black votes and to create obstacles for us to participate on equal footing. It often seems that we are so far from anything resembling democracy. In fact, if you live in a poor black and brown neighborhood, very little seems to change for the better regardless of which party is in power. There are a lot of significant and powerful arguments for why the church ought to choose not to vote and instead to prioritize grassroots justice work.

Before you determine that you will never vote again, let's consider the thoughtful reasons why Christians have decided to vote, even after considering the concerns listed above. Let's start with that last point about the broken electoral process that stifles democracy. The truth is, that alone may actually prove the power of participating in an electoral system. Since formalizing the colonies into a nation-state in 1776, there have been intentional efforts to suppress the votes of particular people groups. Black people, Native Americans, and women of various racial demographics have all experienced extended decades (and often centuries) of laws and customs seeking to enforce the denial and suppression of their vote. If voting were completely meaningless, one would be fair to ask why white Christian men have worked so hard to take away or keep that right from others. The very fact that it has the potential to change how we organize our society is visible through efforts to keep certain people outside the conversation and decision-making process.

While in years past the black community has been denied the right to vote through white supremacist terrorism and intimidation, through laws, through poll taxes, through random and biased registration rules concocted to target black voters, through literacy tests, and so forth, today more sophisticated ways of targeting the black community's access to the voting booth have been practiced. One simple way is by allowing certain states to deny the right to vote to anyone with a past conviction, which disproportionately affects black men, along with many other demographic groups. Secondly, there have been more subtle and devious ways of suppressing black votes, like GOP efforts to create new voter ID laws that knowingly make it harder for many poor black people who do not have a driver's license to easily provide the kind of identification necessary to vote. It is just one more hoop to jump through, despite research which has shown that voter fraud (which is the reason many white people claim the laws are needed) is in actuality extremely rare. There have also been times when entire communities and counties have had voter rolls purged by GOP-controlled lawmakers, and were unable to vote because they had been unknowingly erased and needed to reregister. But probably the most devious and successful way of suppressing the vote and undermining democratic values has been through widespread gerrymandering. White lawmakers have redrawn the lines of districts according to voting tendencies in order to intentionally dilute black votes by including them with larger and larger amounts of white rural voters through strange and awkward mapping. The end result is the further suppression of votes. It has gotten so bad that many states have witnessed an ongoing increase in Democratic votes while white Republicans have actually taken more and more seats in those areas because of undemocratic gerrymandering practices. If the right to vote did not hold powerful potential, all this effort would be for nothing.[12]

On the positive side, we have seen encouraging changes over the years thanks to voting. Electoral officials, although sometimes against their own beliefs or instincts, have created legislation against slavery and Jim Crow and for various civil rights laws. I think most justice-loving people would agree that more policies, rather than less, are needed to create a fair and equitable society. Furthermore, the participation of more and more people of color in government, and through democratic conversation in the public square, has continued to guide our society toward more change and an awakening conscience to other people's lived realities. Consider that many mainstream politicians have openly endorsed the need to explore and pursue reparations for the ongoing impact that slavery and oppression have caused for black people. The growing diversity of legislators right now, and the bold vision for justice that a small handful of them have, bears witness to the possibility that social change is hard but not impossible.

Ultimately, it seems that being pro-voting as a Christian ought to be rooted in the call to love our neighbors, to do justice, and to seek the shalom, or flourishing, of our society. Sometimes Christians use the language of pursuing the common good. Christian ethics turns the church beyond individualistic piety and moralism, against selfish political pursuits, and toward concretely loving our neighborhoods and the people that inhabit them. Voting as followers of Jesus, it can be argued, provides an opportunity for us to humbly participate in the imperfect human institutions we have created while we seek to honor God through how we collectively collaborate with our neighbors while staying awake to God's dream for all of us.

There are convincing pros and cons to voting as Christians. There is no question that electoral politics is about representation, power, and the organization of our society. Whether or not one votes, it should be clear that followers of Jesus care about how our society is governed precisely because we care about the impact that it has on individuals and our neighborhoods. For that reason, all faithful Christians are necessarily political if they are following Jesus through our world and walking in his way.

Some final thoughts on voting and electoral politics are needed. For those who do engage in voting, there is a need to not let the tail wag the dog. The church should not be instructed on its morals and ethics by ruling elites and partisan platforms. We should never be passive and obedient minions to the whims of our political establishments. God reigns and Jesus is preeminent. We pursue the ethics and politics of God through careful and humble discernment. The church is a revolutionary entity that moves on the ground first and foremost, deeply bound to the lived experiences of everyday people, especially those most vulnerable and oppressed. Our concrete love for our neighbors is the beginning of our political action. When the church's unique voice (echoing the God revealed in Jesus Christ) is not distinctly audible, our political imagination has become captive to powers and forces seen and unseen.

Along those lines, we really must rediscover our prophetic witness to the state when we engage the electoral process. Voting should never be the primary political act of the church. The politics of the church is about surrendering our whole lives to God and participating in what our Creator and Liberator is doing in the world. Rather than starting with voting, we must start with our faithful everyday witness to God's desire for humanity and all of creation. Every day it is our responsibility to bear witness to God's greatness and the divine will for actual flourishing for all living creatures. And when our world rebels against the well-being of people and the planet, we must stand strong and speak up within the prophetic tradition of our faith. Therefore, our everyday witness through organizing, movements, nonviolent struggle, prophetic speech, ecclesial counter-witness, and communal discernment ought to always precede electoral politics. If we do those things as people delivered from the captivity and conformity of coercive reasoning, we are better positioned to organically allow our vote (if our church tradition allows it) to flow seamlessly with our actual ecclesial politics. It is when we reverse that approach, and make the vote the starting point, that we lose sight of our first citizenship in God's new society and become puppets to the empire rather than prophets of God.

One way of engaging legislators with a prophetic witness rooted in the church is to discuss the issues happening in your local community (or those of a vulnerable community) with others and then go to legislators and tell them about the injustice happening on the ground. Tell them how it is affecting real people by telling these local stories or, if possible, bringing those most affected to tell their own story. This is bottom-up engagement rather than a passive top-down posture. I have done this on a couple of occasions. I have been to Washington, D.C., to advocate for prison reform alongside other faith leaders from all over the country. We each visited our own representatives and lawmakers in their offices, and made our appeal and bore witness to God's justice on behalf of those most affected. Similarly, I have done this in my own state's capital as well, as part of the effort to address the inequitable distribution of funds for public education in Pennsylvania. To be honest, this is not something I enjoy, and I personally would not find joy in doing this kind of work full-time. But I do think it provides an opportunity for us to actually have a real voice by communicating exactly how we feel, what we have witnessed, the nature of the harm, and the kind of policies that could begin to make things right. In similar fashion, after a candidate has been elected (and especially if we voted for them), we have the sacred responsibility of being a prophetic voice to them while they are seated in a position of decision-making power. That bottom-up approach allows us to be faithful and pragmatic as the church as we navigate the political realities of our democratic republic.

A COLLABORATIVE AND ADAPTABLE HYBRID APPROACH

The church is called to participate in the things that make for peace and justice in our world. But different historical contexts open up a need for reimagining how we do that faithfully as followers of Jesus. This chapter, hopefully, has refused to simply baptize one approach. There are many ways that we can do justice and join in with God's delivering presence. It takes worshiping our Most High God, carefully and humbly immersing ourselves in Scripture, yielding to the Spirit, following the way of Jesus, discerning with the church body, and receiving the sacred voice and stories of oppressed people for us to creatively and wisely plan our next steps toward doing justice.

I already mentioned the Poor People's Campaign, and I think they may be helpful for us to consider a bit more as we conclude this chapter. I have noted the tension and differences that often exist among organizers and movement activists. Sometimes the ideological commitments of either approach can limit the potential for experiencing God's deliverance in society because we have turned our strategy into a sacred idol. I appreciate the philosophy of the Poor People's Campaign precisely because it takes a hybrid approach. There is no question that organizing is central to the kind of ongoing work they are committed to. Yet at the same time, they also engage in nonviolent actions and civil disobedience. They make a lot of room for people who just want to show up for the large protest rallies and marches, but make such events possible through committed participants who are organizing locally and partnering with other organizations across their state and the nation. They have very specific ethical and political goals related to poverty, education, justice and prison systems, ecological devastation, military spending, and livable wages.

They discerned those things together as leaders and are going to their government representatives and reminding them that they have a responsibility to let justice roll down like waters.

I believe that local congregations should have a similarly open approach to doing justice. We do not need to create idols of any specific strategy or tactic. That doesn't mean that there won't be one particular approach that is especially conducive for your community or context. That is inevitable. However, we need to remain open to creatively discerning how to scheme and plot for justice so that we are as wise as serpents yet as innocent as doves. Let's put our brains together so that more and more people can experience God's peace and righteousness.

Also, you may notice that I haven't even mentioned other strategies that the church can do locally. For example, there are mercy ministries like running food pantries, hosting soup kitchens, providing school supplies or other resources to your neighborhood, or even more radical actions like becoming a sanctuary church or hosting "know your rights" trainings. These are all important, and the list goes well beyond this. These are necessary and needed ways for the church to engage local neighborhoods. Some of them are more focused on meeting the needs of individuals than on changing the root causes that allow so many people to find themselves in that position to begin with. I think many churches already have an imagination for doing mercy ministries to meet the needs of individuals; whether they are actually stepping up and doing so is another question. I decided to focus on doing justice that will affect the way our society is organized by policies that produce so many individuals needing help. Nonviolent struggle, organizing, protest movements, and electoral politics all have the capacity to change the root cause. But it should be clear that mercy ministries are important. One can hardly talk about loving one's neighbor if we won't give them food for today because we are solely committed to working on a future world that they may not make it to.

Similarly, I haven't spent much time discussing community development organizations. These institutions are often positioned to do significantly more than just give a handout to someone in need. They often are organized and ready to empower people, and sometimes are working toward some structural changes within their community as well. I deeply believe that community development organizations can play an important role in doing justice locally. The church I'm a part of in Harrisburg has two nonprofits that would be categorized as community development organizations. One is the Brethren Housing Association (BHA), which provides housing, support, training, and trauma-informed care to women and children experiencing homelessness. The second is bcmPEACE, which does a range of trainings and community work. Most notably, it provides an agape-satyagraha nonviolence training for young black and brown youth in our community suffering from cycles of violence. Drawing on the work of Dr. King and Gandhi, youth learn how to break those cycles and work for peace.

Another organization that comes to mind is the Christian Community Development Association (CCDA), which was co-founded by minister and civil rights activist John Perkins. I am not part of this group, but I know many people have learned a lot from this large organization, which equips leaders to do development work. That is a place to start if your congregation is looking to initiate something like that.

As I write this, I am a co-leader for FREE Together, a relational network of Christian leaders in my city that are committed to racial and economic justice in our neighborhood through partnership with faith-based organizers and activists, as well as by doing our own internal trainings and Christian formation for our participants. This approach has allowed us to adopt a very fluid and hybrid approach to doing justice without making any idol of a particular social change strategy. And at the same time we are able to support the important work of organizers and activists in our neighborhood by our participation in and commitment to do the work as it aligns with our own strategies for justice. As local congregations, whether we adopt organizing, protest movement, electoral, or other strategies for doing justice, our priority is to do so as people awakened to God's desires and dreams for humanity and creation.

And then there are other really powerful ways to bring social change. For example, artists and lawyers are positioned to have significant impact on our society. Artists help us to see our world and one another in fresh ways. Thank God for those who write poetry, tell stories, paint, do photography, compose novels, develop films, sculpt monuments, and do so inspired by the reality that another world is possible. Lawyers, obviously, have the capacity to work directly with the legal system, and with a sense of calling can put those skills directly to use to defend the vulnerable and engage the legal system at the policy level. Michelle Alexander is a great example of a lawyer who is using her vocation to fight for justice. I have personally been encouraged by the few times I briefly got to meet Bryan Stevenson at the Equal Justice Initiative, and as he spoke at Messiah College for commencement. What inspired me most was how he didn't stay in his lane. The Equal Justice Initiative engages in legal work, especially for those on death row. And their capacity to overturn wrongful convictions is admirable. But they do much more. They create monuments and museums, resources and films, which all help to tell a more truthful narrative about where our society has been, and where we need to go. Creativity and skill, and the combination of the two, are powerful instruments for social change.

Our means matter because we are called to embody God's future right now in the present at the grassroots level. Our strategies and tactics should make the story of Jesus visible for our neighbors rather than merely reaffirm the physical violence, top-down power, and corrosive partisan obedience that pervades the mindsets of so many in mainstream society. There are things that make for actual peace and that bring concrete justice to our world, so let us become students of Jesus who are as wise as serpents yet as innocent as doves as we seek God's deliverance in our world.

9
THE POLITICS OF LOVE

Saint Augustine, in his writing *On Christian Doctrine*, taught principles to guide Christians in how to read Scripture faithfully for themselves. He made many points, but concluded his argument by summarizing how the Bible ought to point us toward the ultimate goal of the law; to love God and others. For Augustine, "Whoever, therefore, thinks that he understands the divine scriptures or any part of them so that it does not build the double love of God and of our neighbor does not understand it at all."[1] While Augustine is known for innovating Christian teaching (for good and for bad), in this moment he is articulating the heart of Jesus' own teaching in which the summation of the law is described in terms of loving

God with every aspect of our being and loving our neighbors as we would our own selves.

Augustine then provides a great illustration to demonstrate the task of faithful biblical interpretation. He describes someone who is on a journey with a particular destination in mind. However, this man accidentally leaves the road he was on as he is traveling. Augustine assures us that this departure is "by mistake" and not intentional. The man is now on an alternative route and making his way through a field. Thankfully, without knowing it, the field is heading "to the same place toward which the road itself leads" rather than heading in the wrong direction.[2] The man is parallel to the path he should be on. Ultimately, he arrives at the intended destination. Arriving at the right destination matters most.

For Augustine there are two things to understand about interpreting the Bible and Christian ethics. First, he insists that someone who departs from the path but arrives at the intended destination is not wrong. When someone misinterprets or misunderstands Scripture yet ultimately teaches the love of God and love of neighbor, "they do not lie." This is hard for many Western Christians who imagine that there is only one proper way to interpret a text. However, Augustine also recognizes that big detours and departures can eventually result in not arriving at one's intended location (love of God and neighbor). Therefore, the man must "be corrected and shown that it is more useful not to leave the road, lest the habit of deviating force him to take a crossroad or a perverse way."[3] It is vital for Augustine that people find the well-worn path that leads to loving God and loving others. It is the summary, goal, and destination of our faith in Jesus. Through Jesus' faithfulness, and our following after him, we have a road back to this life of love. How might our world be different if we read Scripture through the lens of loving God and loving our neighbor, and we were not satisfied with any interpretation that lacked the capacity to ignite genuine love for others?

THE NEED FOR LOVE IN OUR POLITICAL ACTION

On multiple occasions, I have stood before Christian gatherings delivering unwanted words. It was particularly acute because of the administration in the White House. Present for many people were the expected pent-up anxieties from our corrosive partisan climate and the national scandals happening in the administration. When I defined racism as organizing our society according to the logic of racial hierarchy, the crowds were still with me. When I went further and explained that they too were complicit in racism, and that they had consciously and unconsciously allowed race to organize their lives in relation to their relationships, networks, geographic residence, faith communities, schools, and narratives of others, the audience was (mostly) with me. When I exposed the whitened Jesus that replaced the Jesus described in Matthew, Mark, Luke, and John, or elaborated on how Christendom and colonialism continue to shape the logics and habits of the church today, and when I called them toward counterintuitive solidarity with oppressed people in the way of Jesus, overwhelmingly, people were with me. I have witnessed standing ovations, responses of lament, commitments to study and learn more, and first steps toward taking local action through organizing efforts, all from my challenges. But a metaphorical ankle always gets turned and sprained on one specific topic. With each syllable proceeding from my mouth, I witness visceral discomfort, sometimes shock, and responses that reflect people working through cognitive dissonance. These responses are usually in reaction to when I share the most deeply Christian message imaginable, the call of laboring in love in response to their political enemies.

Sometimes it seems as though there is a naive belief that electoral politics will solve all our problems. Don't get me wrong, electoral politics clearly affect our society significantly. My hope for 2020 included wanting to show Donald Trump the door. On a legislative level, he perpetuated core racist and classist policies. On a cultural level, he revived and deployed racist rhetoric as strategy to instill fear because of the significant demographic changes unfolding in the country. I definitely wanted to be first in line to tell him, "Don't let the door hit ya on your way out." But it is a deep mistake to think that electing a Democrat as president will fix the deep antagonism and hostility that gridlocks our country's future. We have political enemies in this country. The impulses that led some to vote for Donald Trump, and to support the rhetoric and agenda he pursued, will live on well after any administration changes. Donald Trump has no inherent power individually, and he wields no magic. His authority (and ongoing cultural voice) exists only to the degree that he gets support from almost half the country.

Typically, Christians have shallow insights on faithful and effective strategies for social change. Believers often take sides about whether we need to "change laws" or "change hearts." It is a fact that changing laws eventually leads to changes in many people's views. No one is going to suggest that abolishing slavery or passing Civil Rights Acts hasn't significantly changed the lived experiences of many black people and other people of color in this nation. Those policy changes, with enough time, influence masses of people. Only the most corrosive and hard-hearted of Americans defend slavery today and would reintroduce it if possible. When you change the rules of the system, and hold people accountable, they actually live by those changes, and create new habits over time. Policy change doesn't make everyone believe the same thing, but some form of change will come. At the same time, when people's views adapt to policy changes, it doesn't mean they have adopted a truly righteous perspective. Those who practiced slavery *mutated* their views for a new era and went on to justify neo-slavery through convict leasing, peonage, chain gangs, and exploitative sharecropping arrangements under newly legislated black codes and a Jim Crow social order. Anti-blackness still held hands with most white churches like two fifth-graders having their first crush.

The twentieth century is a testament to the power of changing legislation and why, simultaneously, that is not enough. After civil rights legislation took root in the 1950s and '60s, a new backlash arose, such as the prison industrial complex. A change of policies began making an immediate change in our society. However, something more is needed for deeper social transformation that policy can't accomplish. When we keep track of the people directly harmed by newly invented death-dealing legislation, as well as the people who "know not what they do," we must reorient our discipleship back to the heart of the gospel of Jesus, which requires loving our neighbors and enemies concretely.

LOVING GOD AND NEIGHBOR

In Christianity, one indisputable commandment holds special honor as the greatest and most important. When all things fall away, what remains is the commandment to love. Here in this simple four-letter word, *love*, everything hangs in the balance. It is what grounds Christian life. You can achieve everything else, but if you have not grasped hold of love, your life is empty and you really have nothing. How many self-professed Christians go on and on about faith, with sophisticated nuance and distinction, expressing all the theological complexities and ethical ambiguities involved, but are still found wanting in the basic practice of love?

The gospel of John contends that people will know the disciples of Jesus by their love for one another (John 13:34-35). Disciples of Jesus love their neighbor. For John, this is not about whether followers of Jesus *should* love their neighbors. This is what disciples of Jesus do; they love. It is their defining characteristic. They are a community of love. They give, receive, and share love. Love grounds their lives. They practice love and are good at it. They show people the way to live by embodying love. They persevere through challenges with it. It is their lasting mark and eternal legacy.

The reason it is central for followers of Jesus is simple. Disciples seek to obey the great commandment of Jesus. He is the one who passed on to us the vocation of love. The early church passed down several stories that emphasize how central love was for Jesus. In Mark 12:28-34, it is written that an expert in the law came to Jesus, asking which commandment was most important. Jesus, a faithful Jew, took him back to the Scriptures, quoting from Deuteronomy and Leviticus:

> The most important is: "Listen, Israel, the Lord our God, the Lord is one. Love the Lord your God with all your heart, with all your soul, with all your mind, and with all your strength." The second is: "Love your neighbor as yourself." There is no other commandment greater than these. (vv. 29-31 NET)

These lines are often referred to as the Shema, which in English translates as "listen" or "hear." This is something we really need to receive. We must slow down and listen. Hear these words, repeat them, let them soak in until you internalize them and they are a part of your being. They must define your life. Of course, Mark's gospel is not the only one to provide the double commandment of love. In Matthew 22:34-40, we are told that a Pharisee tries to test Jesus, and there at that point Jesus explains that loving God with all your being is the greatest commandment and that the second is to love your neighbor as yourself. For Jesus, "On these two commandments hang all the law and the prophets" (v. 40). Luke's gospel provides us with a different situation altogether but ultimately demonstrates the same consistent teaching from Jesus. This happens in what has traditionally been called the good Samaritan story. Once again, an expert in the law comes to Jesus with a question, but this time it is about what he must do to inherit eternal life. Jesus believes that what is required is already clear in the Torah, and therefore asks him to explain what the Law teaches. The expert in the law replies with the Shema—that is, to love God with all your being, as well as to love your neighbor as yourself, drawn straight from Leviticus. Jesus affirms his answer and tells him to do this and he will live.

Loving God and loving our neighbor is the greatest commandment, standing more important than any other. It is the summation and goal of the first testament, and the most basic characteristic of Christian life. Jesus, in his teaching, fuses together love of God and love of neighbor so that the two are inseparable from one another. Through Jesus' fusion, you cannot love God if you do not concretely love your neighbor in ways similar to how you care for your own body. Likewise, you do not genuinely love your neighbor fully without the love for our Creator seizing you and permeating your life. Early Christian writers rejected the possibility that love for God can be authentic while disregarding the well-being of people in society.

Early Christian leaders affirmed the interdependency of our love of God and our love of our neighbor in Scripture: "Those who say, "I love God," and hate their brothers or sisters, are liars; for those who do not love a brother or sister whom they have seen, cannot love God whom they have not seen" (1 John 4:20). You cannot love God and not seek after the well-being of undocumented people in our country fleeing violence or poverty. You cannot love God and desire to hoard all the financial resources for your already wealthy community while other children's school districts remain dilapidated and underfunded. You cannot love God and remain apathetic when our military uses missile strikes to bomb innocent civilians on the other side of the globe. You cannot love God and allow your silence to deem a black man's life of no value when he is shot in the back by the state. You cannot love God and turn your back on Native Americans who have persevered through ongoing land theft, erasure, and systemic oppression. You cannot love God and remain unmoved when Muslim Americans are harassed in the public square, when LGBTQ people encounter mockery and not Christ's love among believers, when poor people's wages are suppressed, when healthcare and well-being are stripped from the vulnerable for greater corporate profits. You cannot love God and allow black ghettos to be swallowed up by exploitation, mass incarceration, and apartheid educational systems and to be cut off from the opportunities available to most Americans without it breaking your heart and moving you to action.

We must take it one step further: love of God is manifested *through* our love of our fellow humans. By this, I am suggesting that it is more than just an interdependency of love of God with love of neighbor. For too long self-professed Christians have convinced themselves they were loving God while centuries of oppression and exploitation took place in this land. They sang their songs of devotion, prayed with passion, and were moved during deep contemplation. But it is precisely at this moment that Jesus' greatest commandment pulls back the curtain on the whole circus and exposes the hypocrisy and emptiness grounded in disobedience to the great commandment and our disdain for our fellow creatures living before the Creator. Gustavo Gutiérrez explains it this way, "It is not enough to say that love of God is inseparable from the love of one's neighbor. It must be added that love for God is unavoidably expressed *through* love of one's neighbor."[4] If he is right, then there have been many attempts to worship God among church folk that have lacked genuine love for God.

AGAPE IS NOT ABOUT SENTIMENTALITY

When some oppressed people hear Christians talk about love, they shudder in fear because their "love" often results in further harm. The meaning of love has been domesticated and manipulated and is frequently weaponized. We don't know what love is. We don't know what love looks like. Just about anything can pass as love in Christian circles today. Until we have a concrete conception of what it is, we'll continue to be bamboozled and hoodwinked with a counterfeit.

One of the most popular ways that love is domesticated is by equating it with sentimentality. That is, those in power like to pass it off as a mushy feeling. When comfortable people are having their feels, they will suggest that is their evidence of love. For example, I've seen white liberals sit in circles expressing their sadness about the terrible circumstances of some poor black lad whose life has been cut short once again. There are usually lots of tears and white guilt expressed. As they talked it appeared that their emotions and feelings were the work they were called to. That was the end goal. This was their Christian expression of love for others. Unfortunately, for many their sentimentality results in no action on behalf of the one they claim to love. No effort is made to change their situation. Please do not hear me wrong, we should not respond in hard-hearted or apathetic ways to the suffering of others. Our hearts should be soft, and they should break on behalf of others, just as Jesus had compassion in response to the human suffering he encountered. The problem is when all we have is feelings.

Another way love is manipulated is when it is weaponized by those who have power. I have witnessed Christians justify dehumanizing marginalized people by claiming it was all "tough love." Now, any parent can tell you that sometimes you make difficult decisions about what is best for your child, and it often does not include giving in to their every whim and desire. So in one sense there is something about love that may be tough at times. On the other hand, so much that falls under the umbrella of "tough love" has nothing to do with love at all. In fact, not all parents who discipline their children and claim "tough love" are genuinely demonstrating love to those little ones. Countless children are abused physically and psychologically, making them feel belittled, leaving them with deep wounds and scars that will take decades to heal. Bet you those parents are claiming "tough love." Likewise, to deny hospitality and genuine care to people because they are different from you, and then to simply call your rejection, meanness, or bullying behavior "tough love" and for their ultimate best is thoroughly deceitful. We need to be honest when we have failed to authentically care about the well-being of someone else. The real thing has been swapped out for a counterfeit of love; it has become a weapon rather than something for one's actual well-being.

Thankfully, Jesus models Christian love for us, allowing us to clear the table of all the poor imitations. In the life, ministry, and death of Jesus, radical and sacrificial love is embodied on humanity's behalf. Jesus' love isn't mere sentimentality, nor is it a weapon for the comfortable to justify their disregard. Jesus takes on the responsibility for the well-being of those who suffer, those in need, and those captive to the evil forces of sin and death that have entrapped humanity. He responds in such a radical way, as if it were his own suffering, need, and captivity. His love is embodied and therefore costly action. It is costly because love takes risks for others. The truthfulness of his love is expressed through action. Jesus' actions become for Christians the model and measurement for whether love is genuine or fake. Apparently, the early church needed these clarifications as well. First John 3:16-18 explains it this way:

> We know love by this, that he laid down his life for us— and we ought to lay down our lives for one another. How does God's love abide in anyone who has the world's goods and sees a brother or sister in need and yet refuses help? Little children, let us love, not in word or speech, but in truth and action.

There are three things to note about this explanation of love. First, it makes plain that Jesus' laying down his life for us is now our living definition. His example becomes the Christian's new way of knowing love. It isn't assumed that love is "common sense" or something we can take for granted. We do not all innately know what love is, especially since it is so frequently misrepresented and we have too often experienced the pain of false love. We cannot take for granted that our view on love is right. No, our understanding of love itself must die and be resurrected through the revelation of Christ's love.

We know love because Jesus "laid down his life for us." And that is the second observation. It is a radical action. We can understand Jesus' laying down his life in two ways. In a more general sense, he gave of himself by yielding to God's reign and by ministering in life and through his living body. Giving to and blessing others was central to his way of life. At the same time, Jesus accepted death as a consequence of his messianic vocation. This is where he modeled revolutionary love. All the gospels depict Jesus as clashing with the establishment while knowing full well that the powers that be were going to come hard with a backlash. He predicted it, yet while we were still captive to forces of sin and evil and cycles of violence and exploitation, Jesus loved us and laid down his life for us. This revolutionary act conjures memories of courageous ancestors who have laid down their lives on behalf of future generations. And because Jesus is our revolutionary example of love, the logic of discipleship calls us to follow after him: "and we ought to lay down our lives for one another."

Finally, so we don't turn love into a martyr complex, this teaching provides an everyday living example, because the goal is not death but that we all might share in life more abundantly. The question is, "How does God's love abide in anyone who has the world's goods and sees a brother or sister in need yet refuses help?" It is a rhetorical question that needs no answer, because it is impossible for God's love to seize you and for you to remain apathetic to the needs of others. This Christian letter goes one step further just in case you missed the point: "Little children, let us love, not in word or speech, but in truth and action" (v. 18).

In short, love pursues the well-being of others concretely in action. The truth of love is embodied rather than spoken. This is a truth that can only be lived to find its perfection. No words, not even these reflections on this page, can capture the fullness of love. They can only gesture and point you toward the Christian action that embodies God's truth that Jesus laid down his life for us and that we now participate in that very life in Christ. Genuine love is life-giving rather than death-dealing. In living into our Christian calling to love, we seek life, but we do so by regarding the lives of others as if they were our own. When the life of another is threatened and caught between vulnerability and insecurity, we recognize that the greatest expression of God's love is revolutionary, and we are willing to count and accept the costs of imitating Jesus' agape love for us.

If we are going to love our neighbor as God desires, disciples of Jesus must hold tight to the teaching that all humanity is made in the image of God. I've appreciated the way that African American theology has historically emphasized this basic concept amid a long legacy of European racialized frameworks designed to categorize some humans as less valuable than others. Some lives mattered, while others did not. Christian European conquest suggested that some people groups were disposable so that other communities could lord over the earth. But remembering that we are all made in the image of God washes away all the distortions and provides clarity to who you and I, and all of us, actually are. If we are all made in the image of God, then we must recognize the dignity of every person. If we are all made in the image of God, then we must affirm that every single life is sacred. If we are all made in the image of God, then we look deeper and see one another as we are, as invaluable treasures of God. Every person matters.

Each of us a creature of God. Each of us beloved of God. Each of us reflecting God while also having cracks in our image that can only be mended by God. We share in this image-bearing state together. And our capacity to love another person truly will manifest or crumble with our capacity to recognize God's image in all humanity.

This capacity to know one another as people made in the image of God leads us to love more deeply because of our shared humanity. Many forces inhibit all of us from recognizing our shared humanity. When we fail to recognize it, mutual love breaks down. Our society has lots of constructed labels that define for us those who are in our out-group. In-group and out-group behavior is intuitive for humans, and often we do it to provide a sense of safety and to make sense of the world. But too often the categories that humans make to understand the world end up distorting life. They become the tail wagging the dog. We make sense of others through overly simplistic one-dimensional characters. But nobody is actually one-dimensional; we are all complex and multifaceted. Even when humans do terrible and evil things, and need to be stopped and held accountable for those actions, we are all so unpredictably complex, and beyond how we describe our enemies. Fostering mutual love depends on us being delivered from our own human constructions and labels that too often have become our masters.

Yet when we consider how love opens us up to see our shared humanity and creates the possibility for mutuality, we must be careful that we do not use that as a reason to erase actual human differences. It is okay to acknowledge our shared humanity and simultaneously affirm human difference. There is no need to homogenize all of humanity into one bland cookie-cutter mold. There is beauty in the recognition that within our shared humanity exists limitless difference. Human diversity is not a threat when viewed from the vantage point of love. There is something compelling about the human journey in which we can love another person knowing that we share in the human condition on this earth together while also recognizing the mystery of each of us. Our differences are more than our outward physical bodies; they hint at God's creative depth imprinted within each human personality. And so we love others in their difference and the depth they bring as we get to know them, which is once again part of our collective shared human experience as God's handiworks.

Love's goal is nothing short of seeking the fulfillment of beloved community within creation. Beloved community is a term made popular by Dr. King, although he did not invent it. For Dr. King, beloved community had two aspects. The big vision and goal for all his struggles for justice was the emergence of beloved community. In that sense, it was an eschatological vision for creation. That just means it is God's dream, or future, for humanity and the rest of creation. It is where all things are going. In the Hebrew Scriptures this is the biblical vision of shalom. Where the lion and the lamb can lie down together. Where the old sit out on their stoops and children play in the street. Where the ruins and breaches have been repaired, and where justice and peace kiss. It is when God's creatures reconcile and embrace in harmony as God has always intended and desired for humanity.

Of course, this kind of talk sounds great but looks nothing like our current reality. Every tear has not been wiped away and death continues to terrorize our world. For Dr. King, beloved community was not only a future reality, it was also the means by which you get there. Beloved community is something that we can embrace and pursue in the here and now, even if it is a fragile and limited expression of the dream. This is realized eschatology. When Jesus preached that a new reign of God had come, the reality was that the Roman Empire was still standing. Countless more Jews in the first century would be victim to Rome's imperial power and military strength (including Jesus himself). But Jesus proclaimed that the reign of God had come, and that it was there, present among them. Beloved community is another way of talking about the present fragile communities that can emerge when God's delivering presence becomes real in our lives, even amid oppression around us. However, we cannot afford to lose sight of our vision for where we are going. Our goal is shaped by God's dream for us. A community that gives, receives, and shares love. It is to love and to be loved freely and generously in community, knowing that we share in our diversely human life together as image bearers of God. Love of neighbor is ultimately rooted in our inherent interconnectedness as God's creation. This can also be understood through the South African word Ubuntu, which Christians have borrowed to explain our connectedness and communally bounded life together on this earth. Love is the means and the ends because God's future for us has broken into our present.

THE LOVE GAP

Before we adopt the politics of love we must first grapple with "the love gap" that exists in our society. The love gap is a way of describing the human tendency to respond compassionately with and for some people while being socialized to withhold that same compassion and action for other people. Most of us are prone to embrace denial at this point, as if we somehow were above those kinds of social biases and prejudices. Those defensive responses lack self-reflection and honesty. We are all prone to engage in this behavior with particular people groups. We share in the human condition, and this is one of our shared struggles. What matters is what we do with that acknowledgment once we own it. The love gap is my descriptive attempt at revealing how humans are prone to treat some people as worthy of our love and concern while remaining apathetic and unmoved by the suffering of others. A gap exists in our minds between us and other people groups, and this cuts off our potential to be a people that love across all boundaries, especially those we perceive to be most different or even threatening to us. Are we aware of the invisible gap that exists between human groups that leads to immediate compassion or disregard depending on who they are? How should we as followers of Jesus feel and act amid these social patterns?

As a theologian, I am interested in how we describe what Christianity is all about. How we understand Christianity will shape how we love our neighbor, and it can also produce gaps in our love. For example, so much of Christianity has obsessed over claiming themselves to be orthodox. Orthodoxy is about "right beliefs." Christians over the centuries have obsessed over who had the correct doctrine and who did not, and when people crossed a perceived line, they were frequently labeled as heretics. Ironically, those most consumed in heresy hunting and orthodoxy policing have historically caused great harm to others. People have been burned at the stake, drowned, tortured, or run out of town, all in the name of orthodoxy. For some it seems as though they imagine that Christianity is about preparing for a big exam in which we must get all the answers right to pass through death and into a resurrected existence. Of course, there are helpful ways for us to engage the question of right beliefs, especially when we are gracious and dialogical, and when we keep track of a diverse global Christianity that has existed for two thousand years. We can learn many things from the community of saints and the great cloud of witnesses, but simply equating right beliefs with Christianity would be a crude reductionist interpretation.

Not as many Christian communities spend time reflecting on their orthopraxy as they do refereeing other people's beliefs. Orthopraxy is more concerned with "righteous action." It is consumed with the question of how we ought to live as the people of God in the world. The most common and, I would argue, most Christian way of talking about orthopraxy is to tie it to our lived discipleship in the way of Jesus. In 1688, when Western European Christians were engaged in conquest and slavery, a Mennonite and Quaker hybrid group in Germantown, Pennsylvania, wrote an anti-slavery petition rooted in the logic of the golden rule; "Do unto others as you would have them do unto you." In contrast, the majority of Christian traditions that had developed endless theological works and commentaries, nuancing every doctrinal belief, often did not speak up against racialized chattel slavery. Orthopraxy compels us to align our lives with the righteousness of God. Of course, with Christianity being a global faith with a diversity of Christian communities and contexts, there are debates about what is morally and ethically faithful, and people use diverging criteria to discern what is right and wrong. Nonetheless, we can assume that a community that is not introspective about its practices and ways of life will be likely to miss the mark in its attempts at loving others. Orthopraxy orients people to align their everyday life and actions so they can faithfully participate in God's delivering presence in our world.

Finally, only a tiny fraction of Christian communities that recognize the need for faithful orthopraxy also couple it with a robust concern for orthopathy. Orthopathy in this sense has nothing to do with orthopathic medicine. Pathos is about one's feelings. Orthopathy, in the way I am using the word, is about right "internal experience." One could go in several directions when exploring orthopathy and a righteous interior disposition. For example, one might contend that Christians ought always be happy. Or someone might tie it to conversion, like John Wesley, and talk about having your "heart strangely warmed" or some other kind of internal experience. Martin Luther saw grace as freeing him from his overwhelming sense of guilt under the law. These are all different Christian traditions and their way of engaging orthopathy. However, what I'm actually interested in relates to our vocation to love. In remembering 1 John 3:16-18, we are challenged with how someone responds to someone in need. From that passage it appears that there is not only a right action but also a right internal experience that Christians ought to have in response to another's need. We ought to have compassion and be moved internally by the condition that is causing the person's suffering. So, yes, there are a variety of ways the broader historic and global church has framed right internal experience that we cannot evaluate at this time. What I am suggesting is that there ought to be some righteous and faithful internal response to the suffering of others. The love gap remains when we exclude right action and right internal experience from our discipleship in the way of Jesus. Learning systematic doctrine without righteous action and a righteous internal experience will never grow our love for others. Our capacity to love requires radical action and compassionate hearts compelled by God's abundant and revolutionary love toward us.

Now we must consider where we see the love gap frequently reoccurring in our society today. Again, we all have our own tendencies to cut off our love and compassion for some people. When I worked as a youth pastor in Harrisburg and the love gap reared its ugly head in me, I had to intentionally cast out that beast. For example, at one point we had a gym that we rented out on Sunday evenings. Our routine was to give the youth free time to play, then we would do some organized games and activities, and then finally we would seat everyone on the floor in a huge circle and I would give a talk while walking around in the middle. On one particular night as people were settling down for the talk, one of my students—we'll call him Darius—started acting up and giving some of the other teens a hard time. Darius wasn't a bad kid, but he often had trouble interacting well with others. He was a bit socially awkward, his clothes often smelled as though they hadn't been washed, and just about anyone could tell that he had experienced some neglect in his life. So compared to many of the other kids who also lived in a majority black and under-resourced neighborhood, Darius didn't have the easiest life. The love gap haunted Darius.

On that particular Sunday evening, Darius started hitting one of the other teens. None of my other volunteers could get Darius to relax, and suddenly he decided to leave the gym altogether. I was so frustrated. I ended up leaving the group to get Darius and immediately took him home, which meant no talk for the group, since I was the one prepared to give it. On the way to Darius's home, I was mad and frustrated on the inside (talk about an internal experience), and I told Darius that he was banned and could not return. That was the last straw.

The next day, of course, I felt terrible about that decision and saying that to him. I couldn't fathom Jesus turning his back on Darius like I had. And so I decided to meet with him one-on-one for a few months, and then eventually invited him to rejoin the group. I knew that the righteous response to Darius was compassion and concrete love. Jesus, I believe, loved that child so much and would bend over backward for him. I needed to align my heart and my body to that kind of love as well. Sometimes the people we are socialized to demonize or get frustrated with, the ones on the margin, are precisely the ones we are called to love most. I'm grateful that I occasionally see and catch up with Darius around the city, who is now an adult. God continues to crack open my compassion for him even a decade later.

As I mentioned in a previous chapter, I have worked with organizers in my community because Pennsylvania has a racist record for distributing state funds for public education, withholding millions of dollars every year from schools in Harrisburg and Philadelphia and many other predominantly nonwhite school districts across the state. The statisticians have done their work and charted the disparities. Rallies have been held, politicians have been visited, and I have personally explained the problem to many people in my state. When people hear about the resource inequities they are horrified that such a blatant apartheid system of funding could still exist. And they want to know why we can't fix it immediately. I tell them that the real work is not merely explaining the problem, the true work is convincing all the residents of school districts across the state that are being *overfunded* to push to reduce their own state-funded revenue so that other children will be equitably resourced. This problem, as well as changing the broader structure of sourcing education funding from local taxes, is a daunting and difficult sell. The gap that exists is not only in people's comprehension that our system is unjust. The more fundamental gap is one of compassion for children who are not their own. The love gap is prominent among many self-professed Christians who would not dare release one cent from their overfunded financial abundance despite knowing full well about the scarcity deserts that exist for many of our young learners.

Similarly, I was horrified by the lack of compassion in our society when the first news broke about children and parents being separated at the U.S. border. It quickly became a partisan fight, and I couldn't comprehend how someone would want to play party politics instead of ensuring that children were no longer being detained and separated from their parents and guardians. But it should not have shocked me, because I have witnessed this same love gap in response to people's awareness of mass incarceration or while Black Lives Matter protests rallied against police brutality in our communities across the nation. When "Blue Lives Matter" became the response, and Blue Lives Matter merchandise became an instant national industry that raked in large profits, it should have prepared me for the ways we as humans can harden our hearts to the suffering and pains of others. And until that love gap is filled with God's deliverance and compassion, we will continue to see the "soft minds" and "hard hearts" that Dr. King warned about.[5]

The love gap exists in lots of ways. We could talk about inequality in pay and how race and gender affect people's wages. Similarly we could explore, as I have done in other chapters, how we lack love and compassion for poor and working-class people, and are more concerned about the rights of a corporation (which isn't actually a person) than we are about the well-being of the many workers whose wages are suppressed and who are struggling to survive with rising living expenses. In each case, the answer to the problem certainly includes change in legislation. But more than that, we need to fill in the holes in our hearts that are consumed with apathy, disdain, and self-justifications. Followers of Jesus recognize that we too are susceptible to practicing the love gap, and therefore we continually seek for God to deliver us from hard hearts and to break us open toward the communities our own group is least likely to love. The full expression of love toward our neighbor is a revolution in the public square. One might call it the politics of love.

THE POLITICS OF LOVE

In youth groups across the country, American teens are taught lessons about loving their enemies. They are told to write down the name of someone they don't like or someone who teases them, and then they are instructed to pray for them. This is a cute exercise, and we should pray for those we have any ill will toward. However, this kind of teaching lacks the weight of the word *enemy* when used by Jesus in the first century as he expounded and expanded upon whom his followers were called to love. This was not a domesticated lesson on how to love Jessica, a mean girl who is a gossip, or little Tommy who makes fart noises every time you sit down, or the jerk down the block who gives you the side-eye every time you try to say hi. No, Jesus is pronouncing the Father-like love that is turned toward even political enemies that seek to do you harm, that exploit you, that would leave you to suffer and die without any aid. In fact, these enemies are the ones who will drag you into court and instigate the processes that will bring about your destruction. Loving your enemies is extremely political. It is not sentimentality but instead is radical and often revolutionary in character, expressed through action and allowing us to recognize the image of God in another person.

Howard Thurman helps us situate the political character of Jesus' message, helping us to recognize that Jesus' teachings were first and foremost for the one "who stands with his back against the wall."[6] For Thurman, Jesus' message had been domesticated, and it was rooted in forgetting simple realities about Jesus' own existence. He knew he had to "begin with the simple historical fact that Jesus was a Jew."[7] He recognized that severing Jesus from Israel, and the West claiming him as their own, resulted in a long devastating history with centuries of oppression and conquest tied to that history. "The second important fact for our consideration is that Jesus was a poor Jew," writes Thurman.[8] The economic conditions Jesus found himself in aligned him with the masses of poor people in the land. The third point is that "Jesus was a member of a minority group in the midst of a larger dominant and controlling group."[9] Thurman's concern is for us to understand the revolutionary moment that Jesus' people were living in while under Roman occupation. In view of these three things, we can now see how Jesus began his messianic vocation while ministering to a poor Jewish community under Roman rule. In Thurman's words, "His words were directed to the House of Israel, a minority within the Greco-Roman world, smarting under the loss of status, freedom, and autonomy, haunted by the dream of the restoration of a lost glory and a former greatness."[10]

In context, Jesus' teaching on loving our enemies has deep political significance. There are two sides of the enemy-loving coin to explore as we embrace the politics of love. First is the interior work that is done, which makes survival and healing for the oppressed possible while living under an oppressive regime. Once again Howard Thurman can help us explore what Jesus' teaching opens up to those most vulnerable in society. But enemy love has public and political power as well, which moves beyond the internal experience of the disinherited. With this side of enemy love, there lives the potential to transform and convert those who wield political power. To get there we must go beyond Howard Thurman, who never embodied this type of enemy love, and instead we must look to his mentee Dr. Martin Luther King Jr., who politicized Thurman's message. Dr. King fused his inherited black social gospel with the Gandhian method of resistance and then rigged it to the already ongoing black freedom struggle in the United States.[11] With Thurman and King side by side we can see Jesus' teaching of enemy love beyond sentimentality. In its place we revive a revolutionary love that provides healing to the oppressed and simultaneously works for the transformation of society by seeking to change laws and fill the love gap residing in so many people.

To understand the gift that love is for Howard Thurman, we must take note of the three kinds of enemy love one could practice, according to Thurman. "There is first the personal enemy, one who is in some sense a part of one's primary-group life."[12] This aligns with the youth group example I suggested earlier. Here Thurman turns our attention to personal conflicts that arise among those you encounter and interact with in your relational network. "The second kind of enemy comprises those persons who, by their activities, make it difficult for the group to live without shame and humiliation."[13] To explain this kind of enemy love, Thurman uses Jewish tax collectors as an example. He explains the hatred many Jewish people had toward them: "They were despised; they were outcasts, because from the inside they had unlocked the door to the enemy."[14] Basically they were traitors, or what many in the black community call "Uncle Toms," because they are working on behalf of the very people who are oppressing your people. Loving this person is a bit more difficult; in fact, it seems insulting to have to do so. Thurman explains further,

> All underprivileged people have to deal with this kind of enemy. There are always those who seem to be willing to put their special knowledge at the disposal of the dominant group to facilitate the tightening of the chains. They are given positions, often prominence, and above all a guarantee of economic security and status. To love such people requires the uprooting of the bitterness of betrayal, the heartiest poison that grows in the human spirit. . . . But to love them does not mean to condone their way of life.[15]

Finally, the "third type of enemy was exemplified by Rome. . . . Rome was the political enemy." And I believe this category that Thurman identifies is the primary meaning Jesus had in mind when he used *enemy*. For Thurman, the ability to love a political enemy, that is your oppressor, requires that the "Roman had to emerge as a person."[16] We must see their humanity. We must see their personhood. There is no path to loving your enemy without that happening first. When Jesus taught about loving one's enemies, first-century Jews would have known that Jesus first and foremost was talking about the Romans. And that realization turns love into a political act. The more natural response is hatred. But Thurman realized the harm hatred does to the hater. "Hatred, in the mind and spirit of the disinherited, is born out of great bitterness—a bitterness that is made possible by sustained resentment which is bottled up."[17] That, of course, is not the way of Jesus, and the love he turns us toward. At the heart of Jesus' teaching, affirms Thurman, stands the ethic to love one's enemies.

Dr. King also picked up on the harm that hate does as he reflected on Jesus' teaching to love our enemies. "Hate is just as injurious to the person who hates," says King. "Like an unchecked cancer, hate corrodes the personality and eats away its vital unity. Hate destroys a man's sense of values and his objectivity."[18] However, King goes further than Thurman. Yes, he understands that Jesus' message is to the disinherited, but King's understanding of love is more political and revolutionary, and is ready to be radically embodied in the public square in the struggle for justice.

For Martin Luther King Jr., loving your enemy was a powerful instrument for social change. For example, Dr. King also believed "we should love our enemies" because it "is the only force capable of transforming an enemy into a friend."[19] When we respond with hate we are unlikely to get rid of the injustice we face. It just perpetuates the cycles of violence and harm that have already been unfolding. Love attempts to disrupt the cycle through its transformative power. Now, we all should know that love cannot guarantee how someone will ultimately respond. The practice of love during the '60s won some people over but not everyone. Some persevered in their white supremacy and anti-black racism without much of a blink. But hatred never fills in the love gap. It has the worst losing streak in human history. Love has the capacity to convert social and political enemies so that they join the struggle for God's new world. I've seen it happen in people's lives.

Dr. King at times talks about love as a force that can withstand the worst side of humanity. For him, love was not only political, it was something black people could take up in their pursuit for a new society. "Love is the most durable power in the world," he wrote. "This creative force, so beautifully exemplified in the life of our Christ, is the most potent instrument available in mankind's quest for peace and security."[20] Again, for Dr. King, love is revolutionary and not some domesticated sentimental feeling. It has the power to change everything. Our hope depends on our practice of love in the way of Jesus. Its power is tied to the first point, its capacity to transform. Together, we see that the goal of love is not to destroy one's enemies the way regular warfare does. Instead, love in pursuit of justice seeks to destroy the evil and injustice wreaking havoc on humanity. We attack systems and forces of evil that keep people captive and in oppression. In this way, love is not merely an interior response but also a political way of transforming society.

Finally, it must be said that loving enemies isn't about "liking" our enemies or looking the other way in response to real harm caused. Love affirms that they too are made in the image of God and have inherent value, worth, and dignity. Love sees their personhood and complexity and has compassion that they too are in captivity to evil and are in need of God's deliverance. And finally, love refuses to destroy them. This, however, does not take off the table the need for truth-telling, accountability, and ultimately, the responsibility for oppressors to make right the wrongs they have committed. Love is not sentimentality that is unconcerned with the establishment of a just society grounded in God's deliverance.

Some Christians have argued that Christians do not have enemies. They believe that the category of enemy falls away for Christians. No one remains there, is the logic. I disagree. This sounds strange after exploring why enemy love is powerful and even political. I would agree that Christians do not "make" enemies; however, I do think that Christians "have" enemies. Again, if "enemies" is primarily a way to describe a political opponent who seeks to dominate, oppress, exploit, or violate you in any way, then it seems strange to say that Christians by default have no enemies. This logic makes sense only if you are the ones in power. But if you are part of an oppressed community, you know that you can have enemies (people seeking to do you harm through political force) that are not of your making. As Jesus taught his followers, the challenge wasn't to not have enemies, but rather to love them. We should not deny the very real political violence and harm that goes on in society. We must embrace the radical and compassionate love of God that is poised for revolution.

WHEN LOVE AND RIGHTEOUS INDIGNATION KISS

The final component needed to understand the politics of love concerns what disciples of Jesus are to do with anger. I believe that anger is sometimes too quickly aligned with hatred and bitterness. This is a mistake. From my experience there are different kinds of anger, and at least two general categories, if not more, ought to be distinguished. First, as most of us have probably witnessed, there is an uncontrolled and unleashed anger that easily morphs into hatred. This kind of anger is a destructive force that will eat you up from the inside out.

However, that is not the only kind of anger that exists. Not all anger turns into bitterness and hatred. For example, Scripture frequently portrays God as angered by all the injustice and harm that humans have done to one another. Typically, Christians have called this kind of anger righteous indignation. And many have contended that we too ought to have righteous indignation over many things in our world. We should be angry when people are fundamentally violated and not treated with dignity as people created by God.

For this type of anger to not break down into a destructive force, it must be embraced with love so that it can be channeled in creative and constructive ways. Righteous indignation combined with love produces a passion that aligns with God's own responses to injustice and harm. As many frequently pray, we ought to have our hearts break for the things that break God's heart, and we ought to be bothered by the things that bother God. The Prophets reveal that it is idolatry and injustice that bother God most. This concept that all anger is wrong is merely a justification of "civil society" that is uncomfortable with anger and direct confrontation, like the kind Jesus displayed when he flipped the tables in Jerusalem.

Some things ought to make us angry. We ought to get angry when we find out that children are going to bed hungry tonight not because we do not have enough food to go around but because nations and corporations hoard the resources of the earth for personal profit and the accumulation of unimaginable wealth instead of redistributing what was always God's to begin with. We ought to be bothered because two million people are locked in cages in the United States. We ought to have some righteous indignation because we are destroying our planet and causing disproportionate suffering to the most vulnerable people in our world because of our ecological devastation. We ought to be mad when we spend more on our military budget than we do on education, healthcare, and helping people secure adequate housing, and when our ghettos and reservations are still slow-death traps for black and Native American people.

The problem is not that we get angry, but what we do with that anger. We are called to be angry and yet not to sin. We must take our righteous anger against idolatry and injustice and let it converge with genuine love. This will move us from virtue signaling about issues to passionately struggling for the deliverance and well-being of our enemies while refusing to destroy those who do the harm. We fiercely struggle to bring an end to the systems and forces of evil while seeking the deliverance of our social and political enemies. Our anger taps us into the urgency of human suffering while love sustains us to persevere in this work for the long haul.

CONCLUSION: THE PUNCH LINE OF JONAH AND RESTORATIVE LOVE

Jonah's story is such a popular one for many people raised in the church. At very young ages, young disciples are introduced to this fantastic story. And there should be no wondering why that is so—it has all the makings of a great plotline. Jonah avoids God's call to go to Nineveh and takes the first ship heading in the opposite direction. A wild storm rocks the boat to the brink of destruction, until finally he is thrown overboard into the chaotic sea. Then a giant fish swallows him whole. And if that were not enough, Jonah survives in the belly of the fish for three days until it vomits him up. Then, and only then, is he ready to go to those Ninevites, where he gives his best fire-and-brimstone damnation he can muster. In response, the people, and even the animals, repent in sackcloth and ashes. I'm pretty sure this could easily be a Hollywood feature film. If it were done as a comedy, I would like to see Anthony Anderson cast for the role of Jonah. This is a roller coaster of a story line, with multiple plot climaxes that could keep any audience sitting on the edge of their seats if done well.

Ironically, most people familiar with the Jonah story typically tend to miss the punch line of the story. First, for a quick backdrop, we have to remember why Jonah didn't want to go to the Ninevites. The Ninevites were part of Assyria, which was the reigning empire of that time. Any historian can tell you about the brutality of the Assyrians. They were violent, and they thoroughly dominated and humiliated those they conquered. When cities resisted being conquered, the Assyrians often brought them to the ground and left them in ruins. They were especially known for impaling their enemies on spikes. Thousands were usually killed, often including women and children. People were terrified of the brutal methods of warfare the Assyrians used to conquer lands and maintain power. Also bear in mind that they are the ones who demolished and eviscerated the northern kingdom of Israel around AD 722. So when Jonah didn't want to go to Nineveh, you have to understand that they were violent oppressors with a reputation. Understanding this story hinges on understanding Jonah's hatred for these people God was sending him to.

The punch line occurs in chapter 4 after Jonah has preached judgment on the people and they have repented. Jonah is upset because he believes that they deserve punishment, yet because he knows all too well the character of God, he has a terrible feeling about how things will actually unfold. His great nightmare is that God is exactly who he knows God to be, a radically loving God who would extend grace and forgiveness to the Ninevites. Accepting God's radical love extended to these enemies is painful for Jonah because they have done the most inhumane and brutal things to others. Aren't some things unforgivable?

> But this was very displeasing to Jonah, and he became angry. He prayed to the Lord and said, "O Lord! Is not this what I said while I was still in my own country? That is why I fled to Tarshish at the beginning; for I knew that you are a gracious God and merciful, slow to anger, and abounding in steadfast love, and ready to relent from punishing. And now, O Lord, please take my life from me, for it is better for me to die than to live." (Jonah 4:1-3)

Some might be quick to condemn Jonah for this, but I imagine that if you have been on the receiving end of nightmarish evil and violence, or are close to those who have, then you completely understand how Jonah feels. When I am honest, I am able to realize that I often deeply resonate with Jonah and feel that some people who torture and fundamentally violate vulnerable people should get what's coming to them. And then we remember 1 John 4:8: "God is love." We remember the common refrain that threads through the entire Hebrew Scriptures, stating, "The Lord is gracious and merciful, *slow to anger* and abounding in steadfast love" (Exodus 34:6; Numbers 14:18; Psalm 145:8; Joel 2:13; Nehemiah 9:17; my emphasis). In fact, many psalms are organized around God's character and action being rooted in enduring love. The best example is Psalm 136, in which every other phrase says, "For his steadfast love endures forever," as a liturgical song as it recounts the faithfulness Israel has experienced from God. See, Jonah knew all too well exactly who God was. God is love. And God's love and mercy is steadfast, and is slow to anger. God wants to see people repent and turn toward righteous living. Jonah wanted the Ninevites to suffer for their wrong-doing, he wanted an eye for an eye, he wanted eternal torment, he wanted his pound of flesh. But deep down inside he knew how this would all play out.

What the story of Jonah reminds us is that love is capable of transforming political enemies like the Ninevites. However, to seek after that kind of transformation of one's enemies requires that the love of God seize those who have been wronged, so that we first experience healing and so that our ultimate desires will move from punishment and suffering to righteousness and restoration. Righteousness and restoration invite those who have done wrong to make right, through amends and reparations, the harm they have caused and also allow them to become people dedicated to justice and God's deliverance in the world. In the United States, we do not have a framework for this kind of restorative love, because everything is framed around punishment. The politics of love should always prioritize the healing and restoration of victims, but if we desire to participate in God's love, then we also extend an opportunity for violators to repent as well. Of course, repentance does not mean pretending that nothing happened, or not taking proper precautions around violent offenders, and it certainly doesn't mean those who do harm should have their restoration at the expense of the victim's ongoing violation. But it does mean that our imagination for how to engage enemies and violators must be radically reimagined in light of God's faithfulness as an enduring force of love and mercy that seeks conversion of even the most violent and hard-hearted of people.

It is often missed that Jesus teaches that only one characteristic will make us children of our Father in heaven, and that is tied solely to when we love our enemies (Matthew 5:43-48). That act of love gets at the center of God's character and activity. Love of neighbor and enemy alike is vital to the journey on the narrow path toward participating in the delivering presence of God in our world. And it is one of the hardest teachings that I frequently struggle with. Jonah is alive in me, and I often resonate with him. But God's love is greater and more transformative than my momentary resentment and desire that others be punished. Such love has the power to open up transformative dialogue in the public square among often hard-hearted partisan opponents, and it is just as powerful during Thanksgiving dinner when we must speak up and have difficult conversations that expose the conflicts and differences among those in our own family. It has the capacity to transform someone who is actively oppressing others so that they convert and begin working for the liberation of suffering people. And it is even able to change the mind, heart, and practices of those in power. Of course, we are also called to speak truth to power, and at times with righteous indignation, but love is not the opposite of those things. Finally, love is not a magic wand that can guarantee a particular response from everyone. It doesn't work that way. But it still remains the most powerful instrument for creating the possibility of radical deliverance of even oppressors instead of perpetuating cycles of violence and harm. As the church pursues God's justice and deliverance, it must also take seriously the politics of love.

NOTES

INTRODUCTION

1 The black church here is an academic reference to the historic black Protestant denominations, which include black Baptists, black Methodists (AME and AMEZ), and black Pentecostals like Church of God in Christ.

2 Taylor Branch, *Parting the Waters: America in the King Years, 1954–63* (New York: Simon and Schuster, 2006), 728–30.

3 Eschatology refers to the end of this age and the birth of a new age in Christ when creation is renewed and suffering, violence, and death are banished.

4 William J. Barber II, *Forward Together: A Moral Message for the Nation* (St. Louis: Chalice Press, 2014).

5 Alan Kreider, *Patient Ferment of the Early Church* (Grand Rapids, MI: Baker Academic, 2016), 13.

6 *The Complete Writings of Menno Simons: c. 1496–1561*, ed. John Christian Wenger (Scottdale, PA: Herald Press, 1984), 307.

7 Olive Gilbert, *Narrative of Sojourner Truth: A Bondswoman of Olden Time, Emancipated by the New York Legislature in the Early Part of the Present Century; with a History of Her Labors and Correspondence* (for the author, n.p., 1875), 36.

8 Frederick Douglass, *Narrative of the Life of Frederick Douglass, an American Slave* (Boston: n.p., 1847), 118, available at http://hdl.handle.net/2027/uc2.ark:/13960/t9x05zk36.

CHAPTER 1

1 I must note that as far as American exceptionalism goes, we have the most death-dealing systems of military and incarceration that world history has ever seen, surpassing by a long shot the military and prison spending of every other nation that ever existed. With these systems we destroy or diminish the well-being of people made in the image of God on an incomparable scale.

2 Dietrich Bonhoeffer, *Discipleship, Dietrich Bonhoeffer Works*, vol. 4, ed. Geffrey B. Kelly and John D. Godsey, trans. Barbara Green and Reinhard Krauss (Minneapolis, MN: Fortress Press, 2001); Martin Luther King Jr., *Strength to Love* (Minneapolis: Fortress Press, 2010). First published 1977.

3 Ched Myers, *Binding the Strong Man: A Political Reading of Mark's Story of Jesus* (Maryknoll, NY: Orbis, 1988).

4 Ched Myers et al., *Say to This Mountain: Mark's Story of Discipleship*, 1996 (Maryknoll, NY: Orbis, 1996).

5 Different Bibles approach this differently. The more scholarly the Bible, the more likely it will have all the different endings, although it is likely they will have put brackets around the later additions and included a note about its addition to the canon tradition.

6 *We Shall Overcome*, 196.

7 *We Shall Overcome*, 194–96.

8 *We Shall Overcome*, 197.

9 *We Shall Overcome*, 200–201.

10 Myers et al., *Say to This Mountain*, 148–49.

11 Myers et al., *Say to This Mountain*, 148.

CHAPTER 2

1 Some scholars have argued that Christus Victor is the most dominant and ancient atonement metaphor in Scripture.

2 James K. Beilby and Paul R. Eddy, *The Nature of the Atonement: Four Views* (Downers Grove, IL: InterVarsity Press, 2006).

3 David Mathis, "Barabbas and Me," Desiring God, April 5, 2012, https://www.desiringgod.org/articles/barabbas-and-me.

4 N. T. Wright, *The New Testament and the People of God* (Minneapolis: Fortress, 1992), 158–69.

5 Wright, *New Testament*, 170–81.

6 David A. DeSilva, *An Introduction to the New Testament: Contexts, Methods and Ministry Formation* (Downers Grove, IL: IVP Academic, 2014), 161–67.

7 Michael D. Coogan et al., eds., *The New Oxford Annotated Bible*, 4th ed. (New York: Oxford University Press, 2001).

8 Ched Myers, *Binding the Strong Man: A Political Reading of Mark's Story of Jesus* (Maryknoll, NY: Orbis, 1988), 380.

9 See also Coogan et al., *New Oxford Annotated Bible*.

10 See also Coogan et al., *New Oxford Annotated Bible*.

11 See also Coogan et al., *New Oxford Annotated Bible*.

12 See also Coogan et al., *New Oxford Annotated Bible*.

13 Coogan et al., *New Oxford Annotated Bible*, 178.

14 Both men are historical figures who engaged in religious revolt.

15 See also Coogan et al., *New Oxford Annotated Bible*.

16 See also Coogan et al., *New Oxford Annotated Bible*.

17 See also Coogan et al., *New Oxford Annotated Bible*.

18 See also Coogan et al., *New Oxford Annotated Bible*.

19 See also Coogan et al., *New Oxford Annotated Bible*.

20 See also Coogan et al., *New Oxford Annotated Bible*.

21 See, for example, Obery M. Hendricks, *The Politics of Jesus: Rediscovering the True Revolutionary Nature of the Teachings of Jesus and How They Have Been Corrupted* (New York: Doubleday, 2006); John Howard Yoder, *The Politics of Jesus: Vicit Agnus Noster* (Grand Rapids, MI: Eerdmans, 1994).

CHAPTER 3

1 Alan Kreider, *The Change of Conversion and the Origin of Christendom* (Eugene, OR: Wipf & Stock, 1999).

2 H. A. Drake, *Constantine and the Bishops: The Politics of Intolerance* (Baltimore: Johns Hopkins University Press, 2000).

3 John Wesley, "The Mystery of Iniquity," in *Works of John Wesley* 2:463 (Grand Rapids, MI: Baker, 1996), 465, quoted in D. Stephen Long, "Yoderian Constantinianism?," in *Constantine Revisited: Leithart, Yoder, and the Constantinian Debate*, ed. John D. Roth (Eugene, OR: Pickwick, 2013), 102.

4 Peter J. Leithart, *Defending Constantine: The Twilight of an Empire and the Dawn of Christendom* (Downers Grove, IL: InterVarsity Press, 2010), 11.

5 "Romanus Pontifex," *Papal Encyclicals* (blog), June 16, 2017, https://www.papalencyclicals.net/nichol05/romanus-pontifex.htm.

6 Bartolomé de las Casas, *A Short Account of the Destruction of the Indies*, trans. Nigel Griffin and Anthony Pagden (London: Penguin, 2004).

7 Frederick Douglass and William Lloyd Garrison, *Narrative of the Life of Frederick Douglass, an American Slave* (Boston: Anti-Slavery Office, 1847), 118, available at http://catalog.hathitrust.org/Record/009260192.

8 Martin Luther King Jr., *The Radical King*, ed. Cornel West (Boston: Beacon, 2016), 93.

CHAPTER 9

1 ABC News, "Reverend Wright Transcript," ABC News, accessed March 20, 2020, https://abcnews.go.com/Blotter/story?id=4719157&page=1.

2 Philip Gorski, *American Covenant: A History of Civil Religion from the Puritans to the Present*, 2nd ed. (Princeton, NJ: Princeton University Press, 2019).

3 Gorski, *American Covenant*, 17.

4 Gorski, *American Covenant*, 2.

5 Robert Neelly Bellah, *Beyond Belief: Essays on Religion in a Post-Traditional World* (Berkeley: University of California Press, 2009).

6 Gorski, *American Covenant*, 36.

7 Martin Luther King Jr., *The Radical King*, ed. Cornel West (Boston: Beacon, 2016), 204.

8 King, *Radical King*, 178.

9 King, *Radical King*, 91–95.

10 David Walker, *Walker's Appeal, in Four Articles; Together with a Preamble, to the Coloured Citizens of the World, but in Particular, and Very Expressly, to These of the United States of America*, 3rd. ed. (Boston: David Walker, 1830), 39.

11 Walker, *Walker's Appeal*, 45. Emphasis in the original.

12 Frederick Douglass, "What to the Slave Is the Fourth of July?," in *Let Nobody Turn Us Around: Voices of Resistance, Reform, and*

Renewal: An African American Anthology, ed. Manning Marable and Leith Mullings (Lanham, MD: Rowman and Littlefield, 2003), 89.

13 William Wells Brown, "Slavery as It Is," in Marable and Mullings, *Let Nobody*, 65.

14 Henry Highland Garnet, "Let Your Motto Be Resistance!," in Marable and Mullings, *Let Nobody*, 58.

15 Garnet, "Let Your Motto," 63. Emphasis in the original.

16 Henry McNeal Turner, "Emigration to Africa," in *African American Religious History: A Documentary Witness*, ed. Milton C. Sernett, 2nd ed. (Dunham, NC: Duke University Press, 1999), 292.

17 Henry McNeal Turner (speech before the Georgia state legislature, September 3, 1868), available in Marable and Mullings, *Let Nobody*, 134.

18 Ida B. Wells-Barnett (speech before the National Negro Conference, 1909), available in Marable and Mullings, *Let Nobody*, 212.

19 W. E. B. Du Bois, "Returning Soldiers," *Crisis* 18 (May 1919), 14, available in Marable and Mullings, *Let Nobody*, 245.

20 King, *Radical King*, 236.

21 King, *Radical King*, 241.

22 King, *Radical King*, 204.

23 King, *Radical King*, 214.

24 King, *Radical King*, 215.

25 King, *Radical King*, 216.

26 Charles Marsh, Shea Tuttle, and Daniel P. Rhodes, eds., *Can I Get a Witness?: Thirteen Peacemakers, Community-Builders, and Agitators for Faith and Justice* (Grand Rapids, Michigan: Eerdmans, 2019), 124.

27 Marsh, Tuttle, and Rhodes, 122–26.

28 Marsh, Tuttle, and Rhodes, 128–31.

29 Joanne Grant, *Ella Baker: Freedom Bound* (New York: Wiley, 1999), 163.

30 Kelly Brown Douglas, *Stand Your Ground: Black Bodies and the Justice of God* (Maryknoll, New York: Orbis Books, 2015).

31 Douglas, 207.

32 Douglas, 227.

CHAPTER 5

1 Martin Luther King Jr., *The Radical King*, ed. Cornel West (Boston: Beacon, 2016), 128.

2 Khalil Gibran Muhammad, *The Condemnation of Blackness: Race, Crime, and the Making of Modern Urban America* (Cambridge, MA: Harvard University Press, 2011).

CHAPTER 6

1 Michael-Ray Mathews, "Resistance We Can Imagine: Cultivating Ecclesial Imaginations for Racial Justice and Healing in Public Life," in *Trouble the Water: A Christian Resource for the Work of Racial Justice*, ed. Michael-Ray Mathews, Marie Clare P. Onwubuariri, and Cody J. Sanders (Macon, GA: Nurturing Faith, 2017), 4.

2 Alan Kreider, *The Change of Conversion and the Origin of Christendom* (Eugene, OR: Wipf & Stock, 1999), xv.

3 Alan Kreider, *The Origins of Christendom in the West* (New York: T&T Clark, 2001), 24.

4 Kreider, *Origins of Christendom*.

5 Adam L. Gustine, *Becoming a Just Church: Cultivating Communities of God's Shalom* (Downers Grove, IL: IVP Books, 2019).

6 Gustine, *Becoming a Just Church*, 145.

7 Gustine, *Becoming a Just Church*, 150.

8 Gustine, *Becoming a Just Church*, 144–45.

9 Alexia Salvatierra and Peter Heltzel, *Faith-Rooted Organizing: Mobilizing the Church in Service to the World* (Downers Grove, IL: IVP Books, 2013), 94.

10 Salvatierra and Heltzel, *Faith-Rooted Organizing*, 94, 95.

11 Frank A. Thomas, *How to Preach a Dangerous Sermon* (Nashville: Abingdon Press, 2018), 90.

12 Frank A. Thomas, *Introduction to the Practice of African American Preaching* (Nashville: Abingdon Press, 2016), 142.

13 Frank A. Thomas, *Introduction to the Practice of African American Preaching* (Nashville: Abingdon Press, 2016), 87.

14 Stuart Murray, *The Power of All: Building a Multivoiced Church* (Harrisonburg, VA: Herald Press, 2012), 22.

15 Thomas, *African American Preaching*, 137.

16 Murray, *Power of All*, 21.

17 Sandra Maria Van Opstal, *The Next Worship: Glorifying God in a Diverse World* (Downers Grove, IL: IVP Books, 2015), 15.

CHAPTER 7

1 Quoted in Alejandra Crosthwaite, "Latin American Liberative Ethics," in *Ethics: A Liberative Approach*, ed. Miguel A. De La Torre (Minneapolis: Fortress Press, 2013), 9.

2 Quoted in Thomas Aquinas, *Summa Theologiae: Volume 38, Injustice: 2a2ae. 63–79*, ed. Marcus Lefébure (Cambridge, MA: Cambridge University Press, 2006), 282.

3 Quoted in Billy Kangas, "Teachings of the Early Church Fathers on Poverty and Wealth," *The Orant* (blog), August 25, 2012, https://www.patheos.com/blogs/billykangas/2012/08/teachings-of-the-early-church-fathers-on-poverty-wealth.html.

4 Quoted in Kangas, "Early Church Fathers."

5 Quoted in Kangas, "Early Church Fathers."

6 Quoted in Kangas, "Early Church Fathers."

7 Joerg Rieger and Rosemarie Henkel-Rieger, *Unified We Are a Force: How Faith and Labor Can Overcome America's Inequalities* (St. Louis: Chalice Press, 2019), 38.

8 Rieger and Henkel-Rieger, *Unified We Are*, 40.

9 Rieger and Henkel-Rieger, *Unified We Are*, 41.

10 Rieger and Henkel-Rieger, *Unified We Are*, 43.

11 Rieger and Henkel-Rieger, *Unified We Are*, 44.

12 Rieger and Henkel-Rieger, *Unified We Are*, 44–45.

13 Michelle Alexander, *The New Jim Crow: Mass Incarceration in the Age of Colorblindness* (New York: New Press, 2012).

14 Tracy Jan, "1 in 7 White Families Are Now Millionaires. For Black Families, It's 1 in 50.," *Washington Post*, October 3, 2017, https://www.washingtonpost.com/news/wonk/wp/2017/10/03/white-families-are-twice-as-likely-to-be-millionaires-as-a-generation-ago/.

15 Mehrsa Baradaran, *The Color of Money: Black Banks and the Racial Wealth Gap*, repr. ed. (Cambridge, MA: Belknap Press, 2019), 9.

CHAPTER 8

1 Vincent Harding, *There Is a River: The Black Struggle for Freedom in America* (New York: Harcourt Brace Jovanovich, 1981).

2 "The King Philosophy," The King Center, accessed March 3, 2020, https://thekingcenter.org/king-philosophy/.

3 Gene Sharp, *The Politics of Nonviolent Action, Part Two: The Methods of Nonviolent Action*, ed. Marina Finkelstein (Boston: Porter Sargent, 1973).

4 Mark Engler and Paul Engler, *This Is an Uprising: How Nonviolent Revolt Is Shaping the Twenty-First Century*, repr. ed. (New York: Bold Type, 2017), 6.

5 Engler and Engler, *This Is an Uprising*, 109.

6 Engler and Engler, *This Is an Uprising*, 109–11.

7 Engler and Engler, *This Is an Uprising*, 91.

8 Srđa Popović and Matthew Miller, *Blueprint for Revolution: How to Use Rice Pudding, Lego Men, and Other Nonviolent Techniques to Galvanize Communities, Overthrow Dictators, or Simply Change the World* (New York: Spiegel and Grau, 2015), 93.

9 Engler and Engler, *This Is an Uprising*, 92.

10 Nekeisha Alexis-Baker, "Freedom of Voice: Non-Voting and the Political Imagination," in *Electing Not to Vote: Christian Reflections on Reasons for Not Voting*, ed. Ted Lewis (Eugene, OR: Cascade Books, 2008), 31. Benjamin Ginsburg quotation from *Consequences of Consent: Elections, Citizen Control, and Popular Acquiescence* (Reading, MA: Addison-Wesley, 1982), 58.

11 Alexis-Baker, "Freedom of Voice," 25.

12 Carol Anderson and Dick Durbin, *One Person, No Vote: How Voter Suppression Is Destroying Our Democracy*, repr. ed. (Bloomsbury, 2019).

CHAPTER 9

1 Augustine (of Hippo), *On Christian Doctrine*, trans. D. W. Robertson Jr. (New York: Liberal Arts Press, 1958), 30.

2 Augustine, *On Christian Doctrine*, 31.

3 Augustine, *On Christian Doctrine*, 31.

4 Gustavo Gutiérrez, *A Theology of Liberation: History, Politics, and Salvation*, trans. Caridad Inda and John Eagleson, rev. ed. (Maryknoll, NY: Orbis, 1988), 114.

5 Martin Luther King Jr., *Strength to Love*, gift ed. (Minneapolis: Fortress Press, 2010), 1–9.

6 Howard Thurman, *Jesus and the Disinherited*, repr. ed. (Boston: Beacon Press, 1996), 13.

7 Thurman, *Jesus and the Disinherited*, 15.

8 Thurman, *Jesus and the Disinherited*, 17.

9 Thurman, *Jesus and the Disinherited*, 18.

10 Thurman, *Jesus and the Disinherited*, 21.

11 Gary Dorrien, *Breaking White Supremacy: Martin Luther King Jr. and the Black Social Gospel*, repr. ed. (New Haven, CT: Yale University Press, 2019).

12 Thurman, *Jesus and the Disinherited*, 91–92.

13 Thurman, *Jesus and the Disinherited*, 93.

14 Thurman, *Jesus and the Disinherited*, 93.

15 Thurman, *Jesus and the Disinherited*, 94–95.

16 Thurman, *Jesus and the Disinherited*, 95.

17 Thurman, *Jesus and the Disinherited*, 79.

18 King, *Strength to Love*, 48.

19 King, *Strength to Love*, 48.

20 King, *Strength to Love*, 51.

THE AUTHOR

Drew G. I. Hart is a public theologian and professor of theology at Messiah University. He has ten years of pastoral ministry experience and is the recipient of multiple awards for peacemaking. Hart attained his MDiv with an urban concentration from Biblical Theological Seminary and his PhD in theology and ethics from Missio Seminary. He is a sought-after speaker at conferences, campuses, and churches across the United States and Canada. His first book, *Trouble I've Seen: Changing the Way the Church Views Racism*, utilizes personal and everyday stories, theological ethics, and anti-racism frameworks to transform the church's understanding and witness. Hart lives with his wife, Renee, and their three sons in Harrisburg, Pennsylvania.